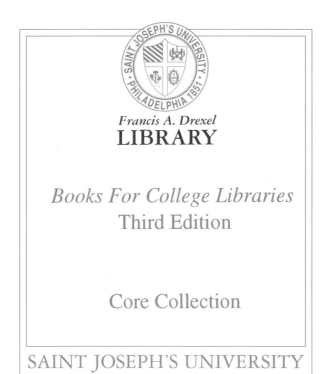

The Emergent Middle School
Second, Enlarged Edition

The Emergent Middle School
Second, Enlarged Edition

WILLIAM M. ALEXANDER
Director, Institute for Curriculum Improvement
University of Florida

EMMETT L. WILLIAMS
University of Florida

MARY COMPTON
University of Georgia

VYNCE A. HINES
University of Florida

DAN PRESCOTT
Emeritus, University of Maryland

RONALD KEALY
University of Florida

HOLT, RINEHART AND WINSTON, INC.
New York • Chicago • San Francisco • Atlanta • Dallas
Montreal • Toronto • London • Sydney

Preface

The Emergent Middle School is intended as a text for students initially preparing for middle school positions and personnel in service retraining themselves for continuing careers in new middle school programs. The book is also intended as a landmark in the developing trend toward middle school organizations differing from traditional 6-3-3, 8-4, and other patterns in the United States. Future middle school programs can both be influenced by, and evaluated in terms of, the descriptions, suggestions, and criteria presented in this first publication of its type on the emergent middle school.

The junior high school was undoubtedly intended by its founders early in this century to be a middle school bridging the elementary and high schools. But the junior high school has generally become a school more like the high school, better geared to the teenager than the "in-between-ager." At the same time children are maturing earlier and knowledge is expanding, and the traditional self-contained classroom organization of the elementary school, with its limited program, seems increasingly inadequate for learners moving toward adolescence. And so, many educators have been seeking a different program and organization focusing on the transitional years from childhood to adolescence. This school should retain appropriate features of the elementary and junior high school, but add other features as needed. It should serve a wide range of individual differences with challenge and success for all. It should be truly in the middle of the school ladder serving the middle range of the school population with a program that is neither elementary nor secondary.

The new middle school, serving children usually enrolled in grades 5 through 8 or 6 through 8, is regarded by many as the answer. A survey very recently conducted by Alexander with the aid of Kealy has identified some 1100 schools in the United States having this grade organization. This number is substantially higher than any prior, partial survey has identified, and is believed to reflect the trend of the past few years away from the 6-3-3 organization. A full report of this survey is reproduced as Part V of this book.

This book deals specifically with middle schools of the emergent type, *not just grade patterns*. Chapter 1 describes the movement toward the new school and states its rationale. Chapters 2 and 3 (Part II) present the case for the middle school from the standpoints respectively of human growth and development and the inadequacies of the 6-3-3 organization. Chapters 4, 5, and 6 (Part III) focus on the program of the new school—its curriculum plan, teaching, organization, and staff. In Part IV, Chapter 7 describes ways and means of evaluating the new school, and Chapter 8 suggests steps to be taken in moving toward it. Part V includes the materials from the research survey cited above: Chapter 9, the survey findings, and Chapter 10, descriptions of illustrative middle schools visited in connection with the survey.

A comprehensive bibliography is included to aid instructors and students in further study of the backgrounds of the middle school, its students, staff, organization, and program. Selected illustrative materials, in addition to those included throughout the text, are reproduced in the Appendix.

The authors are grateful to the middle school faculties we have consulted, to the in-between-agers we have taught as well as students preparing for middle school positions, and to the many associates with whom we have discussed middle school programs. All of these persons have helped us acquire the insights and ideas presented here. We hope that this book will assist all concerned to provide better education for the in-between-agers of the nation.

THE AUTHORS

March 1969

Contents

The Emergent Middle School

Second, Enlarged Edition

PART I

Introduction

Chapter 1

The Movement toward
a New Middle School

Paul Woodring's statement that "it now appears that the 6-3-3 plan, with its junior high school, is on the way out"[1] seemed in October 1965, to be an exaggeration of the facts. Even two years later, however, as this book is in press, Woodring's prediction seems less extreme. There definitely appears to be a rather widespread interest in reorganizing especially the middle division of the 6-3-3 plan into some type of middle or intermediate school different from the traditional grade 7–9 junior high school.

This chapter reviews the rationale, status, and direction of the movement in the 1960s toward a new middle school. Thus it serves also as an overview of the emergent middle school to which this book is devoted.

WHAT IS THE EMERGENT MIDDLE SCHOOL?

The use of the adjective "new" or "emergent" before "middle school" is deliberate and essential. Clearly the junior high school Americans have known in the twentieth century was intended to be a "middle" school. Indeed Samuel Popper's work on *The American Middle School* declares that "what over the years we have come to know as the Junior High School *is* institutionally America's Middle School."[2] To Popper, "What is at issue

[1] Paul Woodring, "The New Intermediate School," *Saturday Review,* 48:77 (October 16, 1965).

[2] Samuel H. Popper, *The American Middle School: An Organizational Analysis* (Waltham, Mass.: Blaisdell Publishing Company, 1967), p. xi.

now in professional dialogue is not whether there shall be a junior high school or a "middle" school, a semantic distinction without a difference, but rather which grades are functionally appropriate for this unit of public school organization."[3]

But to many educators, including the present authors, the issue seems rather to be whether a new program and organization would serve the function of a middle school better than those of the traditional school structures, especially of the upper elementary grades and the grade 7–9 junior high school. The function itself does seem to remain that ascribed by Popper to the pioneers of the junior high school:

> Its pioneers in the United States meant the middle school to serve as a transitional unit between childhood education in the elementary school and later adolescent education in the high school. Pupils between these two stages of maturation, standing at the threshold of puberty, were to be assigned to a middle school.[4]

In our judgment, today's interest in a new middle school stems in part from dissatisfaction with what the junior high school has become, not with the original conception of function. Along with Popper, we would agree that "its unhappy past can well serve as a prologue to a brighter future, provided we cast out from the middle school what has become functionally obsolescent." However, we cannot fully accept as adequate what he proposes (still a grade 7–9 organization, without adequate ties to the levels below and above, we fear) as "a revitalization program" for "the middle school of tomorrow."[5]

The emergent middle school is more than merely a reorganized junior high school. In fact, considerable impetus to a new type of middle school comes from dissatisfaction with the program and organization of the upper years of the elementary school. Some of the data and opinions which point to the need for reorganizing the elementary school are presented in Chapter 3. Too, there is much support for a four-year high school including the ninth grade. Thus the new middle school should be seen more as an effort to reorganize the total school ladder than just one of its levels. It is the 6-3-3 plan, not just one or more of its divisions, that is being reorganized, that may indeed be, as Woodring observed, "on its way out."

We do not conceive of the middle school as serving only early adolescents, unless "early" be regarded as synonymous with the "in-between years." "Middle" here is believed to have two significant connotations which should help to define the scope and limitations of the middle school. In the first place, the youth served are in the "middle," between

[3]Popper.
[4]Popper, p. xii.
[5]Popper.

childhood and adolescence. In the second place, the schools serving them should be in the "middle," between schools for childhood and for adolescent education. Since individual children vary widely in the age at which they attain full adolescence, and since schools are not uniformly and precisely identified as being for childhood or adolescence, overlappings are inevitable and approximations essential.

Thus there is a very real dilemma as to the placement of the middle school in the school organizational plan. The dilemma is heightened by the diverse factors operating in American school districts, which have created every variety of graded structures, including (without reference to pre-grade 1, community junior college, and ungraded structures) such organizations as 1-12, 8-4, 6-6, 6-3-3, 6-2-4, 5-3-4, 4-4-4, 7-5, 7-2-3, and others. Nevertheless, it is clear that before 1960 the most popular organization had become the 6-3-3 one (a reversal in forty years from the 8-4 plan equally popular in 1920) and that the current reorganization movement is one that modifies this pattern. Specifically, the emergent middle school combines into one organization and facility certain school years, usually those in grades 5-8 or 6-8, that have been separated by elementary and junior high organizations under the 6-3-3 plan.

What, then, is the emergent middle school? To us, it is *a school providing a program planned for a range of older children, preadolescents, and early adolescents that builds upon the elementary school program for earlier childhood and in turn is built upon by the high school's program for adolescence.* Specifically, it focuses on the educational needs of what we have termed the "in-between-ager," although its clientele inevitably includes a few children for whom puberty may arrive before or after the middle school period. It is a school having a much less homogeneous population, on the criterion of developmental level, than either the elementary or high school, with their concentration on childhood or adolescence.

Thus, the emergent middle school may be best thought of as *a phase and program of schooling bridging but differing from the childhood and adolescent phases and programs.* This conception assumes that schooling is planned from school exit to school termination with three closely articulated phases or levels: childhood, middle, and adolescent. The decision as to what grades and ages, if any, are to be assigned to specific levels must be, we believe, a decision to be reached within each school district on the basis of local data and experience as to developmental levels of children, existing graded school organizations, and school facilities. We ourselves are inclined to believe that the school level for childhood should generally be designed to serve children until about age ten, and the level for adolescence those who are about fourteen and older, with the middle school designed for those in between these years. We fully recognize, however, both the wisdom and the necessity of disregarding such theoretical norms in a particular situation. The essential point is that there be a planned program of schooling giving due consideration to these three levels of growth and development.

HOW WIDESPREAD IS THE MOVEMENT?

No comprehensive data are yet available to document fully the authors' belief that there is a "movement" toward the emergent middle school as just defined. Indeed the first-named author of this publication is in 1967–1968 conducting a survey funded by the United States Office of Education to determine the number of schools which have recently moved toward an organization and program differing in the middle school years from the traditional 6-3-3 plan and other organizations. He has compiled preliminary data from this survey which clearly confirm partial surveys and estimates by others as to the existence of such a movement. Some related data and observations are reviewed in this section.

Predictions and Observations

Paul Woodring's 1965 comment, noted earlier, that the 6-3-3 plan, with its junior high school, appeared to be on the way out was reflected in a 1966 pamphlet prepared under the auspices of the Twin Cities Metropolitan Area, Incorporated (Minneapolis-St. Paul, Minnesota). In this pamphlet the author, Neal C. Nickerson, asserted that there was a definite move away from the junior high organization toward a different middle school plan, and he enumerated a number of reasons for the trend.[6] This notion of the demise of the junior high school also characterized an unofficial selection of the "Ten Major Educational Events of 1966" for the Educational Press Association, which included the following as one of these events:

Educators became disillusioned with the junior high school and endorsed the middle school as an alternative.

No more exciting concept emerged from the thinking and practice of educators than that of the middle school as a better medium for educating young adolescents than the junior high school . . . .

Although the middle school has been under study since the 1950's, it was only in 1966 that some schoolmen were ready to say flatly: The junior high is on the way out; the middle school is in . . . .

Its objectives were still valid, but, claimed the critics, the junior high school never did meet them. They admitted that there is no guarantee that the middle

[6]Neal C. Nickerson, *Junior High Schools Are on the Way Out* (Danville, Ill.: The Interstate Printers and Publishers, 1966).

school will either. But educationists wanted to try the middle school to make a new start.[7]

Although we see the 6-3-3 plan itself, not just a particular junior high school grade organization, as being "on the way out," such interpretations as the foregoing have undoubtedly caused some defensive concern on the part of grade 7–9 junior high school leaders and proponents. After all, it is this grade 7–9 phase of the 6-3-3 plan that is likely to be most immediately and completely involved in reorganization. It is not surprising, therefore, that certain recent publications sponsored by the Committee on Junior High School Education, National Association of Secondary-School Principals, use both "junior high" and "middle school" in their titles. Thus a 1966 statement of *Guidelines for Junior High and Middle School Education* noted that "the junior high school composed of grades 7, 8, and 9 is the most widespread pattern, but is currently being challenged by 'middle school,' composed of grades 6, 7, and 8, or even 5, 6, 7, and 8."[8] This publication, although reporting that the junior high school principals' consensus favored the three-year school, grades 7–9, stated in Guideline No. 1 that the school program should provide "courses that interest and benefit students in the age range of eleven to fifteen inclusive, with flexibility in admission and promotion policies within the school and at the two extremes."[9] Thus, "flexibility in admission and promotion" would be designed to attain some of the adjustment to individual differences sought in the new middle school plans. The Committee on Junior High School Education of the National Association of Secondary-School Principals also published a statement of its position on "Recommended Grades or Years in Junior High or Middle Schools." The Committee noted a recent focus of interest on the 5-3-4 and 4-4-4 plans of the school ladder, encouraged research to help answer questions relating to the issue of grade organization, and stated this point of view:

In the meantime, every community that contemplates an organizational change is urged to obtain evidence regarding the maturation patterns of its children in deciding whether a 5–8, 6–8, or 6–9 school is likely to be as satisfactory an educational unit as the 7–9 school has been.[10]

As J. Lloyd Trump put it, in reviewing the Committee's stand and certain other publications, the NASSP Committee recommended studies to com-

[7]An unofficial selection for the Educational Press Association of America, by Ben Brodinsky, Editor-in-Chief, Croft Educational Services, and Past President, Educational Press Association of America (mimeographed press release, undated).

[8]Gordon F. Vars (ed.), *Guidelines for Junior High and Middle School Education* (Washington, D. C.: National Association of Secondary-School Principals, 1966), p. 3.

[9]Vars.

[10]*Bulletin* of the NASSP, 51:70 (February 1967).

pare different organizations, "but in the meantime places the burden of proof on those who plan changes in the grade structure."[11] The position of the NASSP Committee on Junior High School Education, representing as it does the junior high school principals of the country, really seems as open-minded to change as could be hoped for from the administrators whose school organizations (mostly grade 7–9) are elsewhere reported to be "on the way out." This attitude may be in part recognition of the fact that a different type of organization and program is already emerging. But it also represents some encouragement toward experimentation in education for the middle school years.

Surveys

The available surveys, as already noted, do indicate that some reorganization has been occurring in the 1960s, although as yet there is little support for the more extravagant statements as to its extent. A survey by the United States Office of Education of a sample of junior high schools in 1959–1960 found that 12 percent of the junior high schools and 15 percent of the junior-senior high schools were planning to change the grouping of grades 7, 8, and 9 with reference to other grades. Of the 79 junior high schools planning to make such changes, 20 percent would convert to plans other than grades 7 through 9.[12]

In his study of changes in junior high schools in the northeastern United States, Zdanowicz found that almost 16 percent had changed from the modal pattern of the junior high school to one which included grade 6 or grades 5 and 6. He identified as middle schools 24 which had grades 6–8 and 13, grades 5–8, noting that 32 of these 37 schools were either newly organized schools or had changed their grade organization within the period 1954–1963.[13] Zdanowicz commented later as follows:

There has been a tremendous increase in the number of intermediate schools in the Northeast, most of which are two- or three-year junior high schools. However, there was a proportionately greater increase in the number of middle schools—the majority of which were recently organized—and some junior high schools were considering changing to the middle school plan.[14]

[11]"Junior High versus Middle School," *Bulletin of the NASSP,* 51:73 (February 1967).

[12]Grade S. Wright and Edith S. Greer, *The Junior High School: A Survey of Grades 7–8–9 in Junior and Junior-Senior High Schools, 1959–60,* Bulletin 1963, No. 32, (United States Office of Education [Washington, D.C.: Government Printing Office, 1963]), p. 4.

[13]Paul J. Zdanowicz, "A Study of the Changes that Have Taken Place in the Junior High Schools of Northeastern United States during the Last Decade and the Reasons for Some of the Changes" (unpublished doctoral dissertation, Temple University, June 1965).

[14]Paul J. Zdanowicz, "Analyzing Trends in School Reorganization: The Middle School and the Junior High School," an address at the NASSP 51st Annual Convention (mimeographed, Dallas, Texas: February 26, 1967), p. 3.

Brod reported in February 1966 that she had received information from over 40 percent of the nation's school systems, and that 10 percent of these had or were moving to either a 5-3-4 or 4-4-4 organization. An additional 1 percent were reported to be considering such a reorganization, and at least 45 of the 50 states were said to have one or more middle schools in operation.[15]

A survey of administrators of schools in New York State employing either the 4-4-4 or 5-3-4 organization reported by Curtis in March 1966 reflected the movement toward middle schools in New York State and a generally favorable attitude of administrators toward this development.[16] Curtis later provided one of the authors a list of middle schools operating in New York State as of May 1966; this list included 33 schools—25 retained "Junior High School" in their name, 5 had a name including "Middle School," and 3 had neither designation.

Although precise data are not available as to the total number of new school organizations developed in relation to the desegregation effort in urban centers, undoubtedly this factor has contributed significantly to the middle school movement. In a 1966 report, *The Schoolhouse in the City,* note was made of the "emergence of the 'middle school' as a replacement for the junior high school"; it was stated that in the cities the real force behind this movement "is the drive to eliminate *de facto* segregation."[17] This report identified New Haven, New York, and Pittsburgh as systems committed to such a reorganization and stated that "similar plans are in various stages of discussion or action in other cities."[18] Other purposes of these reorganizations more clearly relevant to the emergent middle school were also cited in this report and will be commented upon later in this chapter.

A more comprehensive survey was attempted by Cuff.[19] For his purposes a middle school was defined as having grades 6 and 7 and not extending below grade 4 or above grade 8. Information he received from 36 state departments of education and from reports in various publications yielded data about middle schools in 44 states; specifically he reported that 446 public school districts in 29 states were operating 499 middle schools as defined. *The present authors' survey (see Chapter 9) found that the number of schools in 1967–1968 was more than double—about 1100.* Cuff further observed, "The number of middle schools is presently in-

[15]Pearl Brod, "Middle School: Trends toward Adoption," *The Clearing House,* 40: 331–333 (February 1966).

[16]T. E. Curtis, "Administrators View the Middle School," *High Points,* 48:30–35 (March 1966).

[17](New York: Educational Facilities Laboratories, 1966), pp. 9–10.

[18]*The Schoolhouse in the City,* p. 10.

[19]William A. Cuff, "Middle Schools on the March," *Bulletin* of the NASSP, 51:82–86 (February 1967).

creasing, accompanied by a decrease in the number of junior high schools. Several state education officials reported middle schools in the process of planning or construction."[20] However, this survey, and the others cited (but see Chapter 9), did not probe into the reasons for the organizations or reorganizations identified, and cannot be considered as adequate evidence that the new or different grade structures really include a middle school organization and program of the emergent type we identified earlier in this chapter. Cuff did note a trend toward a middle school planning. As to grade organization, he reported these data: 5-3-4, 55 percent; 4-4-4, 30 percent; 3-5-4, 9 percent; 5-2-5, 4-3-5, 3-4-5, scattered.

These various partial surveys, as already noted, give evidence only that there is a movement away from the 6-3-3 and other traditional grade organizations to various other patterns. It is clear that many school districts are seeking, for reasons analyzed here and in Chapter 9, an organization different from the dominant one. In some of these efforts there is believed to be the concern for the "in-betweener" that we consider characteristic of the truly emergent middle school. Varying the grade organization will not alone satisfy this concern, but widespread variations do seem symptomatic of a dissatisfaction with existing school structures, especially in the middle of the school ladder.

This current movement toward diversity in grade plan is well illustrated by this report on "The Schools in Between":

A Richmond, Calif., citizens committee has recently recommended a change-over in that city to a 4-4-4 middle school arrangement to reduce de facto segregation, or, at least, limit it to elementary schools. The Portland, Ore., school staff has submitted a long-range plan to its school board for conversion to a 6-2-4 plan, using 30 of the city's 90 elementary schools as the new middle schools. New York City will have completed changing its junior high schools to middle schools by 1972. And even the small school systems are turning to this new organization— Radnor Township, Pa., has just adopted a five-year plan that will convert old and proposed buildings to a K-5 plan for the elementary schools, and a 6–8 and 9–12 for the remaining grades.[21]

WHY A NEW MIDDLE SCHOOL?

In addition to reviewing such published materials as are available on the theory and practice of new middle schools, the authors have questioned numerous middle school administrators and examined materials from their schools to search out the reasons for their establishment. A plethora of reasons is revealed, usually more than one for the same

[20]Cuff, p. 84.
[21]*Education USA*, April 17, 1967, p. 201.

school. The most extensive such list of beliefs about middle school children and their school we examined includes the following statements, selected by us (from a total of fifteen) as illustrative of the reasons most frequently given:

(2) Rather than consider these years as best for reinforcement, they should be considered as crucial—for at this age the pupil is establishing his attitude towards learning. He must, therefore, be challenged with new and interesting ideas, materials and concepts.

(4) Knowledge has exploded to the point where no one teacher can, or should be expected to teach all subjects. Specialized teachers working in teams provide the best method of educating these youngsters.

(6) The middle school youngster must have an individualized program. Probably at no other time in the educational ladder will one find such a tremendous range of social, physical and intellectual development. Grouping in the middle school must be flexible and suited to the child's educational history and potential.

(8) The middle school allows its pupils to be introduced to new areas at an earlier and more crucial stage in their lives. For example, our sixth graders will start foreign languages, industrial arts, homemaking, secondary mathematics and science, and have the proper equipment and teachers available to them.

(10) The middle school will attract and hold superior teachers interested in being part of an exciting, challenging undertaking. The faculty will consist of subject matter specialists who have the desire and ability to work with growing minds. Although we have only had a middle school for six months we have already attracted the attention of placement officers throughout the area.

(12) The middle school will allow Pearl River to create a four year high school. Traditionally high schools have considered the ninth grade as the beginning of secondary education and educators have long supported this type of organization.

(14) The middle school will help prevent the academic, athletic and social pattern of high school from being forced down on less mature adolescents.[22]

Review of such statements of rationale for numerous middle schools suggests three principal lines of justification which have major, direct implications for the program of the emergent middle school:

1. To provide a program especially adapted to the wide range of individual differences and special needs of the "in-between-ager."

2. To create a school ladder arrangement that promotes continuity of education from school entrance to exit.

3. To facilitate through a new organization, the introduction of needed innovations in curriculum and instruction.

[22]Raymond J. Gerson, "Rationale for a Middle School" (unpublished manuscript, Pearl River, N.Y., Pearl River Middle School, April 1965), pp. 2–4.

In addition to these major, program-related considerations, various specific factors, in some cases almost extraneous to the educational program, have markedly affected the genesis of new middle schools.

Focus on the Individual

The Pearl River statement just cited notes further that: "The focus of the school is on the individual—the program is flexible." This focus on the wide range of individual differences and needs of the "in-between-ager" is stated or implied in many of the plans and proposals for new middle schools. The Educational Facilities Laboratories report, *Middle Schools,* summarized this argument well in this paragraph:

In general, the proponents of the middle school envisage a school adapted to a range of children who, rampant individualists though they are, seem to have more in common with each other than with elementary-school children as a group, or high-schoolers as a group. The school would assume that, in general, its population had some mastery of the tools of learning but was not ready for the academic specialization of high school (and its attendant college-preparation pressures). The school could concentrate, then, on provisions for individual differences, so long touted, so little effected by American education, taking particular account of the increased sophistication and knowledge of today's 10-or-11- to 14-year-olds over previous generations.[23]

The following excellent description of the middle school youngster and the implications of his characteristics for the new Fox Lane School, Bedford, New York, was included in an early report of the original planning for this school:

The Middle School youngster is to be valued in this school for what he is: a preadolescent emerging from childhood in slow stages, sometimes awkward and insecure, sometimes facile and adept, frequently concerned with self-assessment, often amazed by newly-developing powers, constantly in need of appropriate opportunities for exploration and venture, sometimes capable of adult behavior and responses, and frequently in need of opportunities for trial-and-error in situations where error is acceptable.

This implies that the school environment and program must differ in certain fundamental respects from the elementary school of his previous experience and the high school he later will attend. Its facilities must be more varied and complex than an elementary school's, yet they need not be as elaborate nor on the same scale as those of the high school. The atmosphere must be suited to the social as well as intellectual needs of the youngsters, providing more opportunity for social exchange than the lower school but setting more limits than an upper

[23]Judith Murphy, *Middle Schools* (New York: Educational Facilities Laboratories, 1965), p. 15.

school. The total range of academic offerings should, in a middle school, be more readily accessible to the youngsters than in a high school, where a degree of specialization in one or another branch of studies is progressively countenanced.[24]

This rationale of the Fox Lane School was pinpointed in a February 15, 1967, letter to one of the authors from its principal, Neil P. Atkins, in this sentence: "The Fox Lane Middle School was built primarily to promote a more realistic attempt to cope with the enormous educational variability characteristic of 11 to 13 year olds by making instruction more individual than we have been able to do heretofore—at least here in Bedford."

Individualization is also emphasized in a 1966 report of the Barrington, Illinois, Middle School:

In the Barrington Grade School System, K through 5 provides students with the basic building blocks of the educational process. The Middle School, 6 through 8, serves as a catalyst, helping the students use these building blocks in new ways and in new combinations to solve problems; in short, to plumb the possibilities of their own minds and talents. This is easier said than done. Pre-adolescents and young teens are restless, curious and possess extreme differences. Their uneven growth patterns on the physical, mental, emotional and social levels create very real challenges to the dedicated educator. With this in mind, the team teaching concepts are used to meet individual student needs in greater depth. At the same time they sharpen the educational proficiency of individual teachers. In this sense, Barrington Middle School is not a "junior high" school, or a pre-prep school for the university. Rather, it guides students to the discovery of their innate capacities through a more individualized involvement in the learning process.[25]

This first and most significant reason for establishing new middle schools—"focus on the individual," we are labeling it—has two aspects one must understand in analyzing the movement. First, there is the attempt to focus on the population of in-between-agers as they differ from children in the earlier elementary school and adolescents in the later high school. Although this focus is needed and is being sought, we have already emphasized, and will dwell on in Chapter 2, the futility of prescribing an exact age or grade range that would include all in-betweeners. This caution leads to the second aspect, namely, the fact of tremendous variability among the in-between-age population. Thus, individualization because of variability must be coupled with a broad focus on the somewhat unique characteristics of this population. Focus on the individual means then focusing on individual students whose chief characteristic as a group is

---

[24] *Middle School: A Report of Two Conferences on the Definition of Its Purpose, Its Spirit, and Its Shape* (Mt. Kisco, N.Y.: Bedford Public Schools, 1962), p. 19.

[25] *Barrington Middle School: A Report* (Barrington, Ill.: Barrington Public Schools, 1966), p. 5.

that of variability within a wide range of later childhood, preadolescence, and early adolescence.

Greater Continuity

Much of the reasoning behind the establishment of new middle schools seems the same as that originally given for the junior high school. This similarity is particularly striking with regard to the problem of continuity. Increase continuity, decrease the separateness of elementary and secondary education, ease the transition by a junior high school—it was argued. But over a little more than a half century after the first junior high schools were established, there are the recurring arguments that the junior high school has become too much like the high school, that the transition from elementary to junior high school is too abrupt for many children, and that what is needed is a continuous program of schooling as little interrupted as possible by breaks between levels. Hence it is really a complete reorganization of the school organizational ladder that many school systems are seeking, so as to reduce breaks and increase continuity. Note a further statement to this end from the Pearl River Schools:

> The goal of the Pearl River Public Schools is that the separate units (elementary, middle school, and high school) should operate as though they were, in fact, one. Relationships between the units, continuity in program, and intrafaculty coordination should all function so that the transfer of a child from one unit to the next will be a smooth, efficient step for each of our boys and girls. The creation of the middle school has been a significant step in furthering the education of the youth of Pearl River.

The establishment of a K4-4-4 plan several years ago in Saginaw, Michigan, was reported to have been based on study of the best break points in a thirteen-year program of schooling:

> There are those who advocate that the perfect school would be that in which all students, kindergarten through the 12th grade, are present. This theory has obvious merit. Nonetheless, it has certain obstacles. Most school communities must break the 13 year sequence in terms of their ability to finance school facilities in the face of exploding populations.
> As we studied the 320 physical, mental, emotional and social growth characteristics and teaching implications for boys and girls, from kindergarten through the 12th grade, we concluded that there were centers of similarity in this 13 year span that merited close study. We observed that the kindergarten youngster and the first, second, third and fourth grade youngsters had more of these growth characteristics in common. We noted further that the growth characteristics of boys and girls at the age levels represented in the fifth, sixth, seventh and eighth grades also had great areas of similarity. We felt, too, that the age level repre-

sented by the ninth, tenth, eleventh and twelfth graders in terms of those growth characteristics had large areas of similarity.

In addition, there were strong indications from the Edsel Ford Foundation Curriculum Study in Dearborn that the four-year high school (since tradition forces these four years to be considered for college entrance) ought to be under one hat or in one institution, rather than having the ninth grade in a separate institution. These conclusions led us to establish the primary school, which includes kindergarten through Grade 4, the middle school with Grades 5 through 8, and the four-year high school with Grades 9 through 12.[26]

This total reorganization reasoning also involves reconsideration of the place of grade 9 and of grades 5 and 6. As just illustrated, there is substantial support for retaining or returning to the four-year high school which dominated practice until the 6-3-3 plan became more popular than the 8-4 plan it has never completely replaced. Another, practical type of reasoning for returning grade 9 to the high school is stated in this excerpt from a 1967 letter written by a Midwestern high school principal to one of the authors:

We feel that our present 10–12 program would be strengthened by adding grade 9 to the high school. For example, our present junior high school facilities in industrial arts are not large enough to permit a strong 7–9 program. Our senior high industrial arts program is almost non-existent. We do, however, have a very strong trades and industries program throughout grades 10–12. By combining grade 9 with the senior high, it is anticipated that there would be less resistance to providing shop facilities for a comprehensive program at the senior high school.

The authors' information from several school districts entirely supports a summary statement regarding the four-year high school argument, in the Educational Facilities Laboratories report: "A marked tendency among some educators to retain or restore the 4-year high for purely educational reasons also contributes to acceptance of the 4-4-4 concept."[27]

A strong statement to one of the authors by a superintendent of a small suburban school system in the East is an excellent summation of the argument for a different organization to aid the continuity of learning of younger students:

I think the forgotten youngsters in today's educational planning are the ten and eleven year olds—or expressed in grade equivalents, the fifth and sixth graders. The exploratory and extension of skills philosophies have done very well by our

---

[26]George E. Mills, "The How and Why of Middle Schools," *Nation's Schools,* 68:43, 45 (December 1961).

[27]Murphy, *Middle Schools,* p. 7.

twelves, and thirteens, and fourteens, over the past two decades. Our senior high students have always had more than their share at the educational feeding trough.

The tens and elevens, however, suffer from two extremes. On the one hand they are smothered by love from well meaning primary oriented teachers, and on the other they are clubbed by perhaps not-so-well meaning administrators who see preparation for high school, graduation, and admission to colleges as the *summum bonum* of the educational enterprise. Tens and elevens should neither be smothered by today's typical elementary teacher nor educationally browbeaten by the college prep rat race that now and again pops up in our elementary and junior high planning.

What do these kids need then? I'm not certain, but try these for openers:

1. They desperately need an escape from the female syndrome that permeates their early school years. We need more honest to goodness men in these years so that little girls and boys grow up with the clear understanding that education isn't a sex linked trait. Between commuting schedules, cocktail parties, and the ever growing one parent family it is no wonder that children grow up believing in a matriarchal society.

2. The educational development of boys is different from that of girls. An evolving middle school program ought to take cognizance of these differences instead of hiding them in group achievement results to the detriment of both boys and girls. What, for example, would happen if boys began their formal educational experiences one year later than girls?

3. An instructional program for tens and elevens should capitalize upon the highly developed inquisitiveness which these children possess. They are indeed still children, but they are now literate children whose interests and desires to know range far beyond the borough hall and the municipal zoo. We ought to capitalize on their interests through the use of learning resource centers, laboratories, meaningful field trips, etc.

4. All teachers from kindergarten up should be sensitive to learning problems of children and plan for their remediation. However, for those youngsters who reach ten or eleven or twelve and still have learning disabilities the middle school should sharply focus a battery of specialized educational personnel and tools on the problems. This means a substantial increase in specialized services over what we now consider adequate. Perhaps a third of a middle school staff should be composed of such specialists.

If I were asked to name a middle school span in a thirteen year sequence, I would probably divide it five-four-four. This would cluster fives through nines, tens through thirteens, and fourteens through seventeens.[28]

The problem of continuity becomes especially acute as different levels of the school system explore ungraded arrangements. In fact, widespread gropings for ungraded organization would in effect give each individual his own system of rungs on the school ladder. Current theories and practices of continuous progress necessitate a school ladder that lacks definite

[28]Letter dated September 10, 1965, from Bill A. Bost to William M. Alexander.

age and grade breaks. Although few middle schools are without some type of graded organization, their planning may involve a total review of the entire school ladder and the introduction of greater flexibility in the individual's progression. This possibility seems the chief hope of school reorganizers who would work for greater continuity of education from school entry to school termination.

More Rapid Change

The justification of a middle school organization as a means of accelerating the change process in education appears less frequently in the literature and in school reports and other publications. Nevertheless, our contacts with school administrators and other personnel involved in the middle school movement suggest that this is a very real factor in many school districts. The belief that it is easier to innovate in a new than in an old organization is widespread. Thus a release on "Why the Middle School?" from East Orange, New Jersey, stated: "The school organization which we feel will best provide the facilities, flexibility, staff utilization and climate for developing change and to improve the quality of learning and instruction in 5th grade through 8th, is the 'Middle School concept.' "[29] Similarly, a letter to one of the authors from a middle school principal lists this among various reasons for the middle school: "It will provide, if for no other reason, an opportunity to reevaluate our educational philosophy. We can then include those features which are educationally sound and eliminate those which have not weathered the storm."

Other Reasons

Many factors besides the three just described have entered into the establishment of the new middle schools. We have already commented on the use of the 4-4-4 plan in certain Eastern cities, and possibly elsewhere, as a means of desegregating schools earlier. Thus the New York City Board of Education's Statement of Policy on "Excellence for the Schools of New York City" of April 28, 1965, noted that: "The intermediate school will add an extra ingredient of excellence—the sharing of learning experiences and life values with other children of different races, nationalities and economic status."[30]

A very frequent reason, or perhaps it is more an excuse, for the middle school organization relates to building and enrollment problems. For

[29]Joseph Bongo, "Why the Middle School?" (mimeographed, East Orange, New Jersey: The Schools, May 1966), p. 7.

[30]Quoted in *Primary School-Intermediate School-Four-Year Comprehensive High School: Committee Recommendations to the Superintendent of Schools* (New York City: Public Schools, December 20, 1965), p. 32.

example, one account of the Amory, Mississippi, middle school explains its genesis as follows:

> At Amory, discovery of the middle school concept was the unexpected result of a search for solutions to a problem of overcrowding in the existing schools . . . .
> The new school at Amory was designed to reduce the existing elementary and high schools from six to four grades each, with grades five through eight moving into the new facility. But the plan was more than a simple regrouping of classes from a 6-6 to a 4-4-4 pattern; it also represents a rejection of the junior-high concept, and made possible a more widespread use of such experimental techniques as nongraded classes, ability grouping, team teaching and individual self-study.[31]

General observation suggests that, as at Amory, planning for a new building frequently opens a wedge into a new school program. Perhaps the building problem's influence on many decisions toward the new middle school organization may lead to greatly improved programs for "in-between-agers" and also for younger and older groups. However, there are exceptions to such generalizations and hopes; for example, this explanation came from a school district that, after study, chose not at the time to move into a middle school organization:

> We did read a great deal about the middle school, talked to administrators in districts in which they existed, and attended an all-day conference sponsored by the state Education Department. It was a pretty uniform feeling that most schools had gone into middle schools because it seemed the best decision in terms of building needs. A typical case is that of one neighboring district. A new high school was built. Grades 5-8 were moved into the old, but good, high school building. I asked the principal what he felt he was able to offer in the instructional program of the middle school for fifth and sixth graders that he could not offer in the K-6 structure. His answer was that now the kids could take showers and they had a bigger gym. Since we have large modern elementary schools with gyms, showers, and impressive libraries, a change in structure would have no such advantage for us.

One suspects, too, that in some school districts, unlike the one from which we just quoted, there may be a band-wagon factor. Undoubtedly, word of a new middle school in a neighboring community or of some widely publicized middle school program does precipitate discussion of its possibilities in other communities.

However unrelated the original reason for a middle school may be to the educational program, school evaluation and planning can, should, and frequently do accompany reorganization. If so, the new organization and program can be tied to the larger rationale we have suggested. With-

[31]"Amory's Middle School," *Southern Education Report,* 1:27-28 (November-December 1965).

out evaluation and planning, little change or improvement in the total educational program or in that for the "in-between-ager" can rightfully be expected. The authors are inclined to believe that, whether or not new structures eventuate from rigorous evaluation, the evaluation process itself should result in some school improvement. Hence we would list as a major reason for any school reorganization the impetus given to program evaluation, planning, and improvement. The data reported in Chapter 9 tend to support this argument.

AIMS OF THE EMERGENT MIDDLE SCHOOL: SUMMARY

The aims of the emergent middle school, as we have defined it, have been stated or implied, at least in general terms, throughout the previous sections of this chapter. We now summarize these aims, as identified and accepted by the authors:

1. To serve the educational needs of the "in-between-agers" (older children, preadolescents, early adolescents) in a school bridging the elementary school for childhood and the high school for adolescence.

2. To provide optimum individualization of curriculum and instruction for a population characterized by great variability.

3. In relation to the foregoing aims, to plan, implement, evaluate, and modify, in a continuing curriculum development program, a curriculum which includes provision for: (a) a planned sequence of concepts in the general education areas; (b) major emphasis on the interests and skills for continued learning; (c) a balanced program of exploratory experiences and other activities and services for personal development; and (d) appropriate attention to the development of values.

4. To promote continuous progress through and smooth articulation between the several phases and levels of the total educational program.

5. To facilitate the optimum use of personnel and facilities available for continuing improvement of schooling.

TOWARD CHAPTERS 2–10

Based on the definition of the emergent middle school presented in the foregoing pages, the following chapters deal further with its justification, program, and implementation. Part II documents the case for a new middle school as outlined above, by reviewing evidence regarding it in Chapter 2 from the standpoint of human growth and development, and in Chapter 3 from the standpoint of the inadequacies of the 6-3-3 organization. Part III describes existing programs and projects possible new ones in the middle school, with attention in Chapter 4 to its curriculum plan, in Chapter 5 to teaching, and in Chapter 6 to the organization and staff. Part IV looks toward evaluating and developing further the emergent middle school as we have conceived it; Chapter 7 is devoted to its evaluation and Chapter 8 to further implementation of the middle school concept. Part V includes a full report of a survey completed in 1968 of the current status of middle schools, with Chapter 9 presenting the facts and Chapter 10 case descriptions of a sample of these schools.

PART II

The Case for a New Middle School

Chapter 2

From the Standpoint
of Human Growth
and Development

A national ferment is giving rise to new ways of organizing schools to evoke more effective learning among pupils. Nor is the concern only to make it possible for disadvantaged children and youth to compete successfully with their more fortunate classmates. The challenge is to ensure greater learning and a richer, more balanced development for all, with meaningful continuity from the nursery school to the graduate school.

The intensity with which this ferment is coming into focus on pupils who are in transition from easily distinguishable childhood to the reproductive maturation characteristic of entry into adolescence has been documented in Chapter 1. The intent to do a serious job of changing the process by which learning occurs marks this ferment. It is thought that much learning time can be saved. Many pupils may become essentially independent learners. Some will become skilled solvers of problems, others, explorers and creators, in the arts as well as in the sciences.

A truly effective school program, regardless of the level of schooling at which it is directed, must be based on knowledge about the learner who is to be served by the school. The curriculum worker cannot divorce himself from the behavioral sciences and hope, through divine insight, to plan and facilitate an instructional program which will result in the type of end product society seeks. By the same token, those segments of the behavioral sciences which concern themselves with the role of education in human development must align themselves with curricular and instructional specialists in order that their mutual efforts may result in optimum provisions for each and every student.

INCREASING KNOWLEDGE ABOUT THE TRANSITION FROM CHILDHOOD TO ADOLESCENCE

Fortunately, many more validated facts about the genetic, physiological, psychological, and cultural dynamics acting in and upon children going through major transition to adolescence are now available. When the junior high schools were set into motion more than fifty years ago, available facts were of a highly generalized nature. Research data gave the average height and weight, together with standard deviations, of children and youth at each chronological age covered by elementary and secondary education. This succession of averages made growth appear both gradual and even throughout childhood and adolescence. On the basis of these data so fine a scholar as Alexander Inglis,[1] for example, advanced the thesis that gradual and even development of individuals was the factual and reasonable basis for planning the work of both the junior and senior high schools. Inglis' interpretations assumed that normal individual development followed the averages of growth shown by large samples of children and youth at each successive chronological age.

A quarter century before, G. Stanley Hall[2] had studied a relatively small number of persons as they passed from childhood into adolescence. His penetrating observations indicated that this period was one of swiftly accelerated growth, followed by equally swift deceleration of the growth rate. He gathered case data which showed that many young people suffered considerable anxiety about their growth and about their new organic functions during this period. He claimed that his subjects went through times of emotional turbulence, erratic behavior, and independent assertiveness during this transition period. All of these insights were repudiated by educators during the two decades when junior high schools were in their formative period. It was felt that research had validated the idea that transition from childhood to adolescence posed no special problems for the pupils, except as individuals lacked intellectual capacity or carried special personal adjustment problems. A counselor or two could take care of pupils "who had problems."

In the 1920s and 1930s, anthropologists, physiologists, psychologists, and sociologists began new studies of human growth and development. Multidiscipline, longitudinal studies began. Data of many different kinds

---

[1] *The Secondary School* (Boston: Ginn & Company, 1921).
[2] *Adolescence* (2 vols.; New York: Appleton-Century-Crofts, 1904).

were gathered about the same individuals through a period of years. The physical and organic development, the development of interpersonal relationships among peers, the evolution of relationships with families, the learning of reading, languages, and arithmetic skills, the development of intelligence, the expression of emotions, and the evolution of concepts of self—all these kinds of changes in human beings were studied by teams of specialists who gathered data about the same individuals through periods of from eight to thirty-five years. These records of how *individuals* grow, develop, and evolve are now available to us. These records make it possible for us to see how individual persons vary from each other as they go through their transition from childhood to adolescence.

As happens too often in education, there is a twenty-five year lag between the availability of valid scientific knowledge and its functional application in the educative process. This is particularly true if the new information requires a fundamental rethinking of factors that influence learning with consequent changes in ways the learning process is organized, stimulated, and guided. For example, between 1936 and 1966, a number of definitive longitudinal studies of the growth of boys and girls and of concomitant physical, social, and psychological phenomena were published. Almost no perceptible impact on education occurred until the emergence of ungraded, flexibly scheduled and individual progress oriented experimental schools within recent years.

What has gradually become apparent is that childhood is a well-marked period in human development. During this period growth is rather steady in pace, marked by the gradual increase in capacities to learn and to do. The growth and developmental processes impose no dramatic changes in behaviors expected of youngsters and therefore no pressing adjustment problems. Rather, our society imposes the learning tasks. The adjustment problems met are due more to illness, to organic defects, learning limitations, culturally imposed learning demands that are inappropriate to the child's background and capacities, familial disorders, and societal disorders such as social class and caste discriminations.

While all these bases for adjustment problems persist through the period of transition from childhood into adolescence, other very significant behavioral requirements and developmental adjustment problems are imposed unavoidably by the growth process itself and by its outcomes. These new developmental tasks and adjustment problems are caused by physiological changes in the functioning of the body, by changes in perceptions of the self that inevitably accompany these growth and physiological alterations of the body dynamics, by changes in modes of cognitive functioning, and by ways in which home, school, and other social institutions view the individual and deal with these changes.

The transitional period, usually of from a three- to five-years duration, is marked by:

1. Differences in physical maturity levels within each sex and between sexes, as well as changes in physiological functioning, which are greater than those occurring at any other time during the growth cycle.

2. The gradual emergence of a more adult-like mode of intellectual functioning.

3. Psychological and social reorientation more traumatic than that of any similar period of growth.

This chapter intends to look at available scientific data about young persons in transition from childhood to adolescence. The authors agree that an individual is much more than a sum of his characteristics. He is, indeed, a product of the transaction of these several components with the environment. For the purposes of a discussion of the learner, however, it is necessary to segment the contributing characteristics into the three distinct areas alluded to above—physical, intellectual, and psycho-social. Each of these will be discussed in sequence.

PHYSICAL DEVELOPMENT

The Pattern of Growth

There is a blueprint of growth which all human beings follow. This genetic blueprint determines the position and sequence in which each body part is differentiated and in which its growth goes on in relation to all other body parts. The blueprint is the same for all boys and for all girls. But the rate, or speed, with which different individual bodies are built in accord with this blueprint varies tremendously from one family to another. While most people go through this process of physical development at an average pace, other *perfectly normal* persons mature much earlier and other equally normal persons mature much later than the average. Varieties in the rate of proceeding through the blueprint of body growth and development are completely normal and healthy and are caused by inherited factors through family lines coupled with environmental factors such as nutrition, diseases and illness, and exercise.

One of the most conspicuous characteristics of body development is the marked change in the rate of growth that occurs before pubescence and again after pubescence. For some children there is rapid acceleration for one year, a maintenance of the rapid pace during another year, and a gradual decrease over an additional year. For these children pubescence may occur at around the age of fourteen years. For another child of the same sex the pattern may be the same, but the period of time involved may be approximately half that required for some other child—two years instead of four.

Each of the pupils in the Adolescent Growth Study of the University of California at Berkeley went through this pattern of change of rate, with acceleration of growth before pubescence and deceleration of growth following pubescence.[3] The same pattern of growth characterized the young people in the Harvard Growth Study[4] and in numerous other longitudinal studies of physical growth including those reported by Bayer and Bayley[5] and by Shuttleworth.[6] All of these studies corroborate each other in showing that the duration of the period is from three and a half to five years. This is the period during which the greatest amount of physical, psychological, and social change will occur in each individual, along with the natural stress that accompanies these changes.

While this period of transition occurs in all children, its timing, that is, the chronological ages at which it occurs, varies markedly from one child to another.

Early and Late Maturing Patterns

The University of California Adolescent Study indicates differences between the rates of growth for early and late maturing children. The investigators found that some male children entered the period of transition before or by the age of ten years; the transition period for these children continued until the ages of thirteen to thirteen and a half years, when they were designated adolescents. Other boys were found to enter the transitional phase of growth only at the age of thirteen and a half years, reaching pubescence at the age of fifteen or fifteen and a half.[7] In other words, boys are seen to enter the period of transition at ages varying from ten to thirteen and a half years. This means that girls will enter this period from the ages of eight and a half years to eleven and a half years. It also means that transition is begun by the earliest maturing girls in the third grade and by the earliest maturing boys in the fourth grade. Likewise, pubescence is reached by early maturing girls in the fifth grade and by the early maturing boys in the sixth grade. If we regard adolescence as clearly marked from a period of six months after pubescence, then late maturing

[3]Herbert R. Stolz and Lois M. Stolz, *The Somatic Development of Adolescent Boys* (New York: Crowell-Collier and Macmillian Company, 1951).

[4]F. K. Shuttleworth, "The Physical and Mental Growth of Boys and Girls Age Six to Nineteen," in *Monographs of the Society for Research in Child Development,* Vol. IV, No. 3 (Washington, D.C.: National Research Council, 1939).

[5]S. M. Bayer and Nancy Bayley, *Growth Diagnosis* (Chicago: University of Chicago Press, 1959).

[6]Shuttleworth.

[7]Herbert R. Stolz, "An Atlas of Specimen Photographs and Graphs to Illustrate Certain Aspects of Development among Boys during the Cycle of Puberty," (University of California Adolescent Study, on file at the Child Study Center, University of California, and the Division of Child Development, University of Chicago, 1939).

girls end the period of transition only in grade 10 and late maturing boys in grade 12. Obviously, the grades during which virtually all children are at some stage in the period of transition are grades 5 through 8. Since some girls begin the transition period as early as grade 3, and some boys terminate it only in grade 12, variation among pupils in physical maturity level will be greatest in grades 5 through 8, although not all pupils will undergo their whole transition periods within these years. There will be some who terminate later, but a *majority* will go through this period during grades 5 through 8, and *all* will be in some stage of transition during these grades.

Range of Differences in Maturity Level in the Same Grade

Another way of bringing out the tremendous range of differences among children in the same classroom during the transition period would be to note that:

1. Some fifth-grade girls already are biologically and physiologically fifteen years old—usual for girls at the ninth-grade level.
2. Some fifth-grade boys still are biologically and physiologically only seven years old—usual for boys at the second-grade level.
3. Some eighth-grade boys are biologically and physiologically seventeen-year-olds, and some eighth-grade girls, nineteen-year-olds— usual for seniors in high school or freshmen at college.
4. Some eighth-grade boys are only ten years old biologically and physiologically, while some eighth-grade girls are only twelve years old physically and in terms of physiological dynamics—usual for fifth-graders.

These facts show simply that organic maturity in the fifth grade ranges from seven to fifteen years of age, a spread of eight years. In the eighth grade the range covers a span of nine years, from age ten in the earliest maturing girl to age nineteen in the latest maturing boy. In subsequent grades the differences among pupils in organic maturity levels swiftly become less as more and more pupils reach reproductive maturation. The data establish a range of eight to nine years in the physical maturity levels of children in each grade from 5 through 8, with the range of maturity levels decreasing at each subsequent grade level in the senior high school.

Physiological Changes during the Transition Period

The anterior lobe of the pituitary gland, which is located in the head just below the brain, produces several hormones that are of vital importance to an understanding of the "period of transition" through which all children pass in moving from childhood into postpubescent adolescence. This period is launched by an increase in one of these hormones—the growth hormone.[8] This hormone stimulates the over-all growth of bones and tissue which brings each individual to his maximum normal size. If too little of this hormone is produced, one sort of dwarfism occurs. If too much is produced, pituitary gigantism ensues. The increment curves, previously discussed, which showed sharp acceleration in growth in standing height, the maintenance of the fast rate for a year or two, and then the rapid decrease in the rate of over-all growth indicated the external results of a sharp increase in this hormone, its maintenance in the greater amount and then its rapid quantitative decrease. In other words, the prepubescent growth spurt is caused by a considerable increase in the growth-stimulating hormone of the pituitary gland, and the subsequent decrease in the rate of growth is caused by the subsequent slowdown in the production of this hormone by the pituitary.

The second pituitary hormone that dramatically influences the period of transition from childhood to postpubescent adolescence is the gonadotrophic hormone. When the production of this gonad-stimulating hormone is increased, it causes the immature gonads to grow and become fully functioning ovaries or testes. As the gonads grow toward maturity, they, in turn, begin to produce hormones of their own which have their own impact on growth. In the girl the ovarian hormones stimulate the growth of the mammary glands, uterus, Fallopian tubes, and vagina, and axillary and pubic hair and the development of a "feminine figure." The male gonadal hormones stimulate the growth of the male sexual apparatus, including the penis, prostate gland, seminal vesicles, and scrotum. They likewise stimulate the development of secondary male sexual characteristics, such as change of voice pitch, growth of the beard, and the growth of pubic and axillary hair.

As the ovaries approach their full development the menarche, or first menstruation, occurs in girls. At the same developmental stage of the testes, boys begin to experience nocturnal emissions. Thus, both boys and girls have dramatic testimony from their bodies, both through growth phenomena and function changes, that the day when they will be able to reproduce the species is rapidly approaching. Indeed, it is seldom more than a year after the first menstruation that a girl can conceive.

The maturation and full function of the gonads seem also to be the factors that dry up the pituitary growth-stimulating hormone and so check growth in standing height. If the gonads mature early in the person's life and their secretions are copious, therefore, the individual will

[8]W. W. Greulich, "Physical Changes in Adolescence," in *Adolescence,* 43rd Yearbook, Part I (National Society for the Study of Education [Chicago: University of Chicago Press, 1944]).

be relatively short of stature as compared to others with the same family line. Equally, if the full function of the gonads comes rather late, the body, expecially the extremities, will have had a longer period in which to grow, and the person will be relatively tall and long-legged for his family line. Later we shall deal with the relationship of these physiological changes as they relate to psycho-social development during this transitional period from childhood to postpubescent adolescence. Meantime, still other organic changes are occurring.

For example, the full production of gonadal hormones not only checks body growth but it also causes the gradual disappearance of the thymus gland, which lies across the chest of children. With the changes in hormonal balance that accompany the disappearance of the thymus, the full-blown production of gonadal hormones, and some consequent checking of secretions of the anterior lobe of the pituitary gland, changes occur also in thyroid, and possibly in adrenal, functioning. The results are changes in the rate of energy production, or metabolism, changes in blood pressure, and changes in pulse rate. Also, during this transition period there is a progressive rise in systolic blood pressure; this rise stops near the time of the menarche and thereafter maintains a fairly constant level. Pulse rate also rises during the premenarcheal years, reaches a maximum near the menarche, and then decreases. Equally striking is the decrease in basal metabolic rate that customarily follows the menarche.[9]

These organic changes with the accompanying occurrence of menarche and the pubescent growth spurt are appearing at earlier ages than they did at the turn of the century. Tanner[10] reports that the entire growth process has been accelerated. Today's youngsters in the period of transition are much larger than children of the same age some fifty years ago. He reports that data indicate that today's ten-year-olds approximate the size of the twelve-year-old at the time of the birth of the junior high school—1909.

Fluctuation and Change
in the Energy Output Rate

Basal metabolism is, of course, a tricky and somewhat unreliable test to make, especially with young people. However, the data from the University of California Study of Adolescents clearly show the gradual decrease in basal metabolism during the transition period. The average basal metabolism is about 45 calories per square meter of body surface per hour in boys at eleven and a half years of age. By the age of fifteen

[9]N. W. Shock, "The Effect of Menarche on Basal Physiological Functions in Girls," *American Journal of Physiology,* 139:288–291 (1943).

[10]J. M. Tanner, *Education and Physical Growth* (London: University of London Press, 1961).

and a half years this has decreased over 10 percent to about 41 calories per square meter of body surface per hour. Over a four-year period this is a significant decrease in the basal rate of energy transmutation. However, like the changes in rate of physical growth, this gradual decrease in metabolic rate is not characteristic of what happens in individuals. Fluctuations of 5–8 percent occur within a six-month period among some children. The behavioral implication would be that their actions might sometimes show considerable restlessness and at other times a marked listlessness. One should not make too much of this in physiological terms, yet, what seventh- or eighth-grade teacher has not noticed exactly these phenomena in boys or girls during their transitional years? Perhaps what we have tended to make a cause for blame and annoyance actually does have a true basis in fluctuations in physiological functions. When one notes the marked changes in endocrine functions during this period and knows that it is possible to stabilize the hormonal balance only a year or more after pubescence has been reached, it is easier to realize that the marked psychological changes which must occur do so in the context of marked physiological fluctuations coupled with the movement toward a higher level of intellectual functioning.

Tanner[11] reports that the child during the transitional years begins in an apparent state of physical adjustment—a state enjoyed only briefly. The emergence of puberty shatters the stability enjoyed by prepubescent children. The body changes occurring during the fifth- to eighth-grade years cause problems of personal adjustment—especially in a society such as ours in which physical appearance receives such great emphasis. Our physical ideals are constantly brought to our attention through television, movies, and illustrations in novels and periodicals, and even in cigarette and beer advertising.

We have attempted to present a discussion based upon scientific data about the physical development of youngsters as they pass through the transitional period from ten to fourteen years of age. It is essential that the aspects of physical development be borne in mind throughout the ensuing sections in order that an interrelationship between all developmental factors may be recognized.

INTELLECTUAL DEVELOPMENT

The 1960s have witnessed a dynamic increase in the number and quality of contributions of developmental psychologists to our knowledge of the nature of intellectual development. Perhaps the greatest debt owed by educators is that due Jean Piaget and his colleagues for their clinical studies and published reports. A wealth of data is now available as a result

[11] J. M. Tanner, *Growth at Adolescence* (Oxford: Basil Blackwell & Mott, Ltd., 1962).

of the efforts of this Geneva group and the psychologists it has influenced. The developmental psychology of Jean Piaget is a massive contribution which has been reported in great detail in several volumes. Any description of it as a portion of a single chapter must, of necessity, be an overgeneralization. With this limitation in mind, the authors present a discussion for the perusal of those who seek to understand the "middle" school student.

Piaget's translator and interpreter, Flavell, discusses the acquisition of cognitive structures as follows:

> The positive, constructive something which we inherit, Piaget argues, is a *mode of intellectual functioning*. We do not inherit cognitive structures as such; these come into being only in the course of development. What we do inherit is a *modus operandi*, a specific manner in which we transact business with the environment. There are two important general characteristics of this mode of functioning. First, it generates cognitive structures. Structures come into being in the course of intellectual functioning; it is through functioning, and only through functioning, that cognitive structures get formed. Second, and this is a most important point, the mode of functioning which Piaget says constitutes our biological heritage remains essentially constant throughout life. That is, the fundamental properties of intellectual functioning are always and everywhere the same, despite the wide varieties of structuring which this functioning creates.[12]

Piaget views cognitive development as a progression through periods, or stages. The periods are sequential and are invariant in their sequence. Not all persons eventually reach the same level of intellectual development, just as not all persons reach the same level of physical development. Many limiting factors may be involved, including environment, physical development, experiences, and emotions. Movement from one period to another does not occur, therefore, for all people at the same chronological age. The ages Piaget reports as typical of the three periods of development are approximate and are not intended to be conceived as invariant. He divides intellectual development into three periods, or stages: (1) the period of sensory-motor intelligence—birth to two years; (2) the period of preparation for and organization of concrete operations—from two to eleven years; and (3) the period of formal operations—from eleven to fifteen years. Each of these broad periods is further divided into subperiods, which describe the gradual progression from one period to the succeeding one.[13]

We are concerned in a discussion of the preadolescent and the early adolescent with the latter two periods. However, since intellectual devel-

[12]Reproduced from THE DEVELOPMENTAL PSYCHOLOGY OF JEAN PIAGET, by J. Flavell, by permission of Van Nostrand-Reinhold Company, a division of Litton Educational Publishing, Inc., Litton Industries, Princeton, New Jersey, 1963, p. 43.
[13]Flavell, Chapter 5.

opment is sequential and has its roots in the first stage, a brief discussion of the child during this period is apropos. The child in the sensory-motor period develops from the self-world of the newborn infant, characterized by reflex movements and an absence of differentiation of the environment, to a relatively coherent organization of sensory-motor actions. His movements are based largely on trial and error, with success and failure of prime importance. He makes simple perceptual and motor adjustments to things in the immediate environment and has difficulty identifying himself as an entity separate from the objects of his actions. His goals are short-ranged and immediate.

The second of Piaget's stages is that of preparation for and organization of concrete operations. The stage actually begins late in the previous period with the appearance of the first crude attempts at symbolization and concludes during the years of preadolescence with the beginning of formal thought. Piaget divides this period into two major subperiods: (1) preoperational representations—ages two through seven; and (2) concrete operations—ages seven through eleven. During the former, the child begins relatively unorganized and fumbling attempts to come to grips with symbols. Also, during this period the child tends to operate solely in terms of his perceptual field—a type of before-the-eye reality. In the latter subperiod he is beginning to extend his thought from what is viewed as reality to that which is potential reality. He can, for example, anticipate that the sequence of symbols 1, 2, 3, and 4 will be followed by the symbols 5, 6, and 7. His focus, however, is on the immediate present—the world around him. He is, during the latter part of this period—about the ages usually considered typical of grades 5 and 6—making a movement toward the nonpresent or potential. He is beginning to develop the ability to "conserve." He can, for example, recognize that a ball of clay may be changed into a square block of the same substance and contain an equal amount of clay. He cannot, however, conserve weight and volume, even with the same clay object. During the latter subperiod he is beginning to appear as if he possesses a fairly stable and well-ordered conceptual framework which he brings to bear on his immediate environment.

The child in the latter years of the elementary school is not dependent on immediate concrete evidence in understanding and dealing with simple abstractions or ideas about phenomena and objects. Such ideas must be preceded by a background of direct, nonverbal experience with the information from which they are abstracted. Once their meaning is firmly established through past experience, the child is capable of comprehending and utilizing them without any current reference to concrete information. However, he is unable to understand and manipulate relationships between abstractions, or ideas about ideas. Beginning with the period of transition from childhood to adulthood, the child becomes increasingly independent of concrete data and is already into the beginning of the next stage of development.[14]

The period of formal operations—the period of a new and final reorganization—begins at approximately age eleven, for some children even earlier. As was stated previously, the child does not move abruptly from one stage to another. The latter subperiod has provided a preparation and a beginning for the period of formal operations. We again turn to Flavell for enlightenment concerning this transitory route of the child from the subperiod of concrete operations to the period of formal operations:

> Piaget suggests that the route is similar in a general way to that by which the transition from preoperational to concrete-operational thinking was effected: as the child becomes more and more proficient at organizing and structuring problem data with concrete-operational methods, he becomes better and better able to recognize the latter's shortcomings as a device for yielding a complete and logically exhaustive solution. That is, as the child's concrete-operational analyses become sharper and more complete, they present him with gaps, uncertainties, and contradictions which a more impoverished analysis could never have brought to light. Faced with these new problems, the child gropes for new methods of attack.[15]

Most middle school students will either be in the early phases of the period of formal operations or at various phases within the major period itself. The main property of this period is the ability to deal with both the real and the possible. The child considers the problem at hand by first attempting to envision all the possible relations which could hold true in the data. He then attempts, through experimentation and analysis, to seek out the relationships that do indeed hold true. He begins to hypothesize and can go beyond what is perceived as reality to what might be—that which he may discover to be true. He tests hypotheses, discarding those his collected data do not support. From the supported hypotheses other hypotheses are formed and tested. He is able to isolate individual variables and to test combinations thereof.

Flavell enumerates the differences between the periods of concrete operations and formal operations:

> 1. Concrete operations *are* concrete, relatively speaking; their structuring and organizing activity is oriented toward concrete things and events in the immediate present. To be sure, the constitution of concrete-operational systems makes for some movement towards the nonpresent or potential. But this movement is of limited scope and consists mostly of simple generalizations of existing structures to new content . . . . [The concrete-operational child] acts as if his primary task were to organize and order what is immediately present; the limited

[14]Flavell, Chapter 6.

[15]Reproduced from THE DEVELOPMENTAL PSYCHOLOGY OF JEAN PIAGET, by J. Flavell, by permission of Van Nostrand-Reinhold Company, a division of Litton Educational Publishing, Inc., Litton Industries, Princeton, New Jersey, 1963, p. 209.

extrapolation is seen as a special-case activity. What he does not do (and what the [child in the formal operations period] . . . does do) is delineate all possible eventualities at the outset and then try to discover which of these possibilities really do occur in the present data; in this latter strategy, the real becomes a special case of the possible, not the other way around.

2. The fact that the concrete-operational child is still (relatively) bound to the phenomenal here and now results in a second limitation: he has to vanquish the various physical properties of objects and events (mass, weight, length, area, time, etc.) one by one because his cognitive instruments are insufficiently "formal," insufficiently detached and dissociated from the subject matter they bear upon, to permit a content-free, once-for-all structuring . . . .

3. The various concrete-operational systems . . . exist as more or less separate islets of organizations during [this period]; they do not interlock to form a simple integrated system, a system by which the child can readily pass from one substructure to another in the course of a single problem . . . . Just as the various content areas resist a single, one-for-all structuring by the concrete-operational child, so his various cognitive structures—adequate though they may be in their own separate dominions—fail to combine into the unified whole necessary to manage certain complex tasks.[16]

This brief summary of the differences between children in the period of concrete operations and those who have entered the period of formal operations indicates that variations in the present instructional program and its organization should be evolved. Ten- and eleven-year-olds approach problems in a much different manner than do children in the lower elementary grades. They operate on much the same plane as do students in the present junior high school years. It seems logical, therefore, that they be grouped with youngsters in the same general period of intellectual development and that the school program be designed in a manner tailored to their needs and abilities.

A third major category of development involves that which relates to the person as a separate entity in the universe, as well as a person transacting with his environment. It is a matter of personality development which must be viewed within a social milieu.

PERSONALITY DEVELOPMENT

Development of the Self Concept

Combs and Snygg[17] define the "self" as "some unique personality we wish to single out from the rest of mankind. It is a term referring to a specific person and has been indispensable in the historical development of man as a conscious and thinking entity." The term "self concept" is de-

---

[16]Reproduced from THE DEVELOPMENTAL PSYCHOLOGY OF JEAN PIAGET, by J. Flavell, by permission of Van Nostrand-Reinhold Company, a division of Litton Educational Publishing, Inc., Litton Industries, Princeton, New Jersey, 1963, pp. 203–204.

[17]Arthur W. Combs and Donald Snygg, *Individual Behavior* (New York: Harper & Row, Publishers, 1959), p. 123.

fined as an understanding of the self. Although a particular individual may be described from the vantage points of many people—for example, his mother, his brother, his teachers, the scoutmaster, or the children with whom he plays—the self concept is, by definition, based on an internal frame of reference—a perception of the individual confined within the boundaries of his own skin.

The self concept develops from the prenatal period throughout the life span. The prenatal world affords distinct limitations for perceptions. The major development of the self concept begins, therefore, with birth; during the ensuing years, the individual attempts to differentiate the facets of the environment. The first of these differentiations are derived from kinesthetic and tactic actions. The child begins to discern the "me" as opposed to the "not me"—the discovery of self. As language develops, it becomes possible for the child to experience by vicarious means what would otherwise have to be experienced slowly, and often, painfully. As Combs and Snygg point out:

It even makes possible experiences one could never otherwise have. Few of us have the problems of queens or presidents, but we can differentiate and understand them through the spoken or written word. Language provides a "shorthand" by which experience can be symbolized, manipulated, and understood with tremendous efficiency. Above all, the possession of language vastly facilitates the differentiation of self and the world about.[18]

As the developing child experiences the world, his self concept develops. At early ages, his world consists mainly of his home and family. When he enters school, his environment and, hence, his experiences, broaden. Changes in the self concept occur gradually and slowly. At times the individual himself is unaware that major changes have occurred.

The world of the preadolescent and the early adolescent undergoes changes which affect the self concept. The child is in a sort of inbetween world—a world between childhood and adulthood. He begins to view himself as separate from the family and rest of the adult world. Gordon states:

A major task of the preadolescent is to sever his close, dependent relationships with his parents and move out into the world of peers and other adults. This process, begun with entrance into school, assumes more personal significance during the preadolescent years. Going to school was an adult, cultural decision over which the child had no control. Emancipation from the home and defining a new relationship with his parents is the child's decision. This movement away from parents is not completed until the end of adolescence.[19]

[18]Combs and Snygg, pp. 133–134.
[19]Ira J. Gordon, *Human Development: From Birth through Adolescence* (New York: Harper & Row, Publishers, 1962), p. 214.

Teachers are often amazed and concerned by the changes which seem to occur in children during the summer between the fourth and fifth grades. Gone is the child of the fourth grade who accepted the teacher as a supreme authority—an extension of the parents, so to speak. She is no longer a sort of love object to whom the child looks for acceptance and from whom all types of behavior are accepted. In the place of this accepting, loving child is an individual who can differentiate the qualities of teachers he likes or dislikes and can define examples of behavior which result in feelings about teachers. The accompaniment of the severing of the close, dependent relationship with parents seems to be the severing of an accepting and dependent relationship with the teacher. These youngsters are influenced by the behavior of the teachers in terms of the effect of such behavior on them. Each act of teacher behavior directed toward the child affects his understanding of himself—his self concept.

From the viewpoint of the development of the self concept, then, the preadolescent and early adolescent years are related to an expansion of this concept in terms of a shift from parental dependency to the world of adults and the peer group. This is a time of sensitivity and acute perception—a crucial time of preparation for adulthood.

Sex Role Identification

As the developing human being is formulating his self concept, he is also learning what it means to be male or female. It is the basic process through which the youngster learns to think, feel, and act like a member of one sex in contrast to the other sex. In our society children are expected to display certain types of behavior. We define some types of behavior as acceptable for boys but quite unacceptable for girls. The reverse is also true. Boys are expected to be aggressive, rough, unkempt, active, and interested in sports and adventure. Girls, antithetically, are expected to be docile, quiet, ladylike, and interested in things related to domesticity. Aggressive acts such as pushing a classmate, although generally not condoned in school, are expected of boys. The identical act performed by a girl is interpreted as an act of hostile aggression. Tears used by a male child, on the other hand, may be met with parental statements such as, "Only babies and girls cry—not big boys."

The learning of the sex role begins early in life. Boys and girls are treated differently even at very early ages. Little girls are given feminine toys, for example, dolls, playhouses, nurse kits, toy dishes; boys, masculine toys such as trucks, toy soldiers, toy guns, tool kits, and the like. The child who behaves in accordance with the expectations of his sex will hear comments designed to reinforce the desirable behavior, such as: "That's a good girl!" "Don't be a bad boy!" or "That's just like Daddy does it!"

In learning to identify with (to think, feel, and act like) members of one's own sex, the developing child passes through what Freudian psychologists[20] refer to as the Oedipal stage. This term is derived from the myth concerning an individual's erotic love for the parent of the opposite sex. (For females it is sometimes referred to as the Electra complex or stage, a term derived from a similar character in ancient mythology.) At first children of both sexes identify with the mother. It is she who cares for the child. Quite early she appears to the child to be merely an extension of his own body. Around the age of three the male child discovers that his mother's sexual structure differs from his, and girls discover that they lack part of the male anatomy. As children proceed through the Oedipal stage, the boy develops an erotic attachment for his mother, the girl, for her father. Siblings may become rivals for the mother's attention, but the father is the boy's formidable rival who interferes with the boy having the mother all to himself. At about the age of six years the Oedipal stage becomes latent and continues until puberty. The child begins to identify with his same-sex parent—adopts the behavior and attitudes of the parent, strives to become like him, and imitates him. The same-sex parent, thus, becomes a model. If, for some reason, the parent is absent from the home (as in divorce or death), another adult of the same sex may become a substitute model. It is through this process of learning to be a "man" or a "woman" that the child develops his or her concept of the sex role.

With the beginning of the preadolescent period boys reject maternal ties and seek rugged, active, aggressive maleness. The boy feels it is important to disassociate himself from any sign of female interest or control. To be called a "sissy" is extremely degrading. "Maleness" in our society is a much more definitive term than "femaleness." Many girls prefer games which, in the past, have been classified as masculine—baseball, basketball, or soccer. Few boys, however, would admit that they prefer games which are often considered appropriate for girls to play. To be a "tomboy" is acceptable, but to be a "sissy" is to be doomed. Gordon emphasizes the difficulties of preadolescent acceptance of one's sex:

It is clear that the preadolescent period is not one of quiet acceptance of one's own sex. The obviously self-conscious peer grouping of boys with boys and girls with girls does not indicate that there is mutual disinterest. It indicates, perhaps, a heightened self-awareness and a seeking after models and support. Certainly, boys are more outspoken in their rejection of girls, but boys are also confronted with many female models and increasingly restricted avenues for self-expression.

Girls are not content to be girls in the conventional sense; they now feel they can be both girls and little-leaguer simultaneously.[21]

[20]Sigmund Freud, *The Ego and the Id* (London: Hogarth Press, Ltd. and Institute of Psychoanalysis, 1935).
[21]Gordon, p. 244.

Inhelder and Piaget[22] suggest a motivational explanation related to sex role identification in accounting, in part, for the transition from the concrete operations period to that of formal operations. Cultural pressure and the eagerness of the child to assume adult roles (with adult modes of thought) are facilitating factors which contribute to the transition.

One of the major tasks of preadolescence, therefore, is the identification of one's sex role and the accompanying appropriate behaviors. It is a task toward which the younger child has not been required to exert the same degree of effort.

Peer Influence

With the search for identification during preadolescence and early adolescence, the child begins to perceive his peers in a different light. Both boys and girls are keenly aware of sex differences. Boys express a much more negative attitude toward girls, however, than do girls toward boys. Close friends are of the same sex. The peer group seems to offer some degree of security in that the youngster can do "what everyone else is doing," and this statement often accompanies the request for permission he expresses to parents. According to Gordon:

> The preadolescent peer group, through its conformist pressures, its emphasis on the need of children to be accepted, its stereotypes of "good" and "bad" behavior, shapes the external behavior of its members. Even though children may resist inwardly or feel threatened, they attempt to produce the behavior they think the group expects of them. This is particularly true in ambiguous situations. Where what is right is unclear, the group attitude will affect the judgment of the individual child.[23]

The influence of the peer group during preadolescence may disturb the teacher who works with this age group. He will, more than likely, find himself in the role of an outsider in whom the group will not confide. He will also find that a child's membership in the peer group remains unthreatened by open conflict or disagreement with the teacher.

Contrast this youngster with those a year or so younger. The younger child associates readily with both sexes. The boy does not reject play activities in which he may come in physical contact with girls, and the girl appears oblivious to the fact that a boy may have touched her. What a difference in attitude a year or two can make!

---

[22]Barbel Inhelder and Jean Piaget, *Growth of Logical Thinking from Childhood to Adolescence* (New York: Basic Books, Inc., 1958).

[23]Gordon, p. 223.

The Turbulent Emotions

As the individual matures, emotional behavior become more mature. The transitional period, according to Gesell, Ilg, and Ames,[24] is marked by the end of one cycle of emotional organization and the beginning of another. The child is changing from emotional behavior which can be described as contented and amiable to that displayed by an often aggressive, belligerent, and argumentative individual. At times he may seem hurt, sad, jealous, or competitive; at other times, worried, cheerful, affectionate, or timid. The anger of the preadolescent is more intense and deeper than that of the younger child, and he may strike out with more fervor. It takes him longer than the younger child to recuperate from emotional outbursts.

During the years of ages ten to fourteen, the emotional development of the child, if plotted on a line graph, would show many minor peaks and valleys. According to Gesell, Ilg, and Ames:

> The twelve-year-old tends to be outgoing, exuberant, enthusiastic. At the thirteen level there is a calming down . . . . Thirteen is more withdrawn and more thoughtful both about himself and others . . . . His great sensitiveness and even his secretiveness indicate that his emotions are deepening and refining . . . . The full blown fourteen-year-old is a spontaneous extrovert. He does not hold back and brood or feel sorry for himself. He is full of laughter, jokes, and humor . . . .[25]

The full adolescent is quite different—an evident calming down can be observed. He may be very enthusiastic toward school or show resistance. He is beginning a period of self-awareness which continues through the teens.

Learning to cope with his changing body, a new mode of intellectual operations, and the desire to be a person in his own right—independent of familial, and especially maternal, dominance—presents a tremendous problem of adjustment for youngsters during this transitional period. Behavior of an emotional nature can be traced to one or several of these changes. If the transitional years are years of turbulent emotions (and evidence supports the notion that they are just that—turbulent), is it any wonder? During no other period of human growth and development are youngsters required to adjust themselves to so many changes simultaneously.

YOUNG PEOPLE IN TRANSITION: SUMMARY

The physical, intellectual, and psycho-social development of youngsters during the transitional period have been presented in separate sections of

[24]Arnold Gesell, Frances L. Ilg, and Louise B. Ames, *Youth: The Years From Ten to Sixteen* (New York: Harper & Row, Publishers, 1956).

[25]Gesell, Ilg, and Ames, p. 333.

this chapter. The following summary of characteristics of young people during this period is an attempt to demonstrate the interrelatedness of these components and return the reader's attention to the concept of the whole child:

1. The transition period is marked by the necessity for relearning to manage the body skillfully during a period of rapid change in body dimensions and general awkwardness.

2. The transition period is marked by the onset and gradual regularization of menstruation in girls and of nocturnal emissions and more frequent erections in boys. These new physical phenomena bring about the need for learning to maintain standards of health and hygiene. They set up new concepts of self and new problems of social behavior.

3. The transition period is marked by a beginning awareness of new erotic sensations in both boys and girls. It is also marked by an awakening interest in persons of the opposite sex and by the necessity for learning to manage these sensations without undue brashness or embarrassment.

4. The transition period is marked by the necessity for developing many social skills in interacting with persons of the opposite sex. These skills run the gamut—from learning to use cosmetics, or to choose and wear clothing that will attract the opposite sex, to learning how to receive and give caresses related to the erotic drive and to manage and check one's partner in these activities.

5. The transition period is marked by dramatic changes in the activities of the peer group and in what is required to maintain belonging to the peer group. Learning to dance, to talk the current slang, "to kid" and to accept "kidding," to joke and to accept practical jokes played on one, and perhaps to drive a car are examples of peer group activities during this period.[26]

6. The transition period is marked by an important evolution in relationships with parents. These include the ways in which love is expressed between the young person and the parents, the assertion by the rapidly developing person of his right to make many more decisions about his own behavior, his own social life, his own management of money, his own choice of companions, and so on. Some psychologists consider this as rebellion, or a drive for independence. It seems more likely to be an attempt by the youth to secure for himself the right to make more decisions about his own behavior. It is not a desire to be free of parents but the need to

[26]Caroline Tryon, "Summary of Material Presented to Members of the Collaboration Center by Herbert R. Stolz," in summaries of Presentations of Consultants to the Collaboration Center, Vol. 9 (mimeographed, [Chicago: Division of Child Development and Teacher Personnel, Commission on Teacher Education, American Council on Education, October 15–December 11, 1939]).

have them accord him the right to test his own choice-making under the new circumstances in which he is living.

7. The transition period is marked by a tremendous change in the individual's perception of himself and, consequently, in a quest for a satisfying concept of himself. Who am I? What am I able to do? Where do I fit into the social world? Into the vocational world? Into the spiritual world? Into the political world? Where do I belong? What do I believe about life and death? If finding the answers to these questions are required of the developmental periods of adolescence and adulthood, the framing of the questions and the exploration of where and to whom to look for answers are among the requirements of persons in transition from childhood into adolescence. Sometimes this is done overtly. More often, perhaps, the young people reveal what is on their minds by frank criticism of adult behavior, by challenges to established mores and ideas. Some show it by quiet withdrawal that finds the teacher or parent suddenly aware that this person has asked no sincere or penetrating questions for some months. For before the affirmation of a new concept of self-becoming can be made, there is the period of uncertain fumbling, the period of confusion about what the right questions are.

8. The transition period often is marked by the necessity of redefining what is right and what is wrong. Evidence of organic maturation confronts the individual with many complex choices about how to behave. Are the next-older peer group, the young postpubescent adolescents, right or wrong in what they do, or claim to do? Is what a person feels as conscience only the memory of what parents and teachers told him when he was too young to be able to decide for himself? How can a person tell? Many a parent thinks of his child in transition as an "innocent child" and is horribly shocked to discover that he has been exploring some undesirable behavior "to find out whether it is really wrong or not."

9. The transition period is marked by the development of a new mode of intellectual operations—a movement away from a dependence upon what can be perceived in the immediate environment to a level of hypothesizing and dealing with abstractions. It is an establishment of a level of adult-like thought (when the adult is his logical best) and a willingness and desire to test ideas. It is manifested in a youngster's dealings not only with what is normally conceived to be activities directly related to so-called school work but also with all facets of his everyday life.

These changes that occur during the period of transition from childhood to adolescence should be reflected, we believe, in a transitional school program. The program for the "in-between-ager" should be developed with direct concern for his characteristics as just summarized. This transitional period is unique in the developmental sequence—a uniqueness which renders children and young people at this stage of development as quite different from those in the first few years of school and those in the high school years.

Does the present school program reflect our knowledge about the transition from childhood to adolescence? As we shall note in Chapter 3, the organization breaks sharply from grade 6 to grade 7, in the very middle of the transitional period of most children's lives. Indeed, Dacus' study[27] of social, emotional, and physical maturity, and opposite sex choices of pupils in grades 5 through 10, found that the differences were *least* between pupils in grades 6 and 7 and pupils in grades 9 and 10—the present break points! The present organization tends to be based on the scientific data related to human growth and development which was available more than fifty years ago. Furthermore, the program of present schools, however organized, rarely focuses during the in-between years on these developmental characteristics, which would seem to be logical priorities. In Chapter 3 the present program provided for youngsters during this transitional period will be critically examined, as a further justification for a new program in the emergent middle school.

---

[27]Wilfred P. Dacus, "A Study of the Grade Organizational Structure of the Junior High School as Measured by Social Maturity, Emotional Maturity, Physical Maturity, and Opposite-Sex Choices" (doctoral dissertation, University of Houston, Abstract; *Dissertation Abstracts,* 24:1461–1462, 1963).

Chapter 3

From the Standpoint
of the Inadequacies
of the 6-3-3 Plan

EVOLUTION OF THE PLAN

The predominant pattern of school organization in the United States today is the six-year elementary school, the three-year junior high school, and the three-year senior high school. It is a product of twentieth-century America. The elementary and high schools had European antecedents and were largely the result of an American effort to pattern our educational system after European plans—specifically, the Prussian system. The junior high school is, however, uniquely American and renders the 6-3-3 plan uniquely American. The present 6-3-3 plan had its beginning some three score years ago with the establishment of the first junior high school.[1]

Contributions of Early National Committees

The 6-3-3 plan did not evolve as a result of the careful scrutiny of the characteristics of the children who were to be served by the three institutional segments, nor was it based on knowledge of human growth and

---

[1]See William Van Til, Gordon F. Vars, and John H. Lounsbury, *Modern Education for the Junior High School Years* (Indianapolis: The Bobbs-Merrill Company, Inc. 1967), pp. 5–21.

development. On the contrary, the most fertile seeds of discontent with the 8-4 plan were sown by university administrators who were concerned with lowering the age of college entrance. Their counterparts in the universities of Europe were admitting students at an earlier age, and, thus, graduates were proceeding to professional endeavors earlier.

A series of committees appointed by various departments of the National Education Association met between 1892 and 1918 to attempt to find solutions to the problem of what to do in order to redesign the elementary and secondary programs. Among the various recommendations reported were:

1.   Extending the secondary program downward to encompass grades 7 and 8, which would become an intermediate school to serve a bridge function between elementary school and the high school.[2]
2.   Retaining the eight-year elementary school, but introducing a few high school subjects in grades 7 and 8.[3]
3.   Establishing a six-year secondary school beginning with grade 7 in order to assure earlier specialization of subject matter.[4]
4.   Providing a separate program for grades 7 and 8 as a part of the six-year secondary school.[5]
5.   Dividing the secondary school into two distinct administrative units—a junior high school for students from twelve to fifteen years of age and a senior high school for students from fifteen to eighteen years of age.[6]

Rapid Acceptance of the 6-3-3 Plan

Following establishment in 1909–1910 of junior high schools in Columbus, Ohio, and Berkeley, California, other school systems began to give consideration to the reorganization of the secondary program. By 1917 there were at least 272 junior high schools in operation throughout the United States.[7] This number included only those institutions enrolling stu-

[2]National Education Association, *Report of the Committee of Ten on Secondary School Studies* (New York: American Book Company, 1894), pp. 51–52.
[3]National Education Association, *Report of the Committee of Fifteen on Elementary Education* (New York: American Book Company, 1895), p. 95.
[4]National Education Association, "Report of the Committee on College Entrance Requirements," *Journal of Proceedings and Addresses,* 659–660 (1899).
[5]National Education Association, "Report of the Committee on Six-Year Courses of Study," *Journal of Proceedings and Addresses,* 625–628 (1908).
[6]Commission on the Reorganization of Secondary Education, *Cardinal Principles of Secondary Education* (Bureau of Education, Department of the Interior, Bulletin 1918, No. 35 [Washington, D.C.: Government Printing Office, 1918]), pp. 12–13.
[7]Thomas H. Briggs, *The Junior High School* (Boston: Houghton Mifflin Company, 1920), p. 32.

dents in grades 7 through 9 in a separate building with its own administrative and instructional staff and thereby meeting the definition of the organizational plan of the junior high school today. Undoubtedly, there were many programs in operation for grades 7 through 9 which, at that time, remained a part of the six-year high school program.

In the fifty years since the 1917 survey of junior high schools, there has been a shift nationally from the 8-4 and 6-6 to the 6-3-3 plan of school organization. Vestiges of the earlier patterns are found in some suburban areas wedded to the 4-year high school and especially in rural areas lacking financial resources and a large school population. Often, however, in these districts differentiation is made in the curriculum for students in grades 7 and 8 which separate it from that provided for younger and older students. In the nation as a whole, however, the junior high school as a separate administrative unit is well entrenched. The 6-3-3 pattern is predominant in all fifty states. Indeed, by the year 1960 the separate junior high school enrolled over 80 percent of the nation's students in grades 7 through 9.[8]

During those fifty years the purposes of the junior high school have also been altered. In addition to its original function of providing secondary education for youngsters at an earlier age, the purpose of the junior high school was to provide: (1) a bridge between the elementary school with its self-contained classroom and the highly specialized program of the senior high school; (2) exploratory experiences for its students in order to allow youngsters to sample various subject areas before making a commitment to a specific program in the senior high school; and (3) guidance services as an aid in academic, vocational, and personal matters.

Had the junior high school really achieved these purposes, and had the elementary school program provided adequate adaptations for its older pupils, the 6-3-3 plan might have had little challenge. But today the plan is being challenged, and its inadequacies in practice are being exposed.

THE 6-3-3 PLAN AND THE "IN-BETWEEN-AGER"

The major inadequacies of the 6-3-3 plan lie in the inconsistency of its assumed functions and its modes of operation in light of what we presently know about the "in-between-ager." There are individual schools which are making supreme efforts to provide adequately for the youngsters they serve. However, when one views the three institutional segments nationally, the problem is evident. Recognizing full well the fine contributions which have been made generally by elementary and secondary schools, the authors agree that current dominant practice under the 6-3-3 plan tends to

---

[8]For a more thorough treatment, see Van Til, Vars, and Lounsbury, pp. 39–59.

neglect learners in the middle school years. This critical view of most frequent practice, supported as possible by research and other observations, is plainly stated in the following pages as a basis for readers' evaluations of the schools they know.

The Upper Elementary Grades

Today's six-year elementary school is characterized by the dominant pattern of the self-contained classroom, with one teacher assuming the responsibility for an instructional program for one group of children during a major portion of the day. In the typical elementary school this is true whether a child is six years of age or twelve. The older children, those between childhood and adolescence, may be taught as "little children" too long.

The Self-contained Classroom

Proponents of the self-contained classroom stand firm in their belief that all elementary students need the security of one teacher in a "home base." They feel that the mother image (or father image) is essential for the provision of an atmosphere of acceptance and guidance in which learning can take place. They seem to feel that this will occur simply by the nature of the school organization, without any emphasis being given to the preparation and personality of the teacher in this classroom. The provision of a self-contained classroom organization for all six grades suggests that the characteristics of the eleven-year-old child differ only slightly, if at all, from the emotional, physical, and social characteristics of the six-year-old. Even the casual observer of children can present evidence to the contrary. The six-year-old (unless he has experienced a year of kindergarten) is in a formal educational environment for the first time in his young life. The eleven-year-old has experienced at least five years of institutionalized education, varying tremendously among youngsters in both quantity and quality. In many instances the girls are already pubescent by the time they enter grade 6 and many of the boys are rapidly approaching pubescence. They are no longer little children, and they resent being treated as such. Their interests differ tremendously from those of first-graders. Yet, they are housed under the same roof and are subjected to an instructional program which does not differ in the main from that of the early elementary grades.

The theory of the self-contained classroom is not as much at fault as is the general practice in the classroom. More often than not, within the classroom the subjects are not integrated. Instead, there is, for example, a distinct break between the teaching of reading and the period devoted to the social studies. It may even be as abrupt as a statement by the

teacher to "put away your readers and take out your geography books."
In reality, therefore, there is a great deal of departmentalization of subject
matter within the so-called self-contained classroom. Frequently, this can
be noted in the nature of the teacher's schedule, which is recorded in the
daily plan book and/or posted on a wall for all to see. Many teachers who
fragment the elementary curriculum in such a manner appear to be oblivious of their actions, and many are staunch supporters of the self-contained
classroom—and, therefore, opponents of any type of departmentalization
in the elementary school.

With the separation of subject matter—regardless of the amount of
subtlety with which it is disguised—within the self-contained classroom
there is not an accompanying competency on the part of the teacher in all
the subjects he is required to teach. No teacher can be a specialist in all
subject fields, and yet, in most elementary schools, this is the role he is
expected to fulfill. In this day of rapid change in all areas of specialization,
it is difficult for even a subject matter specialist to keep abreast of all
the material in his own field. Our present teacher education programs
are focused on the preparation of elementary generalists—with a few
courses included in the program which are aimed at special methods of
teaching for the various subject areas. Many of these so-called methods
courses must, of necessity, include a high concentration of subject content
because of a lack of previous preparation by these students in the various
content areas, and usually evolve into courses in elementary mathematics,
science, English, or the like, providing only incidental information pertaining to instructional methods.

What usually happens in the self-contained classroom of the elementary
generalist is that the only subject area given any true emphasis is the program of language arts. It is the curriculum area with which the teacher
feels most secure and that in which she probably does the most competent
job of instruction. Unfortunately, the other subjects are relegated to whatever portion of the school day is left after the language arts program is
completed. It is little wonder that boys in the upper elementary grades,
who characteristically lack both facility and interest in language arts, become bored and frustrated.

Is Some Specialization Needed?

It seems apparent that in this day of rapid and mass news media the
upper elementary child's knowledge of his world far surpasses that of a
child of the same age only one generation ago. It is no longer adequate
for the teacher to prepare his lesson plans in order to keep just ahead
of his class. He cannot anticipate all the penetrating questions likely to be
raised pertaining to all the various subject fields included in the curriculum
of the upper elementary grades. It is also difficult for him to keep abreast

of the myriad resources to which he can direct a child for answers to questions the teacher cannot himself answer. One view of this inadequacy follows:

The present system of elementary school organization . . . attempts to give every teacher the same number of pupils, the same schedule and curriculum, and the same responsibility, regardless of his or her special training, experience, skill, or capacity for taking responsibility. In addition, many elementary school teachers are overwhelmed with nonprofessional duties. Up to 40 percent of their time is spent in keeping attendance, collecting milk money, typing stencils, correcting routine tests, supervising playground and lunchroom activities, etc.[9]

The argument is often presented that instruction by specialists in the upper elementary grades tends to fragment the curriculum. But within the self-contained classroom the curriculum is already fragmented—often as much as that in a departmentalized organization. The major difference between the two organizational plans is that in the self-contained class-room instruction in the various fragments is not accomplished by teachers with the necessary depth of knowledge in the subject fields.

Another argument which is raised by the advocates of the self-contained classroom is that children in the upper elementary grades lack the psychological maturity to learn in separate classes taught by specialists in the various subject fields. There is evidence to the contrary. Studies were conducted in 1960 in the public schools of Tulsa, Oklahoma, by Broadhead[10] and Livingston,[11] utilizing fifth-grade students who had experienced a semidepartmentalized program in grades 3, 4, and 5. The definition of "semidepartmentalized" used in these studies was as follows: one teacher providing basic instruction in reading, writing, spelling, language arts, and social studies; instruction by specialists in the subjects of science, mathematics, art, music, speech, physical education, and library science. In the studies conducted by Broadhead, findings indicate that the semidepartmentalized group showed better social adjustment than did the sample of students in the self-contained classroom. Livingston studied fifth-grade children who had experienced the semidepartmentalized program during each of their four previous years of schooling, children who had been in self-contained classrooms for the first two years of school and in the semidepartmental organization after that time, and children who had been in self-contained classrooms for all five years. His findings indicate that the group which was best adjusted was that which had spent

[9]Philip Lambert, "Team Teaching for the Elementary School," *Educational Leadership,* 18:85–88, 128 (November 1960).

[10]Fred C. Broadhead, "Pupil-Adjustment in the Semi-departmental Elementary School," *Elementary School Journal,* 60:385–390 (April 1960).

[11]A. H. Livingston, "Does a Departmental Organization Affect Children's Adjustment?" *Elementary School Journal,* 61:217–220 (January 1961).

all five years in a semidepartmental program; the next highest group was that which had spent only the first two years of school in the self-contained classroom; the lowest group was that which had experienced the self-contained classroom all five years.

Gibb and Matala[12] studied the use of special teachers of science and mathematics in grades 5 and 6 in an attempt to determine if science and mathematics could each be taught more effectively by special teachers than by the regular classroom teacher and if the intellectual level of the children being taught made a difference. Their experimental study, conducted over a period of two years, ended in 1961. They found, among other things: There was evidence that children learn science more effectively with special teachers than in the self-contained classroom; there was no evidence that either pattern was more effective in the teaching of mathematics; use of special teachers in science can result in more effective learning by all children regardless of intellectual ability; both the fifth- and sixth-grade groups preferred being taught by specialists.

In schools in which instruction by specialists is available, the specialist is often not accepted as an instructional team member responsible for participating in the planning of the total curriculum for each child. It is not surprising that there appears to be little integration of subject matter within the departmentalized program. In a minority of the schools in which departmentalized or semidepartmentalized programs for the upper elementary grades has come about through careful study and planning on the part of the entire staff, there is no distinct break between language arts, social studies, science, music, art, physical education, and the like because the format has been planned by a team of instructional specialists with a central focus.

There is research evidence which indicates that not only can children in the upper elementary grades benefit from instruction by subject area specialists, but programed instruction and independent study by children as young as the fourth-grade level were found to be effective. The teaching of multiplication of fractions in grade 6 by means of programed materials was investigated by Arvin.[13] He found no significant difference in the achievement of sixth-graders taught by programed materials and those taught by the teacher. However, the group utilizing programed instruction needed only about one-half the amount of time utilized by the conventional group in accomplishing the same purposes. Research conducted by

---

[12]E. Glenadine Gibb and Dorothy C. Matala, "Study on the Use of Special Teachers of Science and Mathematics in Grades 5 and 6," *School Science and Mathematics*, 6:565–585 (November 1962).

[13]Charles Arvin, "An Experimental Study of Programed Instruction in Multiplication of Fractions" (unpublished doctoral dissertation, Colorado State College, 1965).

MacGregor[14] indicated that children as young as those in grade 4 can work as well independently as in a group situation if they are able to see themselves as exerting some control over their work and relying on their own standards of judgment rather than upon the judgment of others.

Self-containment and Guidance

A final word about the elementary school program and its characteristic self-contained classroom should be said pertaining to its claim for the provision of guidance activities. The elementary teacher in the self-contained classroom truly has the opportunity to know his students well and to provide both personal and academic guidance. However, his day is so crowded with the various subject matter fields that there is little time left to provide any form of guidance. The teacher in the self-contained classroom in the upper elementary grades is an extremely busy person. The conscientious teacher, who is likely to attempt to provide guidance for his students, must spend a major portion of his time trying to provide instruction in all the various subject areas for the many levels of ability within his classroom. Most guidance is incidental. At the other extreme, the teacher who is not conscientious and merely "puts in his time" in the classroom does a poor job of providing learning activities for the many student levels, and guidance of any sort is likely to be nonexistent.

Manolakes views the inadequacy of the present-day elementary program thus:

> With few exceptions, the elementary school of today . . . continues to be organized primarily for the teaching of subjects. Thus, teachers and administrators find themselves in the rather contradictory position of functioning within a structure that is designed to promote the coverage of content while they are also striving to meet the personal-social needs of the learners. Frequently these viewpoints are incompatible. Many goals of the elementary school that reflect a concern for children have been regarded as pious platitudes and have been supported only as far as the objective of teaching subjects permits.[15]

In light of what is presently known about the child in the upper elementary grades as discussed in Chapter 2, the elementary school program as presented here is inadequate to meet the needs of the children it serves. Fifth- and sixth-grade youngsters differ greatly from children in grades 1 through 4 and from one another within these two years. It is this great

[14]Mary Jo Lee Smith MacGregor, "Originality and Role Perception in Elementary and Junior High School Children" (unpublished doctoral dissertation, George Peabody College for Teachers, 1964).

[15]George Manolakes, *The Elementary School We Need* (Washington, D.C.: Association for Supervision and Curriculum Development, 1965), p. 3.

variability which makes imperative an administrative organization and school program designed to provide for this individuality.

The "Junior" High School

Perhaps the most publicized and valid indictment of the program of the junior high school is that it mimics that of the senior high school. The name itself implies that if there is a "junior" version of an institution, there must also be a "senior" counterpart. Almost from the time of the establishment of the junior high school protesting voices have been raised against its name.[16] For the past fifty-odd years the protest has continued. What is there about the junior high school that approximates the senior high? There are many such characteristics—not all are found in every junior high, but these practices are sufficiently spread throughout the country to indicate that they are typical. Varsity teams in football, basketball, baseball, and track are to be found in most junior high schools. The accouterments—marching bands, cheer leaders, pep rallies—also approximate those of the high school. In most instances high school athletic coaches and band directors look upon the junior high school as a training ground for their future teams and bands. Even the names given junior high school athletic teams may indicate this concept. For example, one of the authors taught in a junior high school which calls its teams the "midshipmen." The senior high school the students attend upon completion of the junior high school program calls its teams the "sailors." Athletes in junior high schools may even receive varsity letters, an indication of prestige. The student body is expected to look upon these youngsters who are physically gifted as individuals who are a cut or so above the average student.

Eichhorn[17] asserts that although our culture places great emphasis on the person who has outstanding physical ability, educators should be cognizant of the emotional dangers that face older children, preadolescents, and adolescents who are incapable of meeting the standards of exceptionality. He supports, instead, well-conducted intramural athletic programs in which all students may attain some degree of success. James B. Conant, in the report of his study of the junior high school, says:

> Interscholastic athletics and marching bands are to be condemned in junior high schools: there is no sound educational reason for them and too often they serve merely as public entertainment. Community desires to glorify the role of the "senior" in the junior high school must also be watched carefully . . . .[18]

[16]Samuel H. Popper, *The American Middle School: An Organizational Analysis* (Waltham, Mass.: Blaisdell Publishing Company, 1967), p. 7.

[17]Donald H. Eichhorn, *The Middle School* (New York: The Center for Applied Research in Education, 1966), p. 59.

[18]James B. Conant, *Education in the Junior High School Years: A Memorandum to School Boards* (Princeton, N.J.: Educational Testing Service, 1960), p. 42.

Another marked similarity between the program of the junior and senior high schools is the offering of organizations and clubs. Very few are designed specifically for children in this age group; most are junior versions of those offered in the high school—language clubs, dramatics clubs, choral societies, cotillions, science clubs, and the various service clubs found in high schools.

In all too many junior high schools the termination of the school year calls for a prom and a formal graduation, sometimes with academic gowns and mortarboards. This has been known to occur even on the elementary school level—and worse yet, on the kindergarten level. It would seem that most of the excitement would be missing from these activities for high school seniors because they have experienced them earlier in their academic lives.

Departmentalization

The most flagrant similarity between the programs of the junior and senior high schools is the curriculum and its organization. With the exception of the relatively few schools utilizing some type of true "core" approach (not just two periods taught as separate subjects by the same teacher) and those employing true team teaching (not mere "turn teaching"), most junior high schools use a strict subject fields curriculum organization in which separate classes are provided for each subject field. Teachers are assigned to a subject area department whose chairman may either be appointed by the administration or elected by the department membership. The chairman typically is responsible for administrative tasks and performs no supervisory duties. There is little or no interdepartmental planning; no individual teacher is, in reality, responsible for aiding the student and his parents in the selection of courses in the usually limited exploratory program. The typical junior high teacher feels responsible for only his own particular area of specialization and the instruction in this subject for the students assigned him for the various periods of each school day. The teacher may teach as many as six sections of the same course during the typical school day. Naturally, repetition occurs.

Team Teaching May Be Better

Team teaching has proved quite successful in many junior high schools. This success has been based largely on careful planning by the school staff. Klausmeier and Wiersma[19] compared achievement in seventh-grade

---

[19]Herbert Klausmeier and William Wiersma, "Team Teaching and Achievement," *Education*, 86:238–242 (December 1965).

English and social studies when taught by a team and when taught in separate classes. They found that students of low ability did better work in English under a team teaching plan than in regular classes and as well as students in regular classes in social studies. The group of average students in team teaching experienced greater achievement in both English and social studies than did students of the same ability in regular classes. Students who were superior in ability experienced greater achievement in social studies and did as well in English as did students in regular classes. Sweet and Dunn-Rankin[20] found that seventh-grade students taught by a team of teachers in mathematics achieved equally as well as students of similar ability in regular classes. Students, however, expressed a decided preference for instruction by the team method.

The Exploratory Program

Lounsbury and Marani,[21] in their report of a "shadow study" conducted under the auspices of the Association for Supervision and Curriculum Development, pointed to the inadequacies of the junior high school program along several different lines: The learning environment lacked stimulation, the program of required subjects was not diversified, and there was little provision for individual differences among pupils. In addition, they found that although the exploratory purpose of the junior high school was evident, the full possibilities of such a program were not being exploited. This is true, as well, in the seventh and ninth grades of the junior high school. Even in some of the large metropolitan junior high schools, the range of exploratory experiences tends to be extremely narrow. All too often this range is limited to one or two subject areas. For example, a seventh-grader may be given the choice of general music or band for half of the school year. These may be the only electives open to him for the entire school year. This hardly constitutes an adequate program of exploratory experiences for any junior high school student.

Junior High School Staff Problems

What of the junior high school teacher? Is he a specially trained professional who possesses an abundant knowledge of subject matter coupled with an equally sufficient knowledge of the characteristics of the preadolescent and early adolescent students he has been assigned to teach? Unfortunately, an emphatic response in the negative is the only honest one

[20]R. Sweet and Peter Dunn-Rankin, "An Experiment in Team Teaching Seventh Grade Arithmetic," *School Science and Mathematics,* 62:341–344 (May 1962).

[21]J. H. Lounsbury and J. V. Marani, *The Junior High School We Saw: One Day in the Eighth Grade* (Washington, D.C.: Association for Supervision and Curriculum Development, 1964).

which can be given to such a question. Until recent years there have been no programs of teacher education specifically designed for the preparation of junior high school teachers. Teachers holding teaching certificates in elementary education were presumed to be equipped to teach grades 1 through 8; those with secondary certificates, grades 7 through 12. Many of the programs in existence today offer only a course or two pertaining to curriculum and instruction for the junior high school grades. Because of the lack of special preparatory programs for junior high school teachers, administrators usually are forced to recruit from the ranks of the elementary and high school staffs. Given the choice, administrators in the high schools and elementary schools rarely recommend the transfer of their more successful teachers. On the contrary, those transferred usually fit into one of three categories: (1) those who have been unsuccessful at their own teaching level; (2) those who are not fully accepted by the staff and the administration; or (3) those who are being "groomed" by the system level administration for future positions as supervisors or administrators and for whom a few years of teaching experience on the junior high level may prove advantageous in providing them with a broader view of instruction. When the teacher in the high school or elementary school is given the choice of a position in the junior high school, he may choose to transfer for a variety of reasons: (1) he may have a genuine desire to teach that age group; (2) he may view it as a means of "saving face" by moving from a teaching level at which he has been unsuccessful—and, thus, avoiding dismissal; or (3) he may very well be an elementary teacher who views a transfer to the junior high school as a step upward in prestige. The teachers who fit the second and third categories often find that adjustment to junior high school teaching is difficult; for many it is impossible. The authors of the ASCD pamphlet, *The Junior High School We Need,* expressed the following view of the problem of staffing the junior high school:

> For some junior high school teachers, their service in this institution is considered as a way-point on the path "upward" to senior high school assignments. They may have inadequate preparation for junior high school work and little patience for working with young adolescents. Their eyes are directed toward the high school, where they believe higher status may be found, and toward the presumably easier-to-work-with students they hope to discover there.[22]

Teachers who are new to a school system may find themselves placed in a junior high school position because of overcrowded conditions and an accompanying shortage of staff at the junior high school level. It is

[22]Jean D. Grambs, Clarence G. Noyce, Franklin Patterson, and John Robertson, *The Junior High School We Need* (Washington, D.C.: Association for Supervision and Curriculum Development, 1961), p. 11.

apparently easier for school administrators to relocate new staff members than to endure the trauma associated with attempting to persuade tenured staff members in the high schools and elementary schools to agree to transfer.

The junior high school principal is also a professional who has been prepared for an administrative position in either the high school or the elementary school. Those who accept the position may even be athletic coaches or other specialists who, because of the "leadership" nature of their former positions, are identified as potentially good administrators for the junior high school. Often they know little or nothing about administration and even less about curriculum planning. The junior high school principal who has received college preparation for administration may view his administrative position as a training ground and a stepping stone for administrative positions in the high school. This is particularly true in school systems which differentiate between salaries paid elementary, junior high, and senior high school principals. According to Popper:

> . . . In all too many districts, the junior high-school principalship is still a way station in the frenetic climb from the classroom to high-school administration. It is rare to find in such districts talented aspirants for administrative posts who are willing to accept the junior high-school principalship as a lifetime position . . . .[23]

Articulation and Guidance

Junior high school staffs rarely have an adequate knowledge of the programs of both the elementary school and the high school. Usually, articulation between the three levels—when it exists at all—is weak. The total range of school experiences for children is, thus, divided into three distinct segments—each with its isolated program, seemingly oblivious to those of the other two. The break between the elementary school and the junior high school is usually that which is most abrupt. The high school feels that it has a vested interest in the junior high and is much more cognizant of the program of the latter as preparatory for high school. Therefore, the articulation between these two levels is accomplished to some degree at the insistence of the high school. The traumatic break between the elementary and junior high school programs for the youngsters entering the junior high is obvious to anyone who has observed seventh-grade students on the first day of school. These youngsters are lost and frightened in an unfamiliar world. They try vainly to fight back tears when they cannot find their classes or, when they have finally located them, they are reprimanded by the teacher because they are tardy.

Articulation between the junior high school and the educational levels

---

[23]Samuel H. Popper, "Another Look at the Junior High School Principalship," *Bulletin of the National Association of Secondary-School Principals,* 44:125–27 (November 1960).

above and below it is within the realm of guidance. The junior high school student needs to have some indication as to what to expect when he leaves the environment of the self-contained classroom at the elementary level and finds himself in a departmentalized institution which is totally strange to him. Equally as important is the need for attention to be given to the student entering the high school with its highly specialized atmosphere. In short, the provision of guidance counselors at the junior high school level to deal with students who are disciplinary and/or emotional problems, execute the testing program, assume the responsibility for the permanent records for each student, and produce the master schedule for the administration is not sufficient to serve the student population. There must be someone to whom each student feels he can turn for help with a personal problem—someone in whom he can confide. His problems may not be such that he needs to secure an appointment to talk to a guidance counselor. Every classroom teacher needs to be prepared to help students with personal problems. By the very nature of the position every teacher is a guidance worker, whether he identifies himself with that role or not.

The student at this age has a multitude of personal needs and emotional reactions created by his rapid physical growth and the physiological changes which accompany it. He requires a close relationship with a member of the adult staff of the school—a relationship characterized by mutual acceptance and trust.[24] The provision of a homeroom period for one-quarter or one-half hour each day, packed with administrative chores such as attendance-taking, issuing of report cards, and making school-wide announcements is not sufficient, even when it is used by teachers who can steal a few minutes for counseling students.

The observations made by one participant in the ASCD "shadow study" express the predominant view of those who participated in the study and serve to highlight the inadequacies of the junior high school. These comments relate specifically to the eighth grade, but they seem to pertain to the entire junior high school. The participant stated that he would not want to be an eighth-grader.

. . . on such a tight schedule; . . . when I was not involved in planning what was to be done and/or how this would be done; . . . where most teachers lectured and treated us as sponges; . . . where my interests and needs were not considered in planning the curriculum; . . . where I could "get by" very nicely just by being quiet, orderly, and following directions; . . . where my learning was bookish, fragmentized, and purposes were not clear; . . . where I had no opportunities for "me" to grow.[25]

[24]Eichhorn, p. 59.
[25]Lounsbury and Marani, p. 51.

In summary, the program of the junior high school today is not providing adequately for the in-between-aged student. It is too fragmented, too rigid, and it lacks a staff with the professional competencies and personal characteristics needed by educators whose goal is the provision of a program specifically designed to meet the multivaried needs of students in this age group. The junior high school has too long been the stepchild of the public school program and the "little brother" of the high school. It lacks an identity of its own as the segment of the educational ladder with a unique program for the students it serves.

Grade 9

The ninth-grade student may find himself on the horns of a real dilemma. Many ninth-grade courses carry Carnegie unit credit. The student must weigh his choices carefully in order to assure acceptance of his elective courses upon entrance into the high school. The senior high school, thus, feels that it should be consulted by the junior high school in the course offerings for ninth grade—even to the point of impinging some control over the course offerings. Many junior high school teachers and administrators are sympathetic with the requirements of the high school and are willing to relinquish the choice of curriculum planning for grade 9 to the staff of the high school.

Grade 9, for purposes of state and regional accreditation, is included in the reports of the senior high school program. The provision of Carnegie unit credits for grade 9 similar to those of grades 10 through 12 places a burden on the high school to either accept these credits when the student enters the tenth grade or to attempt to exert some influence on their provision in the junior high school. More often than not, the latter is the course of action taken. Students in the ninth grade like to consider themselves as high school "freshmen," and thus not really a part of the junior high school student body. Indeed, as stated in Chapter 2, their physical, emotional, and intellectual characteristics more closely resemble students in grade 10 than those in grade 8. They desire the quasi-adult treatment afforded students in the high school but are, instead, assigned a role they view inferior as junior high school students.

Many educators believe that the high school, therefore, should have all of its program under one administrative organization. In view of the available research information it can be concluded that students in grade 9 do differ substantially from those in the other two junior high school grades. A four-year high school program would more adequately serve ninth-graders by grouping them with students of similar needs and interests. It would also render unnecessary the pressures now being exerted by the high school on the junior high school through the offering of courses in grade 9 for which Carnegie unit credit is provided, and thereby forcing a high school schedule on the entire junior high school.

SUMMARY

The 6-3-3 plan as it exists today does not seem to meet adequately the needs of the in-between-aged student. The upper elementary program tends to be a patchwork of separate subjects, usually under the guise of the self-contained classroom, where the teacher is required to provide instruction in subject fields for which he may have had little preparation. It treats fifth- and sixth-grade youngsters in very much the same way it provides for the first-grader. The junior high school is, in many ways, a mimic of the senior high school. Its program is fragmented and rigid. Its teachers and administrators too often feel they are there on a temporary basis and have received little or no training specifically designed for teaching at that level. The high school impinges on the program of the ninth grade because of the requirements of the Carnegie unit schedule.

The purposes of the 6-3-3 plan as viewed in the literature have been eclipsed by administrative efficacy. The group which suffers most by this inadequacy is the in-between-aged students. They have been forced to the background in the planning of the school program.

We view the 6-3-3 plan in modern education as an anachronism analogous to the horseless carriage in a time of focus on a race for space. It is time to change to an organization and a program designed to care for *youngsters in the middle years,* too, as well as the younger and older ones.

PART III

The Program of the Middle School

Chapter 4

The Curriculum Plan

In the latter 1960s the curriculum of the emergent middle schools in the United States is being, but is not as yet, planned for most of these schools. Indeed, the authors hold that any curriculum plan should always be tentative, in the process of becoming a plan. However, it may be the status of their current construction and planning rather than a philosophy of curriculum which is keeping many middle schools from having fully developed curriculum plans available for review.

Some elements of a curriculum plan for the middle school, and of its development, are reviewed in this chapter. Illustrations of such aspects of the authors' plan as are available are used, and suggestions offered as to problems and procedures for full development of an always tentative operational plan for a middle school curriculum.

A CURRICULUM PLAN FOR *EACH* MIDDLE SCHOOL

Several factors suggest that *each* middle school should have its own planned program of learning opportunities, that is, its own curriculum plan. In the first place, we view the middle school program as one uniquely arranged to serve the educational needs of a population exhibiting a very wide range of differences on many traits. The flexibility required for serving such a population in a particular school is bound to result in a pattern of learning opportunities that is different from the pattern developed by another faculty for another population in another school. The alternative, which we consider undesirable, is to try to fit youngsters into

a closed pattern developed without real reference to the unique characteristics of the particular school and, quite likely, ill-fitted to its facilities,
faculty, and students.

Furthermore, it is especially necessary for the program of a particular
middle school to be fashioned with respect to the elementary program
which precedes and the high school program which follows. Actually, the
middle school curriculum plan must be a large slice of a total plan
developed for schooling from entrance to exit in a particular community.
Variations in grade structure from one community to another, differing
philosophies of education, and different school populations suggest the
virtual impossibility of these curriculum "slices" looking very much alike
as one views them from community to community.

Inevitably, too, physical facilities and faculty competences and interests
do affect the learning opportunities provided by a school. Ideally, the
building should be designed to offer whatever learning opportunities the
faculty can plan, but many middle schools do and will inherit their
facilities from schools originally planned for other levels. Their faculties,
too, cannot always be recruited to fit a program designed prior to faculty
procurement, and the opportunities the school offers are restricted to
those the faculty can adequately supervise.

These arguments do not add up to a conclusion that the middle school
can have no curriculum plan. To the contrary, they underline the necessity for each middle school to have a plan, tentative and open as it should
be. But the plan must be one, we think, that fits into the community's
total program of schooling, anticipates the characteristics of the population served, and squares with the realities of personnel and physical
facilities. Thus, it is best made by the faculty of a particular middle school
for that school.

A CLASSIFICATION OF LEARNING OPPORTUNITIES

Another publication in which one of the authors collaborated describes
a curriculum plan as a group of decisions which define "the nature of the
educational experiences to be provided pupils, the methods of selecting
and organizing the elements of the curriculum into a coherent and unified
program of education, and the place in the education of the child and the
sequential arrangement in which the elements of the curriculum are to be
developed."[1] This publication further describes the scope of a curriculum
plan as including these aspects:

---

[1] J. Galen Saylor and William M. Alexander, *Curriculum Planning for Modern Schools*
(New York: Holt, Rinehart and Winston, Inc., 1966), p. 269.

    1.   The class program of the school, which utilizes bodies of content selected and organized on some predetermined structure

    2.   Extraclassroom activities

    3.   Services provided by the school, such as guidance, health, library, food, and transportation services, and special services for exceptional children

    4.   The social life of the school and the interpersonal relationships among pupils and teachers

    5.   Organizational policies and procedures for providing the instructional program[2]

The more traditional classification of learning opportunities is that of "curricular" and "extracurricular." This designation really gives second-class status to learning opportunities which fall outside the traditional program of studies, and we therefore reject it. Considering, as we do, the total program of learning opportunities to be the curriculum, the term "extracurricular" is not really an appropriate category for any learning opportunities.

The functions of the middle school as described in our first chapter suggest another classification of learning opportunities which we consider more useful. This classification permits inclusion of all learning opportunities and at the same time facilitates a relation between purpose and curriculum organizations. The classification, which is developed more fully in following sections of this chapter, is:

    1.   Personal development

    2.   Skills for continued learning

    3.   Organized knowledge

There is some overlapping between these categories, of course, but the general factor which separates learning opportunities is their purpose. Thus, an opportunity which is planned to develop the learner's "self concept" is differentiated from one planned to assist his use of the library and still another, aimed to assist his understanding of basic concepts in science.

THE PERSONAL DEVELOPMENT AREA

The personal development area of the middle school curriculum encompasses the many learning opportunities which relate to the individual student's development as a person, exclusive of those opportunities directly aiming at his development of cognitive abilities. Thus, this area

[2]Saylor and Alexander.

includes opportunities for counseling, for the development of values, for health and physical development, and for exploration of many interests.

Counseling and Referral

The middle school child needs and should receive counseling on many matters. Hopefully, each of his teachers counsels him at times regarding his learning opportunities and progress in the respective curriculum areas. In addition, he needs one adult at school to whom he can go for information and assistance regarding any problem which relates to his participation in the school program.

In view of the numbers problem which plagues schools at all levels, there seems little hope that the middle school can have sufficient trained counselors to provide a ratio of counselors to children small enough that each child can have immediate and extended access to his counselor. Furthermore, we see value in a relationship of teacher and pupils which involves a teacher in the initial counseling of each child. Hence a plan whereby each child is a member of a home-base group led by a teacher-counselor seems desirable.

This plan must be perceived as different from the self-contained classroom of the elementary school and the administrative homeroom of the junior high school. In the middle school the home-base group is seen basically as an arrangement which assures each child a center which is his school home and in that center an adult who is watching out for his welfare at school. The home-base group has a regular period, usually daily, in which group activities may be carried on, and also in which the teacher in charge has opportunity to talk with individual pupils, to meet with small groups with similar problems or tasks, and to arrange schedules for both group and individual activities.

In such an arrangement, the home-base teacher becomes the first counselor and the referral agent for the members of the group. Appointments are made for interviews with the school's full-time counselor. Special tests are given or arranged for. Children needing specialized help in reading, speech, language, or with special health problems are referred to the services available. Conferences with parents are arranged. If special case investigations are needed, the teacher takes the first steps necessary for their arrangement.

Thus, the middle school child can have as much assistance in his personal development as the counseling and other services of the school provide. The center through which these services are arranged, the home base of the child, is a magnet drawing to each child the assistance of the teacher's data and perceptions as to his advisee.

Development of Values

The middle school child's values have been developing long before he left the elementary school, but continued and intensified focus on them in the middle school seems essential as the youngster approaches adolescence, with its challenges and perils. Certainly every learning opportunity in the middle school may condition children's attitudes and values, but some opportunities need to be especially arranged to guide the formulation of positive, persisting values.

Again, the home-base group provides an excellent setting for this purpose. Here, such issues as the following ones—highly provocative of discussion as to the consequences of alternative actions—are naturally considered:

1. Individual behavior in the school and its relation to the welfare of other persons;
2. The preparation of one's own school assignments and the taking of examinations;
3. Use of school and personal property;
4. Personal dress, mannerisms, and language;
5. Individual services to groups and to the school;
6. Role of students in school government;
7. Relation of students to events in the school, the community, and the nation and world;
8. Conduct of assemblies, recreational activities, and social affairs in the schools;
9. Selection of recreational reading, television programs, movies, and community cultural opportunities.

Such issues and others arising almost daily in the lives of middle school children are treated in various ways in the home-base group. Total group discussions may at times be desirable, usually preceded by an analysis of the issue through pupil or teacher presentation, a film or other aid, or the services of resource persons. Small groups within the home-base group may be formed to analyze each issue, with resultant total group consideration of alternative positions. Committees functioning on a continuing basis may bring periodic reports to the total group. The essential points are that issues which are real to the students be identified and considered, that alternative positions be fully explored, and that the consequences of preferred positions be clearly understood.

Health and Physical Development

The unique nature of the middle school program for health and physical development was characterized as follows by one group planning a new middle school:

The wide range of physical, emotional and social development found in youngsters of middle school age has particular significance for instruction in health and physical education and strongly suggests a diverse program. During this period, the child undergoes several stages of changing attitudes toward others. He also faces the physical and social problems brought about by his rapidly developing body. Too, the degree and range of hand-eye-foot coordination and large muscle development among the pupils is extensive. It is the relationship of attitude and physical skill that must be carefully considered in the physical education program if it is to be consistent with the concern for growth toward independence in learning which will pervade this school.

It has been estimated that by the time a youngster enters the ninth grade, he has developed seventy percent of the physical skill which he will ever possess. The emphasis of the program for the middle school pupil will not only be upon the development of fundamental skills but also upon extending the variety and number of physical activities in which these skills may be used. Such a program will include, for example, fundamental body movement, soccer, modern dance, badminton, tumbling, and aquatics. At the same time, the program will recognize the transitional nature of the physical and social needs of both sexes by offering co-educational experiences like ice skating and dancing.[3]

Health education. The program for health education of the middle schooler may be developed through a special time allotment and instructional situation, or by a shared plan including physical education, science, and the home-base group, or by some other plan developed for the school by its faculty. Whatever the plan of scheduling and presentation, it is essential that emphasis be given to the health requirements of the growing body of the "in-between-ager," to the development and complexities of the human reproductive system, and to health and safety practices appropriate to this age.

In a "*Time* Essay" of June 9, 1967, it was commented that "sex education has moved forward at startling speed" in the preceding three or four years and reported that "experts estimate that two years from now, 70% of the nation's schools will have broad, thorough sex-education programs."[4] Undoubtedly, the middle school is a major point, probably the first in many school systems, for specific attention to the sex-related aspects of growth from childhood to adolescence. The *Time* report cited

[3] *Middle School: A Report of Two Conferences on the Definition of Its Purpose, Its Spirit, and Its Shape* (Mount Kisco, N.Y.: Bedford Public Schools, February 26, 1962), p. 34.

[4] "On Teaching Children about Sex," *Time*, 89:36 (June 9, 1967).

as exemplary the program at Anaheim, California, noting that instruction there "begins in the seventh grade, covering parent-child and sibling conflicts, physical changes in adolescence, and masturbation. The eighth grade takes up more physical changes, 'problem-solving techniques,' and dating"; other topics are cited for higher grades.[5]

Physical education. The following description of the physical education program needed in the middle school suggests appropriate emphases:

The physical education program of the middle school is designed to promote the physical, social, and emotional well-being of the individual. It develops physical skills, and maintains and increases physical efficiency through a balanced, challenging and developmental program, stressing individual accomplishment with competition in team sports through an intramural program.

The program includes these activities which foster skills in rhythms and/or calisthenics, team and individual sports, social and folk dancing. Additional exploratory and recreational activities might be included (gymnastics, swimming, tennis, bowling, billiards, golf, modern dance, ballet) which would allow for individual accomplishment and pleasure now as well as in later years as an adult.

This program develops worthy ideals and habits along with a sense of achievement, fair play, control of emotions through group relations, powers of observation, judgment and decision. It should contribute to and foster the growth of student confidence, leadership, sustained effort and enjoyment considering at all times the individual's limitations as well as capabilities.[6]

Health services. The health services program provides for systematic identification and follow-up of health and physical deficiencies, including vision, hearing, teeth, malnutrition, and other difficulties. Hopefully, each middle school can have adequate facilities and arrangements to provide for continuing identification and follow-up services, as well as for emergency and corrective problems.

Individual Interests

The middle school program is expected to offer a wide range of special interest activities designed both to awaken and deepen interests of children most of whom are having a first opportunity to participate in school experiences outside the elementary school program of studies. This offering may be of several types.

The dominant plan in junior high schools has been that of courses offered on both elective and required bases, primarily in the fine and practical arts. Practice varies widely as to the length of such courses;

[5]"On Teaching Children about Sex," pp. 36–37.

[6]"Program of the Middle School: A Working Paper," prepared by participants in the Middle School Institute (mimeographed, University of Florida, 1967), p. 3.

some initial offerings may be as short as 6 weeks, although 12 and 18 weeks' courses are more common. Other courses, hopefully elected after some briefer exploratory experience, are full-year ones.

In addition to regular courses, both middle and junior high schools offer a variety of clubs and other occasional activities that provide for the exploration and development of interests not provided for in the regular class structure. Thus a description provided the authors by the Alvord Unified School District, Riverside, California, lists the following clubs and activities that "should supplement the general instructional program:"

1. Active Student Council
2. Archery Club
3. Rifle Club
4. Photography Club
5. Pep Club
6. Song and Cheer Leader Groups
7. Boys' Cooking Club
8. Art and Poster Club
9. Rocket Club
10. Song Club
11. Chemistry Club
12. Square Dancing Club
13. Rock Hounds Club
14. Model Club—airplanes, boats, cars, etc.
15. Radio Club
16. Electronics Club
17. Ceramics Club
18. Code Club
19. Language Clubs—Spanish, French, German, etc.
20. Aeronautics and Space Club

The authors suggest a pattern of special interest activities for the middle school that has these three aspects:

1. *Exploratory experiences.* Each middle schooler should have an opportunity to learn enough about his interest in such areas as the following, to decide whether to participate for an extended period: art, dance, drama, foreign language, home arts, industrial arts, journalism, music, typing, and various school work projects. Exploration might be done through very brief survey-type introductory courses, possibly arranged for small groups working in the laboratory involved over a period of one to three weeks.

2. *Laboratory courses.* One or more full-year experiences should be available for the interested student in each of the areas named and prob-

ably others as student interests and facilities are developed. Several of these areas might well develop such laboratory experiences in more than one aspect; thus the music program may include special interest opportunities in band, chorus, and orchestra; the art and industrial arts program opportunities in woodworking, ceramics, crafts, and painting, in addition to the general programs; and the foreign language program opportunities in several languages.

3. *Activity program.* A variety of special interest clubs may be provided on an occasional basis through some scheduling arrangement that gives each student a chance without enforcing uniform participation. Clubs should be voluntary and open to all students. Their successful existence would depend on the availability of resource leadership from the faculty or community. Usually they would meet during the school day, with children who do not participate having the activity period free for work in classroom or library or another study center. Under this arrangement a student may participate in only one club at a time, although club meetings may alternate to allow each student to be involved in more than one activity.

It is recognized, too, that many student interests are related to the development of greater competence in learning skills and to certain areas of organized knowledge. These interests are served through the other curriculum areas to which we now turn attention.

SKILLS FOR CONTINUED LEARNING

Learning skills introduced in the elementary school require further instruction in the middle school, and here additional skills are required. The further career of the child as a learner—a career that needs to be lifelong—may be virtually settled in these middle school years. If the child enjoys learning, if he becomes skilled in its processes, then a lifelong pursuit of learning may be assured. If learning is distasteful, if he lacks basic skills, he will likely drop out of school long before completing college, possibly during the high school years, and grow into an adulthood marred by ignorance and inability to adjust to new conditions and situations.

The program of learning skills development is uniquely a responsibility of the entire faculty. Every instructional situation is an opportunity to make learning both attractive and possible. But the significance of this area is such that the curriculum plan cannot leave it to chance. Thus the middle school faculty may well develop its own plan of identifying and teaching learning skills. Such a plan would probably include several of the provisions now described.

What skills? The curriculum plan should define and describe the learning skills to be emphasized. Such a list would undoubtedly include the following:

1. Reading;
2. Listening;
3. Asking questions; interviewing;
4. Viewing films, television, and so forth;
5. Using library tools and resources;
6. Observing the natural and social environment;
7. Organizing information;
8. Generalizing from observation, incidents, reading, and the like;
9. Evaluating information, opinion, observation, and such;
10. Problem solving.

Learning skills in every classroom. The middle school faculty will need to determine which skills are to be emphasized in all learning situations and which in only certain situations. Thus, it has to be decided where reading skills will be developed, and where and on what bases special reading instruction is to be given. Decisions may be reached, too, as to responsibility for direct instruction in such particular skills as listening, viewing, and using the library; is this to be done in all language arts classes, for example, or by the librarian in a special series of instruction, or by some combination approach?

Specialized instruction in learning skills. The middle school is certain to have a considerable number of students who need direct instruction in reading and other skills. Decisions need to be reached as to the use of a reading laboratory—who is to direct it? When and for how long shall children needing specialized instruction go to the laboratory? Can programed instruction be used, and under what conditions? The faculty may well consider, too, the advisability of setting up a composition or writing laboratory in which tutorial or other assistance may be given children needing special help in organizing information and ideas into written form.

Among other possibilities for specialized instruction in learning skills, the following may merit faculty consideration:

1. The establishment of study-skills centers supervised by teachers interested in helping children develop improved study skills;
2. The development of a series of training sessions for teaching such skills as interviewing, problem solving, evaluation, and group discussion;
3. The use of high school students as tutors for middle schoolers;
4. The use of automated programs of instruction in skills areas for which these are available.

Independent study. The middle school may be the first opportunity for many students to have experience in independent study. We refer here to learning activity largely motivated by the child's own intellectual curiosity and carried on independently of a class or other group, with the teacher serving as a resource person rather than as the director of learning activity. Such activity may be in the nature of individual projects undertaken by some members of a class, or it may be a plan of study developed for exceptional children judged by a teacher as needing independent rather than group instruction, or it may be a seminar-type program in which the major learning activity for all members consists of special, individual projects, readings, papers, or investigations.

Such independent studies usually emanate from one of the fields of organized knowledge. However, they might also be used in connection with the development of special interests or learning skills. For example, a student seeking to improve in his reading and other information-getting and organizing skills and having some particular hobby interest might be guided by his home-base or reading teacher to do independent study in the interest field.

A coordinated program might also be planned by the faculty to provide special arrangements for a group of students selected from volunteers for independent study cutting across conventional subject lines. These students would be given special schedules allowing them time to pursue their investigations in the school library or laboratories or elsewhere as arranged with the faculty coordinator.

THE AREA OF ORGANIZED KNOWLEDGE

The curriculum of every middle school is expected for the foreseeable future to provide systematic instruction in the subject fields generally provided in all schools and at all levels: English, mathematics, science, and social studies. Undoubtedly, the specific organizing centers determined within these fields and the specific content chosen around these centers will and should vary from school to school. An indication of the variations and yet of common emphases is revealed by examination of curriculum descriptions contained in reports and recommendations of middle school programs. Such materials for three middle school situations are excerpted here.

A Middle School in a Suburban Area

The 1966–1967 *Student Guide* for the Pearl River Middle School (grades 6–8) of Pearl River, New York, includes descriptions of the various curriculum areas. The excerpts cited are for the areas of present concern.[7]

Mathematics.   Every student should have a practical understanding of the basic concepts of mathematics and he should be helped and encouraged to develop and use all of his innate capacities.

The mathematics program will place a great deal of emphasis on the "new" mathematics. However, the traditional goals of mastery of computation and manipulative skills are still stressed. Modern mathematics deals with the basic concepts that explain the rules and serve to unify the branches of mathematics. The goal is for you to grow in understanding the basic mathematical ideas and to see the connections that exist among some of them so that there will be greater flexibility and creativity in application.

In the sixth grade you will continue practice in fundamental operations with natural numbers, decimals, and fractions. You will extend your understanding of measures and continue to build and refine quantitative terminology.

In the seventh and eighth grades you will be expected to experiment with ideas and to figure problems out for yourself. You will make discoveries in mathematics and will be given new insights into how a mathematician functions. The principal function of the teacher is to carefully set the stage for learning in an organized fashion so that you will "discover" for yourself the fundamental concepts involved. These concepts are those which you will use as you continue your study of mathematics.

Language Arts and Social Studies.   In most classes these subjects are taught together by the same teacher so that you can see the relationships that exist naturally between language arts and social studies.

Students who take a language may take these courses with separate teachers. However, these two teachers will work together closely to see that work in each course is related.

In language arts you will study grammar, acceptable English usage, good writing style, and literature of all types. The literature and reading programs are closely related to materials studied in social studies.

In Grade 6, for example, your literature study will include reading of myths, stories, and legends from early times. These readings will tie in with your social studies topics: the story of man, his way of life, his struggles, and his accomplishments. This study traces the highlights of man's development from his origin to modern times, with an emphasis on selected modern cultures.

In Grade 7 your literature will focus on the themes of "Courage" and "Man and His Environment." These themes are related to your social studies units, which will explore the local community and New York State with an emphasis on the Iroquois Indians and the "Age of Homespun."

In Grade 8 literature is related to social studies explorations of American history from the Civil War period to the present day.

Science.   The three units of science have been worked out to help you gain useful information about the world in which you live. They are also designed to give you knowledge and abilities to carry on successfully in a world that is science oriented.

[7]Excerpted from *Pearl River Middle School 1966–67 Student Guide* (Pearl River, N.Y.: Union Free School District No. 8), pp. 2–4.

In the sixth grade, you will study astronomy and geology. Here you will find the earth's place in the universe and how it probably came to be as it is today.

In the seventh grade you will study the life sciences. You can learn all about the plant and animal kingdoms and how each one depends upon the other in the balance of nature. You will also learn a great deal about yourselves, how your body functions, and how you can keep yourself in good health.

In the eighth grade you will be looking at the physical sciences and covering such topics as water, sound, heat, electricity, light, and many more.

This program is designed for you to learn through investigations as individuals or in groups, both in school and at home.

Two Middle Schools in a Small City

Two Dover, Delaware, middle schools are organized on a grade 5–8 basis. Material describing the program of these schools includes the following statements relevant to the subject fields of English, mathematics, science, and social studies.[8]

Mathematics. Dover Middle Schools' mathematics program is designed for children in grades 5 through 8. The program is continuous over this four-year period of time. A child beginning sixth grade continues his studies in mathematics in the unit in which he was working when he finished fifth grade. The same is true of the seventh and eighth grade pupil. A teacher who teaches mathematics in Dover Middle Schools is not limited by a basic textbook. The teacher has available a large resource of mathematics texts and enrichment materials from a variety of publishers. Each fifth grade math teacher has fourth, fifth, and sixth grade materials with which to work; each sixth grade teacher has fifth, sixth, and seventh grade materials, etc. The total mathematics program is outlined in a thorough curriculum guide.

Portions of the following units are now being taught at each grade level: Numeration Systems, Base Number Systems, Mathematical Systems, Problem Solving, Rational Numbers, Ratio Proportion, Measurement, Geometry, and Percent.

Humanities. The humanities program encompasses the subject areas in English and social studies. The objective in combining these two areas is to correlate the social and behavioral sciences with language arts, employing man's creative expressions in literature, music, and fine arts, and the performing arts. Through this emphasis the pupil is better able to understand man in his individuality and in his culture. Past, present, and future are treated not as separate entities but as spatial units with reciprocal relationships. The pupil is brought into contact with other communities, countries, and cultures as well as with his own personal sphere of experiences. People and their ways of living are presented through an examination of:

1. Environment: climate, location, resources, geographic determinism
2. Institutions: family, economy, government, education, religion

[8]"Teaching in the Dover Middle Schools," prepared by Alex M. Gottesman, Assistant Superintendent (mimeographed, Dover, Delaware, Schools, Spring 1967).

3. Values, goals, beliefs
4. Creative expressions

The fifth grade curriculum approaches American civilization through a study of geographic regions and important individual contributions. The sixth grade curriculum is American neighbors exploring Canada, the West Indies, Mexico, Central and South Americas. The seventh grade curriculum presents the concepts of social studies and stresses cultural anthropology with an in-depth study of various cultures. The eighth grade curriculum returns to American civilization. After the acquaintance with other world neighbors and cultural groupings, the pupil examines the development of a national image through its historical processes. With this basic social studies curriculum the language arts is a most flexible complement and necessity to enrich the pupil's usage and application of the English language as the key to communication.

Science.   The guiding philosophy behind the science program of the middle schools is to provide an activity centered course at the pupil's level in order to facilitate a unified understanding of scientific conceptual schemes and concepts. An attempt is made to employ a type of curriculum presenting scientific ideas in a logical order so as to have continuity and to avoid repetition. A special attempt is made to provide a wide variety of meaningful laboratory experiences, reports and/or projects throughout the curriculum which suit the interests, needs, and abilities of the pupils.

The following areas are presented in grades five through eight:

Our Living Environment
Our Physical Environment
Life Science
Earth and Space

Children explore living things in their environment which is facilitated with the use of science laboratories, equipment, and community resources. Some of the areas that are explored are as follows: characteristics of living things, invertebrates, vertebrates, simple plants and higher plants, the human body, and the interdependence of living organisms.

Physical science concepts are discovered through the use of the laboratories and a variety of other activities. Some of the areas explored are: measurement, chemistry in the child's environment, electricity and magnetism, light and sound, simple machines, and communications.

Life science is taught in the regular science laboratories. A broad use of community resources is encouraged. Explorations include: biology as a science, interrelationships and interdependence of living things, continuation of life (reproduction), simple plants, higher plants, lower invertebrates and vertebrates, higher invertebrates and vertebrates, human biology, and problems in human biology.

Earth and space science is presented through a variety of learning experiences. Some of the areas that are explored are as follows: the nature of matter, measurement, mineralogy, the study of rocks, fossils, mountain building and related topics in geology, oceanography, meteorology, conservation, astronomy, and space science.

Middle Schools
in a Large Urban System

In connection with the shift to a 4-4-4 plan in New York City, a set of Committee Recommendations to the Superintendent of Schools, dated December 20, 1965, included recommendations as to various curriculum areas. Those pertaining to English, mathematics, science, and social studies are excerpted here:[9]

English. Instruction will be differentiated for pupils of various levels of achievement, with major consideration given to the child's status in reading. Articulation will be closely maintained with the Primary Schools and the High Schools. A structured, sequential program will be built, level by level, in each of the language arts areas. The approach to teaching will be integrative, fusing pupil language arts experiences.

A concerned effort will be made to meet the reading needs of all students. Reading skills will be taught directly as well as incidentally. In this pattern, after spending some classroom time on skill-building activities aimed at developing children's insights into the reading process, teachers will seek to reinforce this learning by emphasizing wide reading, in and out of class, both for enjoyment and for appreciation.

Pupils' capacities in speaking and listening will be developed through a newly-established sequence of activities calling for specific areas of concentration at each ability level based on sequential skills. Although skillful participation in round table discussions and in public speaking will be an objective for those children able to function successfully in such activities, the main objectives for all pupils will be that of enabling them to speak with ease and clarity. Standard American speech will be taught, but recognition will be given to the role of regional and dialectal patterns.

Emphasis will be placed on the teaching of composition skills and on improving competence in writing. Teachers will guide pupils through the complete composition cycle of preparation, writing, proof-reading, evaluation, and revision for each major writing assignment.

The literature program will aim at a balance in the study of literary types and will furnish, in part, a basis for a course in humanities. Allocations of time will be assigned for the novel, the short story, the play, the biography, the essay, and the poem. This will provide a common core of modern and traditional "classics" to be given intensive classroom treatment.

For the content of their writing, children will frequently use their own experiences, stimulated, if necessary, by the teacher's motivation.

Grammar, usage, spelling, handwriting, and word study will be emphasized. The language program will continue to reflect experimental work and new developments in such areas as grammar, spelling, linguistics, semantics, and others.

---

[9]From Committee Recommendations to the Superintendent of Schools, *Primary School— Intermediate School—Four-Year Comprehensive High School* (New York City: Public Schools, December 20, 1965), pp. 40–43.

Mathematics. The program of mathematics for the Intermediate School will be built on the basic content or common body of knowledge developed in the Primary School. At the intermediate level, differentiation of content will be presented to meet the individual needs of pupils whose varying rates of growth and academic achievement become more marked at this stage.

Mathematics for Grades 5, 6, 7 and 8 will include the development of fundamental concepts and skills of arithmetic as well as the basic concept of metric and nonmetric geometry; newer concepts of sets, numeration, inequalities; and the structure of arithmetic, all of which will be needed to prepare children for modern High School mathematics.

Science. The approach to the teaching of science in the Middle School will emphasize the theory and methods of inquiry, and the discovery of concepts through direct and individualized laboratory-centered science experiences. The program will be built on the foundation laid in the Primary School.

The program's stress will be on the development of science as a method of critical thinking, of investigation, and of operation. Discrete blocks of subject matter from the various science, mathematics, and social science disciplines will be integrated in terms of their suitability for the development of concepts and generalizations. An individual-laboratory approach will also allow the pupils to learn from first-hand experience at their own pace. Scientific attitudes, particularly as they apply to human relations, will be stressed.

Social studies. A revision of the K–12 History and Social Science program based on sequential development of concepts is now underway in the city schools. The program for the Middle School will draw on this new curriculum. This program will unify and develop curriculum concepts spirally from all related disciplines (history, geography, economics, sociology, political science, anthropology, archeology, psychology, and others). An appreciation of the values of all cultures and ethnic groups will be stressed. The study of civil rights, civil liberties, civic responsibility, and human relations will furnish a persistent theme throughout the intermediate grades. Correlation of this course with literature, and with the history of art, music, religion, and philosophy as part of a humanities course will be made the basis of pilot projects.

Common Goals and Content

These illustrative descriptions of plans for the four major curriculum areas indicate not only some difference in approaches but also some commonality of goals and content. The following common emphases seem especially significant in the middle school curriculum:

1. The importance of the student's own investigations that lead him to understand basic concepts in the various disciplines and especially in mathematics and science;

2. The application of mathematics and language skills and of basic concepts in science and social studies to everyday activities and problems;

3. The relationships of people and cultures to each other, to their institutions, and to their environment;

4. The significance of organized knowledge, especially of major generalizations in the various fields, to the understanding of people and their ways of living;

5. The role of literature and the arts in the development of communication and culture;

6. The individual's mastery of such ways of thinking about and attacking questions and problems as will yield reliable answers and solutions.

CRITERIA FOR EVALUATING AND DEVELOPING THE CURRICULUM

Among many criteria which might be used in evaluating and developing the middle school curriculum, several considered especially appropriate are briefly stated in the following paragraphs.

Is the Curriculum Balanced?

Balance has at least two dimensions: the school's program and the individual's own program, that is, the curriculum "planned" and the curriculum "had." As to the former dimension, curriculum planners and evaluators would answer such questions as these:

Are learning opportunities provided in each of the three major aspects of the curriculum sufficiently broad and varied to provide for the total school population?

Do the school plant, facilities, and schedule facilitate attention to each aspect of the curriculum?

Is the curriculum plan sufficiently structured that progression is assured without unnecessary duplications from year to year?

Are learning experiences so planned as to provide a variety of learning activities with adequate time for both "doing" and "reflecting" activities?

Attention to the balance of learning opportunities in which each individual becomes involved necessitates consideration of such questions as these:

Is each student counseled periodically by his home-base teacher or other counselor as to his choice of optional opportunities?

Does the cumulative record of each student reflect his total program and progress from year to year, and is it consulted by his counselors?

Is each student helped to have both breadth and depth in his program?

Is Continuity Provided?

The middle school program is uniquely situated to bring about continuity both in the total school program and in each student's own program. Among many related problems for curriculum planners and evaluators are these:

Is there an organization for curriculum planning which facilitates review and evaluation of the total program and each of its major aspects for the entire period of schooling?

Are there provisions for the smooth transition of students from one level to another? One year to another?

Do teachers of the same students, especially team teachers, exchange information regarding these students' experiences with their past and present teachers?

Do teachers representing the same field of specialization plan periodically so as to maintain a curriculum structure that has continuity?

Do teachers systematically consider the past experiences, present interests, and current learning status of their students in planning instructional sequences?

Is each student's daily and weekly schedule planned to minimize unnecessarily sharp breaks in learning activities and unduly short or long periods of the same type of activity?

Is the Curriculum Plan Flexible?

The best plan for a middle school's curriculum breaks down if ground-to-be-covered and other expectations restrict teachers' initiative in changing plans to fit situations as they arise. For example, flexibility is called for by these questions:

Can teaching teams develop their own schedules for the curriculum areas they represent?

Can needed and available learning resources be utilized at the time they are needed?

Can teachers arrange for longer periods of work with pupils when needed? Can individual pupils be scheduled for independent study when its use is indicated? Can teachers work out plans to visit each other's groups?

Can individual students be moved from one home base or other organization to another when teachers agree on the need for such movement?

Can new content be substituted in curriculum syllabuses as it becomes available?

Are teachers encouraged and helped to work out instructional units for testing experimentally in their classrooms?

Is Curriculum Individualization Provided?

Throughout our discussion of the middle school program we have emphasized its justification for attending to the wide range of individual differences among the middle schoolers. This emphasis may be tested by such questions as these:

Are self-direction and independent study emphasized in both counseling and instruction?

Do home-base teachers have adequate opportunity, and do they use it well for helping each student in planning his own program?

Are students given adequate guidance in selecting and carrying on their individual learning activities in each learning situation?

Are such problems as underachievement, poor behavior, irregular school attendance, and disinterest studied for clues as to program planning for the students concerned?

Is each individual's record in the personal development and learning skills areas analyzed by his teachers and counselors as a basis for ensuring his optimum progression?

CONTINUING CURRICULUM PLANNING

We see as essential to the maintenance of a good curriculum in the emergent middle school, a set of provisions for continuing curriculum planning. Even if the school begins operations, as it should, with the finest of well-formulated, comprehensive plans, continued curriculum planning is necessitated by the very nature of the middle school program, as well as by the facts of an ever-changing society and body of knowledge. To ensure such continued curriculum planning, the following provisions are suggested:

1. Complete, as fully as is possible before the school opens, a plan of the general design of the curriculum in its major aspects.

2. Schedule provisions whereby the following groups can meet regularly for curriculum review and evaluation: some faculty group representing each major aspect of the curriculum at all levels; teachers most involved in the personal development aspect of the curriculum; teachers most involved in the learning skills aspect; teaching teams working in the organized knowledge aspect; and groups of teachers with specialized com-

petence in English, mathematics, science, and social studies, and perhaps other areas.

3. Provide services to assist teachers in keeping their own knowledge updated about their students and their teaching specialties: inservice education activities, meetings with guidance and child development specialists, library of curriculum and instructional materials, and advice of curriculum specialists.

4. Establish a program of coordination of curriculum planning and evaluation by a curriculum coordinator, who provides an input of ideas and materials, assists planning groups in developing their own materials, and arranges for articulation of middle school planning with that for the lower and upper levels.

5. Provide for representation of the middle school on vertical curriculum planning committees for the total school program and its major aspects.

Chapter 5

Teaching in the Middle School

Teaching in the middle school is a challenging and rewarding experience for those who enjoy working with older children and younger adolescents. The extreme variability among these "in-between-agers" demands a staff of adults possessing a wide variety of skills, abilities, and talents. The nature of the middle school student is, in reality, what differentiates teaching in the middle school from teaching at any other level of the school organizational ladder. These pupils, who are no longer children but are not yet adolescents, need the guidance and stimulation of teachers who see as their main goal the full development of the creative potential of every individual in the middle school.

The goal of "full development of the creative potential of every individual" is admittedly too broad to suggest specific teaching practices, but it does provide a perspective from which to view approaches to teaching. For example, the curriculum plan described in Chapter 4 provides for "systematic instruction" in such subject fields as English, mathematics, science, and social studies, but the aim of the systematic instruction is to enhance the individual's perception of his competency as a learner, *not* to reach some arbitrary grade level mastery in the subject. This attitude toward teaching is inherent in the functions of the middle school which have been stated or implied throughout this book.

TEACHING IS RELATED TO THE SCHOOL'S FUNCTIONS

A teacher behaves in the classroom, in large part, according to what he believes to be the important functions the school is to serve. When the transmission of knowledge is viewed as the primary function of the school, the teacher's task is to organize the content of the fields of knowledge, present the content to the pupils, assign the materials to be drilled and learned, and, finally, test the pupils for mastery of the subject matter content. When the school's functions are broadened to include the development of attitudes and understandings, as well as the accomplishment of certain developmental tasks of youth, the teacher's role is broadened accordingly. The broad functions outlined in Chapter 1 for the emergent middle school include the following: (1) *to provide a program for a range of older children, preadolescents, and early adolescents;* (2) *to emphasize individualization and continuity in the educational program;* and (3) *to accelerate the acceptance of promising innovations in the educational process.* The three-way classification of curriculum opportunities described in Chapter 4 is designed to carry out these functions. A statement of purposes of teaching in a school serving the above functions should be formulated by each middle school. We propose the following guide:

1. *The middle school aims to help the pupil understand himself as a unique human individual with personal needs and shared social responsibilities.* Thus the teacher in the middle school must be a skilled worker able to help older children, developing into adolescents, to examine, understand, and accept new roles and changing relationships. In fulfilling this role, the teacher becomes a *teacher-counselor* with responsibility for knowing the student well enough to give individual educational guidance and to coordinate all of the various components of the individual student's total program. The teacher needs to learn to work effectively with small groups, encouraging pupils to pursue openly the questions of personal meaning to them and to see these questions in the wider context of adolescent developmental tasks. A knowledge of the principles of group dynamics and a thorough understanding of the nature of preadolescent and early adolescent behavior are essential for successful performance of these roles.

2. *One purpose of the middle school is to assure every pupil a degree of success in understanding the underlying principles and the ways of knowing in the areas of organized learning.* In fulfilling this role, the teacher must become a *subject specialist* in one or more areas of organized knowledge. For a middle school teacher to become a "specialist," it is not necessary for him to become a renowned scholar or a sophisticated researcher. The middle school subject specialist should identify with one of the basic academic disciplines, pursue advanced study beyond the general education level in that field, and attempt to keep informed about the field by participating in the appropriate professional association, reading the journals in the field, and sharing with his colleagues the important developments in his chosen area of specialization. It is important to note

that the aim of the curriculum in the area of organized knowledge is to assure every pupil a degree of success in understanding the big ideas of the subject field. This is considerably different from saying that some minimum standard of mastery of some stated quantity of content is to be required. The goal of success for every pupil at an appropriate level demands a teacher who knows a subject well enough to see and to express the premises at the core of every organized discipline. Such a teacher is better able to help students see relationships among their school subjects and to discover relevancies to significant areas of their present and future lives. And, even more importantly, only a teacher who is enthusiastic about what he is teaching is likely to transmit an enthusiasm for learning and scholarship to his students.

There is a danger that some will misinterpret this purpose and use it as an excuse to return to subject-centered teaching. Indeed, the effect of some of the national curriculum projects in many instances has been to introduce subject matter earlier, stressing *the* program and over-emphasizing grades. Nothing could be further from the aims of the middle school envisioned in this book. What is envisioned is that by varying the time allotted and the techniques used, every child will come to see that as man has tried to make sense of the world around him, he has organized his knowledge about the world into "disciplines" or "subjects." Through active involvement with the materials, methods, and major ideas of the disciplines, the middle school child can learn how knowledge is produced as well as how it is systematically organized. In short, the middle school strives for the intellectual development of all pupils, not just those who in the past have been early identified as "college bound." Furthermore, the goal of intellectual development is not pursued at the expense of the social, emotional, and physical development of the individual. The curriculum plan described in Chapter 4 promotes a balance among these developmental goals. In today's world, the citizen who is not minimally competent to understand the contributions of the organized disciplines to man's progress is at a serious disadvantage.

3. *Another major purpose of the middle school is to promote maximum individual growth in the basic learning skills.* These include communication and computation, social and civic competence, and continued learning. Such skills can be taught, in part, in various types of learning laboratories, special resource centers, and independent study centers. A wide range of programed instructional materials and electronic and other newer media will be utilized. New teaching positions, as well as new teaching strategies, will be created for work in this area of the school's program. Many of the basic skills will be developed in the regular classroom under the direction of the teacher-counselor or the subject specialist as well, but the work of these teachers will be augmented by specialists

who can diagnose specific learning problems and prescribe individual remedial and developmental programs.

4. *A significant purpose of the middle school is to foster independent learning on the part of every pupil.* Pupils begin to learn to work independently from the very earliest school experiences, but at the middle school level independent learning skills and habits become major curriculum emphases. Teaching strategies to encourage and facilitate independent learning must be identified and practiced. The curriculum plan should not leave independent study to chance, but rather it should make provision for such study in the schedule of each student. In working with independent study plans, teachers must learn to give students freedom in choosing the project and guidance in carrying through with the study. For example, teachers in this area of the curriculum need to gain skill in helping students define the problem and state the objectives. It is often much easier to do this for the student, but the goal of giving the student the thrill of proposing his own plan of study is then thwarted. In the beginning stages, the student will need fairly definite steps to follow during the independent study, including an understanding of what questions he is trying to answer, where he might start his search, when his study is to terminate, and what procedures will be used to evaluate the study. Initial independent study projects should be short-term affairs. As the student develops confidence in studying independently, he should be given increasing freedom to design his own study plans. Not all independent study will be individual study. Often, two or three students working together on a project of mutual interest will stimulate each other to very high quality performance. Also, some of the independent study learnings can grow out of student seminar-type programs. Teaching in seminar-type settings requires teachers who can foster interaction among students as well as student-teacher dialogue.

5. *The middle school aims to permit wide exploration of personal interests.* The exploratory function of the junior high school has typically been met by requiring a series of courses in such subject areas as the fine arts, music, home economics, industrial arts, commercial subjects, or others, depending on the outlook of the school community. In many communities today's "in-between-agers" have already had rich experiences in the areas in which they are asked to take "introductory" courses. The middle school program should provide the scheduled time, plant facilities and equipment, and trained resource personnel to allow boys and girls to pursue academic and avocational interests beyond the beginning stages. Teaching in this area of the curriculum may at times be done by citizens in the community who possess particular skills and abilities. They may be volunteers who can devote only a few hours a week or month to the program, or they may be employed by the school as technical aides to work with certificated teachers.

UNIQUE QUALIFICATIONS
OF MIDDLE SCHOOL TEACHERS

The above list of functions and purposes of teaching in the middle school does not attempt to be comprehensive; rather it is illustrative of those purposes most distinctive of the emergent middle school. What kinds of persons should be selected to serve the functions and carry out these purposes? Are there desirable personal characteristics for middle school teachers which might be different from teachers of other levels? Unfortunately, research is not much help in answering this question. While it seems reasonable to look for such qualities as warmth, supportiveness, empathy, responsiveness, and the like rather than for their opposites, Getzels and Jackson reviewed the literature in this field and concluded:

> Despite the critical importance of the problem and a half-century of prodigious research effort, very little is known about the nature and measurement of teacher personality, or about the relationship between teacher personality and teaching effectiveness. The regrettable fact is that many of the studies have not produced significant results.[1]

Obviously, those responsible for staffing schools cannot wait for research results to tell them what types of teachers to employ. A more promising approach than merely listing desired qualities to be sought in teacher candidates for the middle school may be to spell out as precisely as possible the demands of the job and then let the teachers select themselves. A person who is comfortable working all alone in a self-contained classroom with approximately thirty pupils may not find it easy to deal with the greater numbers of pupils he will have to face in most middle school plans. On the other hand, the teacher who is accustomed to a departmentalized junior high school may find it difficult to adjust to the greater blocks of time with a single group of pupils and the resulting greater responsibility for planning and evaluating a larger portion of the instruction for the group. The middle school teacher may require more specialization in subject matter than an elementary trained teacher usually possesses and, at the same time, more general knowledge of a large number of areas that a secondary trained teacher typically handles. The middle school teacher must work with pupils who are not as dependent on the teacher as younger children, and yet not as capable of independence as older secondary youths.

Until better instruments for predicting teacher effectiveness in particular situations are developed, a teacher's expressed desire to work with

[1] J. W. Getzels and P. W. Jackson, "The Teacher's Personality and Characteristics," in N. L. Gage (ed.), *Handbook of Research on Teaching* (Skokie, Ill.: Rand McNally & Company, 1963), p. 574.

middle school age children in an innovative organization is as significant as any other personal quality that can be identified at this time. Indeed, that the teacher's attitude toward an organization is a critical factor in the success of the organization is the position of a recent UNESCO institute publication. The report states:

> It is not an exaggeration to say that teachers have the power to ensure or to jeopardize the success of any particular form of organization. We are not suggesting that they indulge in acts of sabotage as a reprisal against authorities who impose grouping practices with which they disagree. Teachers obviously have too deep a sense of professional responsibility to indulge in behavior of this kind. What clearly happens, however—and there is abundant evidence to support this contention—is that the success of any form of educational organization assessed in terms, for example, of the progress and achievements of the pupils concerned is less dependent on the form of that organization, *per se,* than on the attitude of the teachers who function within its framework.[2]

What this suggests is that, assuming appropriate professional credentials, enthusiasm for working with "in-between-agers" and a positive attitude toward innovation and flexibility are good recommendations for successful teaching in the middle school. It should be added, however, that even the most enthusiastic and well-qualified teachers must have the support of a congenial organizational framework, abundant resources, pertinent inservice programs, and appropriate evaluation procedures to assure continued optimum performance.

SELECTING THE MOST APPROPRIATE TEACHING METHODS FOR MIDDLE SCHOOLS

The treatment of methodology in the history of American education has followed an interesting progression. From an earlier period when a single method, such as the Morrisonian Unit Plan, might be recommended for all of education, there was a shift toward the position that method was an outgrowth of a teacher's personality and that a teacher should find the method he was most comfortable with and perfect it. A newer view of methodology is that an effective teacher is adept at using a variety of teaching methods for different purposes and for different kinds of learners. While teachers have always adapted their particular choice of method to suit the demands of the situation, the writers of the following description had in mind something more than merely modifying a single method to suit varying conditions:

[2]Alfred Yates (ed.), *Grouping In Education* (New York: John Wiley & Sons, Inc., 1966), pp. 83–84.

While we are not at all certain what combination of events makes a good lesson or what combination of qualities makes a good teacher, the potentially better teacher is one who is able to plan and control his professional behavior—to teach many kinds of lessons, to reach many diverse learners, to create different social climates, and to adapt a wide range of teaching strategies to constantly changing conditions. The reason the teacher must possess a range of teaching strategies is simply because different styles or patterns of teaching behavior are useful for different educational purposes, and every teacher seeks educational ends that demand more than one way of teaching. Sometimes students are unruly, and the teacher must shift his strategies to develop a cooperative social system. Sometimes students are bold thinkers who challenge the teacher to lead them in the exploration of content that interests them. Other students are conforming thinkers, reluctant to venture original ideas. They need to be induced to stop seeking "right" answers and develop an intellectual autonomy. There are learners lacking important basic skills, who need direction and protection until they can acquire them. Each student is a unique combination of needs and abilities, and each class a unique combination of individuals. The teacher learns to recognize differences between students and between groups of students and adjust his strategies and style of teaching as he turns from one to another.[3]

It is interesting to note that in the above description the word *method* is not present; instead, such words as *strategies* and *styles* are used. This is not merely a difference in terminology; a shift in thinking about the function of teaching has taken place: Teaching is not considered as the application of a method or methods but rather the making of decisions about organization, activities, materials, strategies, and evaluative procedures to accomplish instructional goals. Nevertheless, teacher behavior can be classified broadly into one or another of several methods, and it is usual to find some methods recommended and others looked upon with disfavor in pedagogical journals and texts. For example, the *lecture* method is usually compared unfavorably with the *discussion* method; *deductive* approaches are thought to be inferior to *inductive*; and, currently, *discovery* methods are much preferred to *expository* techniques. Such *either-or* dichotomies are unwise. Despite a plethora of "studies" purporting to compare the relative efficacy of various methods, an exhaustive survey of research on teaching methods led Wallen and Travers to conclude that rigorous well-defined "research has produced no results favoring any particular pattern of teaching."[4]

Teaching strategies or methods should be selected because of their relevance to a particular instructional objective; they should not be selected or rejected because of a naive position such as: Student-led discus-

[3]Bruce R. Joyce and Berj Harootunian, *The Structure of Teaching* (Chicago: Science Research Associates, Inc., 1967), pp. 94–95.

[4]Norman E. Wallen and Robert M. W. Travers, "Analysis and Investigation of Teaching Methods," in *Handbook of Research on Teaching,* pp. 458–505 (see also page 451).

sions are always "good"; or teacher-conducted lectures are always "bad."
Since the pupil population of the middle school brings to the classroom
a variety of learning styles, and since the program of the school has
varied educational goals, the position that teachers should utilize a range
of strategies or methods appears very sound. The problem is complicated,
however, if teachers do not know how to use a variety of teaching styles
suited to particular conditions. Observation of teaching in many classrooms often leads to the conclusion that professional teachers are limited
in the range of teaching methods or strategies which they can use at will.
Flanders' research team tabulated over 1,250,000 teacher-student inter-
actions at all grade levels and concluded that what teachers do is very
similar from day to day and school to school. He reported:

> Common practice in today's classrooms with regard to teacher influence can be
> expressed by the "rule of two-thirds." Two-thirds of the time spent in a class-
> room, someone is talking. Two-thirds of the time someone is talking, it is the
> teacher—for the teacher talks more than all the students combined. Two-thirds
> of the time that the teacher is talking, he is lecturing, giving directions, or
> criticising the behavior of students. One-third of the time he is asking questions,
> reacting to student ideas, or giving praise.[5]

When teachers are confronted with verbatim transcripts, or audio or
video tapes of lessons they have taught, they frequently express disbelief
and chagrin at the discrepancies between their *intended* methodology and
the *observed* methods being employed. Classroom teachers are generally
very desirous of using "newer" methods, but their own background often
has not prepared them to be able to analyze, evaluate, and adopt as their
own the target method. If middle school teachers are to develop skill
in using a variety of teaching strategies and methods, appropriate inservice programs must be set up for this purpose.

Using the Methods of Discovery and Inquiry

There is currently much interest in the so-called discovery and inquiry
methods. In the generic sense of the words, *discovery* and *inquiry* would
appear to be essential in a middle school program aimed to produce
autonomous learners. If learners can be systematically trained in discovery approaches and inquiry techniques, the student can be expected to
assume greater responsibility for his own intellectual development. There
is promising evidence that inquiry training and discovery learning may
produce more autonomous, self-directed, and successful learners.

[5]Ned A. Flanders, "Teacher and Classroom Influences on Individual Learning," in
A. Harry Passow (ed.), *Nurturing Individual Potential* (Washington, D.C.: Association for
Supervision and Curriculum Development, 1964), p. 58.

The use of the term "discovery" as a label for a specific approach is often associated with certain of the national curriculum projects, especially those in the field of mathematics. An excerpt from a brief description of the University of Illinois School Mathematics Study Group illustrates the importance attached, not only to the content of the field, but to the method of learning the contents:

> The committee set out to present mathematics as a consistent, unified discipline; to lead students to "discover" principles for themselves; and to assure the development of those manipulative skills necessary for problem solving. The UICSM program emphasizes "learning by discovery," with the student *doing* (rather than being told about) mathematics. The student need not verbalize his discovery; in fact early verbalization is discouraged for fear that premature or incorrect verbalization of a generalization may hinder its use. . . . Verbalization, for communication and proof, is to come after the student has become thoroughly familiar with the generalization and has had adequate opportunity to test it and refine it.[6]

The idea of the discovery method is that students can learn to work much in the manner of the scholars who produce the knowledge of the disciplines. When the student is confronted with a problem situation, he is expected to use the available data, draw on his store of accumulated knowledge, hypothesize a solution, test it out, refine it, and finally state the solution as a principle or generalization. It may help clarify the discovery method to compare it with the expository method. In studying the Missouri Compromise in a United States history unit, the teacher using the expository method would discuss the background of the compromise (cause) and then present the document itself, or at least the major provisions (effect). The students would then "study" the compromise for the purpose of answering questions about it on a test. Countless thousands of American citizens have "learned" their history in this fashion. If the teacher used a discovery approach, he might give the students some information about the social and economic conditions of the cotton-producing South and the industrial North. A number of biographies of Daniel Webster and Henry Clay would be available, along with copies of speeches entered into the Congressional Record of the time. Some students would read essays by leading abolitionists and perhaps some of the fiction of the age. After the students had gained a background of knowledge about the issues, they would then be asked to write their "own" Missouri Compromise. Then, and only then, would they examine the original, compare it with their own, noting and speculating about points of difference and similarity.

[6]John I. Goodlad, *School Curriculum Reform in the United States* (New York: The Fund For The Advancement of Education, 1964), p. 14.

Some advocates of the discovery method would use it to the virtual exclusion of all others. They argue that a student learns science only by acting like a scientist; that mathematical principles are understood better, remembered longer, and applied more readily in new situations if the learner has "discovered" the principles for himself. Jerome Bruner sees the method of discovery as a part of the structure of the discipline itself; that is, a subject is not truly known until the learner knows how to discover it. He claims the benefits of "increased intellectual potency, intrinsic rewards, useful learning techniques, and better memory processes" from the experience of learning through discovery.[7]

The *inquiry* method is in reality the same thing as the discovery method, even though some writers argue about shades of differences.[8] An inquiry is a question, a search, an investigation. The inquiry method is essentially a method which relies on using the learners' questions (not the teacher's) as an effective way of learning. J. Richard Suchman, an investigator who has developed a specific program for training children in the process of inquiry, states that:

> There is a wide range of cognitive skills involved in the inquiry process. This includes the gathering, organizing, and processing of data, the trying out of conceptual models, the restructuring of these models to accommodate the new data, and the testing of models for validity. At times it is necessary to use exacting methods of sampling, control and analysis. At other times a wild, intuitive leap might be the operation most needed. There are broad strategies and special tactics that help to make inquiry more productive. The one most dependable quality of inquiry is that there is no one fixed method of operation.[9]

The key sentence in the above passage is, "There are broad strategies and special tactics that help to make inquiry more productive." Suchman has developed an "Inquiry Training Project"[10] to try to identify the effective strategies and techniques. His pilot studies had indicated that elementary school children in the intermediate grades were generally unable to inquire systematically or productively when made curious by a puzzling episode and given freedom to ask questions. Their questions tended to seek explanations from the teacher rather than information which would help find an explanation. They were very dependent on the teacher and accepted teacher responses rather uncritically.

[7]Jerome S. Bruner, "Structures in Learning," *NEA Journal,* 52:26 (March 1963).

[8]See, for example, J. Richard Suchman, "In Pursuit of Meaning," *The Instructor,* 75, 1:32, 70 (September 1965).

[9]J. Richard Suchman, "The Child and The Inquiry Process," in A. Harry Passow and Robert Leeper (eds.), *Intellectual Development: Another Look* (Washington, D.C.: Association for Supervision and Curriculum Development, 1964), pp. 68–69.

[10]J. Richard Suchman, *The Elementary School Training Program in Scientific Inquiry,* Illinois Studies in Inquiry Training (Urbana: University of Illinois, 1962).

In the Inquiry Training Project, the students are shown a brief film of a physics demonstration. They are then asked to find out why the events in the filmed episode occurred. The children may obtain additional data from the teachers by asking questions, but they may not ask for generalizations or explanations. The questions should be answerable by "yes" or "no." The inquiry session is tape recorded, and some time after the session, a critique is held in which the children observe the effects of various types of questions. The aim of the method is to increase the learner's ability to ask the right kinds of questions. While all of the results are not in, preliminary findings are very promising.[11]

Middle school teachers will find many uses for the discovery and inquiry methods in helping students to learn how to learn, in building the learner's confidence in his ability to cope with his environment, and in stimulating excitement in the processes of learning. There are certain cautions to be observed, however, in considering these methods. First, it should be recognized that effective use of discovery approaches is a complete undertaking, and most teachers will need expert guidance in developing skill in the method. Second, it must be recognized that these approaches are time consuming. One investigator, after studying the various curriculum projects based on discovery methods, concluded:

This requires a very carefully detailed curriculum, an extremely knowledgeable instructor, and, some believe, a pliable and alert group of youngsters. Given these, the demonstrations can be quite remarkable indeed. Whether they are efficient is another matter. The efficiency of the discovery method in education is likely to be a source of continuing controversy for the next decade.[12]

Many other writers have discussed the pros and cons of the use of discovery approaches in learning. One statement that puts the limitations and the potentials in good perspective is the following:

Only a small part of the school curriculum or of a single subject can be treated through the discovery approach. Limits of time, inaccessibility of certain kinds of materials and experiences, and restrictions of the pupil's own ability and research techniques make it impossible that he rediscover all that he needs to know of science, history, or any other field. Nor can he learn through direct experience all that he can usefully comprehend about methods of inquiry in the various fields.

Fortunately, the benefits of learning through discovery probably can be gained through relatively occasional use of this approach. Discovery situations placed at intervals in the sequence of each subject field can be used to maintain interest

[11]J. Richard Suchman, "The Child and The Inquiry Process," *The Elementary School Training Program in Scientific Inquiry,* pp. 73–75.

[12]James D. Gallagher, "Research On Enhancing Productive Thinking," *Intellectual Development: Another Look,* p. 46.

and illuminate meaningful presentations of other kinds—information and explanations provided by the teacher, reading materials, or films, for example.[13]

Most middle school teachers will see many similarities between the discovery approaches discussed above and the techniques of the problem solving method with which they are already familiar. Despite the difficulties and limitations of such methods, they appear to be appropriate to many of the aims of the emergent middle school and should be added to the teachers' repertory to be used along with other methods and strategies.

Signs of Creative Teaching

Whatever method is chosen, care should be taken that it is not applied mechanically. This is a potential danger in some of the programs which restrict the learner's questions and probe to a very narrow range of possibilities. It is very possible for the "discovery" method to degenerate into a game of discovering what is in the teacher's mind. As teachers work to develop skill in using various strategies to achieve specific objectives, they should keep in mind the broader aims of instruction. A list such as the following may help teachers evaluate their methods in terms of the goals of creative teaching:

Less teacher domination; more faith that children can find answers satisfying to them.

Less teacher talk; more listening to children, allowing them to use the teacher and the group as a sounding board when ideas are explored.

Less questioning for the right answer; more open-ended questions with room for difference and the exploration of many answers.

Less destructive criticism; more teacher help which directs the child's attention back to his own feelings for clarification and understanding.

Less emphasis on failure; more acceptance of mistakes—more feeling on the part of the child that when he makes a mistake it is done, accepted and that's it. As one child said, "She doesn't rub salt in."

Children's work is appreciated, but praise is not used to put words in the mouths of children.

Goals are clearly defined; structure is understood and accepted by the group.

Within appropriate limits, children are given responsibility and freedom to work. "For once a teacher told us we could do it ourselves and really meant it."

Children are free to express what they feel and seem secure in their knowledge that the teacher likes them as they are.

Ideas are explored; there is an honest respect for solid information, an attitude of "Let's find out."

[13]NEA Project on Instruction, *Deciding What to Teach,* Dorothy M. Fraser (Washington, D.C.: National Education Association, 1963), pp. 39–40.

There is a balance of common tasks and individual responsibility for specific tasks which are unique and not shared.

The teacher communicates clearly to children that learning is self-learning. Faith is demonstrated that all children want to become and pupils show satisfaction as they become aware of their growth.

Evaluation is a shared process and includes more than academic achievement.

Motivation for learning is high and seems inner-directed; pupil activity seems to say, "I've got a job I want to do."[14]

If teaching in the middle school is going to achieve the aims implied in the three-way classification of curriculum opportunities of personal development, continued learning, and organized knowledge, teachers must be given freedom to experiment with creative approaches and must be provided with resources to evaluate the results of their experimentation.

TEAM TEACHING IN THE MIDDLE SCHOOL

While team teaching is not an essential feature of the middle school plan, many middle schools use team teaching arrangements for at least a portion of the instruction. A more extensive treatment than is possible in this section will be found in several recent books on the subject.[15] Additionally, team teaching is primarily an organizational arrangement, and the organizational aspects are discussed in Chapter 6. Here we consider briefly only those aspects of team teaching that can be seen to make new demands on the teaching personnel involved.

New Teaching Roles

As teaching roles are recast in team teaching, some teachers may feel a loss of autonomy and personal freedom. The individual teacher's ideas about what is best for a particular group may have to be sublimated to the will of the team group. Even teachers who have found it feasible to work cooperatively on curriculum plans at the school-wide level may find it difficult to submit to a group plan at the classroom level. There is the question of what happens to an individual's self concept when he no

[14]Arthur W. Combs (chm.), *Perceiving, Behaving, Becoming: A New Focus for Education,* 1962 Yearbook of Association for Supervision and Curriculum Development (Washington, D.C.: National Education Association, 1962), p. 237.

[15]For an extended discussion and comprehensive bibliography of team teaching see the following: Medill Bair and Richard G. Woodward, *Team Teaching in Action* (Boston: Houghton Mifflin Company, 1964); David Beggs, III (ed.), *Team Teaching, Bold New Venture* (Indianapolis: Unified College Press, Inc., 1964); Nicholas C. Polos, *The Dynamics of Team Teaching* (Dubuque: William C. Brown Company, 1965); and Judson T. Shaplin and Henry Olds, Jr. (eds.), *Team Teaching* (New York: Harper & Row, Publishers, 1964).

longer has full responsibility for "his" group of students. Some teachers may have to face the possibility that they do not possess the personal qualities to become effective team members without a great effort to make the necessary accommodations. When teachers are aware of the demands of team teaching, it is very likely that they will be able to meet these demands if they see team teaching as a desirable means of achieving their instructional goals for boys and girls.

The varied leadership roles place new demands on the professional skills of teachers. The *team leader* must schedule and direct team planning sessions, coordinate the work of several professional and nonprofessional staff members, see that materials and resources are available at the proper place and time, and ensure that appropriate evaluative procedures are followed. Sometimes the team leader is responsible for observing teachers and making supervisory judgments. In addition to these or similar duties, the team leader must plan and teach classes.

The degree of formal team structure may vary from plan to plan, but in any case, there are special demands on team members. If there is a hierarchy of ranks such as senior teacher, associate teacher, assistant teacher, and the like, appropriate duties and relationships must be spelled out. Plans must be written out in detail when they are to be shared with a group. A team member may be asked to serve as a resource for a particular task; on some teams certain members take major responsibility for large group instruction, and others specialize in small group work. If the team includes teacher aides, the teacher must develop the new skill of directing the work of such assistants.

New Demands on Time

In almost every evaluation of team teaching projects, the need for more time for cooperative planning is mentioned. Not only do the team planning sessions themselves require time, the preparation for the planning session is likely to take more time than teachers are accustomed to giving to lesson planning. If the team planning involves the regrouping of pupils for special purposes, or the scheduling of special instructional materials or spaces, time is required.

New Demands on Evaluation

While team teaching may trace its antecedents to the platoon plans, the Winnetka Plan and the Hosic Plan of earlier times, in its present manifestation, team teaching must be considered innovative and experimental. As such, it places special demands on its practitioners to evaluate rigorously the relevance of the plan to the goals of the institution. Not all middle schools will be able to mount sophisticated, controlled research studies of team teaching, but every staff planning to try team teaching should know exactly what it expects team teaching to do to improve instruction and should have a clearly understood plan for collecting evidence as to whether or not their expectations are being met.

THE PROFESSIONAL PREPARATION OF MIDDLE SCHOOL TEACHERS

There is a continuing controversy over what constitutes an adequate preparation for teaching at any level. It is not likely that the issues will ever be settled, nor is it desirable that the search for better ways be ended. Guidelines for programs to prepare teachers should be planned with reference to the aims and functions of schools in which they will teach. Leslie J. Bishop, Executive Secretary of the Association for Supervision and Curriculum Development, has proposed that a good preservice program for teaching at any level should have the following characteristics:

Supervisors, curriculum workers, and public schools should insist that pre-service programs equip teachers to know the structure of, and to have experienced, an area or discipline; that they understand children and the difference between the normal curve and a unique individual; that they know the new curriculum and media developments and their consequences; that they know and experience the appropriate methods of inquiry and the development of knowledge; that they have an opportunity to develop some coherent set of beliefs about education, about learners, about self; that they know that their professional education has just begun, that it is not complete.[16]

Whether such a program can be accomplished in the usual four-year baccalaureate program is not clear; what is clear is that such a program is needed. Where there are gaps in the teacher's program, both graduate study and inservice programs are necessary.

Present teacher education programs are slanted either toward preparation for teaching in the elementary or secondary programs. Of course, there are many common elements in the programs of both levels. If a middle school teacher is studying in an elementary program, he should build as strong a minor as possible in one of the teaching fields. Those in the secondary program should strive to achieve a good background in the nature of older childhood and preadolescence, and they should add courses in the teaching of reading.

[16]Leslie J. Bishop, "Challenges for Supervisors," in *The Supervisor: Agent for Change in Teaching* (Washington, D.C.: Association for Supervision and Curriculum Development, 1966), p. 98.

Programs Designed Especially
for the Middle School

In recognition of the movement toward the middle school reorganization documented in Chapter 1, the future may see the development of special preparation programs for many specialties in the middle school. During the 1966–1967 year, the authors were associated with an institute supported by the United States Office of Education; it was held at the University of Florida to retrain personnel from the public schools of Atlanta, Georgia, Dade County (Miami), Florida, and Montgomery County, Maryland, for middle schools in these systems. An outline of this year-long program is presented below.

The participants in the Florida program were experienced teachers with elementary and junior high school teaching and administrative backgrounds. The program consisted of three basic elements: (1) a common core of especially designed professional education course work; (2) an individually selected sequence of courses in the participant's academic teaching field; and (3) a practicum on teaching in the middle school.

The common core of professional education courses. A special year-long study of the problems of curriculum and instruction in the middle school was developed with the participants. This course met in a three-hour block weekly, and additional meetings were scheduled routinely. An intensive study was made of the rationale and philosophy, the organization of and the interrelationships among the various components of the curriculum, the roles of the various staff members, the instructional organization, and means for implementing and evaluating the program of the middle school.

The participants' understanding of the middle school child was deepened by a six-months course in the dynamics of behavior of the preadolescent as viewed from a perceptual and humanistic orientation. The course was designed for and limited to institute participants. Intensive study was given to the questions of how the preadolescent develops, what he is like, what he is trying to do, and what he is trying to become. Methods of change in the behavior of the preadolescent were considered, as well as ways of helping him become a more adequate person.

Additionally, each participant had three months of intensive work in measurement and statistics designed to provide sufficient statistical and theoretical background for constructing tests and for using and understanding commercially prepared tests. Special emphasis was given to the preparation, selection, and use of evaluation instruments suitable for the middle school population.

In order to see the middle school as a part of the total educational program, the participants enrolled in a graduate level study of the school curriculum. The course emphasized recent trends and developments and proposals for change in the curriculum from kindergarten through community junior college.

Study in the academic disciplines. The participants were expected to enroll in a minimum of one and a maximum of two graduate level courses in the regular university curriculum each trimester. In those cases where the participants did not have the undergraduate prerequisites, special independent study plans were worked out with the participant's academic advisor. In addition to the regular classwork, each student participated in a content seminar for the purpose of relating the work in the discipline to teaching in the middle school.

The practicum on teaching in the middle school. The P. K. Yonge Laboratory School of the College of Education at the University furnished a model of a middle school in development. An interdisciplinary team of four teachers and approximately 120 pupils from grades 6 and 7 gave the institute participants ample opportunity to test their ideas against reality. The organization of the P. K. Yonge team is described in Chapter 6. The work of the practicum was correlated with the middle school curriculum and instruction course work. In preparation for the practicum, the participants engaged in seminar study of such topics as: Instructional theory and research on teaching; nongrading and continuous progress plans; team teaching; and evaluation of individual pupils' programs.

A CHECK LIST FOR PROSPECTIVE
MIDDLE SCHOOL TEACHERS

Throughout this chapter it has been maintained that no single set of personal or professional characteristics can be determined which will guarantee successful teaching in the middle school. Indeed, it is expected that a wide range of teacher personalities and teaching styles will be desirable in the emergent middle school. This is not to say that every one will be successful or happy teaching at this level. It should be possible for a prospective middle school teacher to get an idea of his potential for success at this level by attempting to compare his known strengths, weaknesses, and personal preferences against a check list of demands of middle school teaching similar to those set forth earlier in this chapter. Teachers who can give an affirmative answer to the questions listed below very likely possess the ability to make a significant contribution to teaching in the middle school.

1. *Do I enjoy working with older children and younger adolescents?* Middle school age pupils are searching for new identities and new re-

lationships and they need the guidance of adults who have a strong, secure sense of self. The insecure teacher may feel that his best efforts to help are often rejected and rebuffed. The successful middle school teacher will take satisfaction in seeing dependent children grow into self-reliant young adolescents. A former middle school administrator recently stated that:

> No test can select such an individual with a 99.99 percent level of confidence, but the kind of teacher needed by the middle schooler can be defined. He will enjoy students who are active, energetic, and loud, and will take teasing in stride. He will be flexible and sensitive to quick changes of moods and needs, and will sense group feeling and student interaction.[17]

2. *Do I have the interest and the ability to develop scholarship in one of the areas of organized knowledge?* The teacher who is developing his own scholarship in a particular field will have more respect for scholarship in general and will be better able to stimulate his students to take delight in their studies. Teaching in the middle school will demand more specialization than has been typical of elementary schools, but subject-centered teaching must be avoided. The middle school teacher-specialist is as concerned about the attitudes of his students toward the areas of organized study as he is about their mastery of the content and skills of the subject.

3. *Am I willing to learn to use a wide variety of diagnostic instruments, automated aids, and programed materials to help students develop basic learning skills and the skills of continued learning?* In general, educators have lagged behind industry, government, and business in harnessing the developing technology to aid in the accomplishment of instructional goals. Because the emergent middle school is developing at a period when the ways of utilizing the newer media and the newer programs have been demonstrated in prototype programs, middle school teachers should be expected to take advantage of promising innovations in this area.

4. *Can I learn to work effectively in close collaboration with my colleagues in cooperative planning and team teaching?* The demands of team teaching have been discussed earlier in this chapter. Some educators who have been optimistic about the potentials of team teaching for improving instruction have become pessimistic about the ability of the teaching profession to take advantage of these potential opportunities. The traditional role of the teacher has stressed individual teacher autonomy, and conventional teacher preparation programs reinforce this pattern of behavior. Accordingly, teachers have had little experience in the complex management of affairs demanded by real team teaching. In spite of these

---

[17]M. Ann Grooms, *Perspectives on the Middle School* (Columbus, Ohio: Charles E. Merrill Books, Inc., 1967), p. 46.

obstacles, the majority of middle schools will attempt some form of team teaching, and prospective middle school teachers should resolve to give team teaching a fair chance to succeed.

5. *Do I have an open mind toward innovation and change?* Many teachers are uncomfortable in an atmosphere of continual search for new and better ways to organize, direct, and evaluate instructional procedures, but the new middle school is committed to an innovative approach. Teachers in the middle school will be expected to try out many new plans, materials, approaches, and techniques. The process of change can be very stimulating, but it is also very demanding. The prospective middle school teacher should face candidly the question of whether he prefers the stimulation of challenge to the security of a comfortable routine.

Chapter 6

The Organization and Staff

Previous chapters in Part III have described the curriculum plan and teaching practices in the middle school program. The present chapter treats the organizational arrangements and the staffing patterns characteristic of presently existing middle schools and suggests desirable practices for the emergent middle school of the future.

DIMENSIONS OF ORGANIZATION

The purpose of any plan of school organization is to facilitate the achievement of the stated aims and objectives of an educational program. In determining what plan of organization is most appropriate to the goals of a school program, three dimensions of organization are typically considered: the dimension of the *age-grade range* of the pupils included in the school; the *horizontal* dimension, which consists of the arrangements for grouping pupils for instruction and other school-directed activities; and the *vertical* dimension, the arrangements for moving pupils through the program from entrance to exit.

AGE-GRADE RANGE

The most visible dimension of school organization is that of the age-grade range. Indeed, this is the feature most often used to identify a school as an elementary school (grades K–6), a junior high school (grades 7–9), a senior high school (grades 10–12). It is not surprising, then, that planners of new middle schools are nearly always asked, "What grades are included?"

Two prevailing patterns can be observed in presently existing middle schools. Typically, the middle school program is either a three-year program including grades 6–8, or a four-year program encompassing grades 5–8. Several variations from the 6–8 or 5–8 organization were identified in Chapter 1. Some communities have found it either expedient or desirable to keep the ninth grade with the reorganized middle school, resulting in either a 5–9 or a 6–9 middle school program. A few middle schools are two-year (7–8) schools, while some 7–9 organized junior high schools have so successfully endeavored to design a program and facilities appropriate for early adolescence that they meet the standards set by the definition of *middle school* presented in Chapter 1.

What Grade Organization Is Best?

Research on school organization does not demonstrate the clear superiority of any one organizational arrangement over all others. Many authorities would agree with Mauritz Johnson, Jr., who observed:

The decision as to form of organization will have to be made on practical grounds and on the basis of social and administrative viability. Any pattern is satisfactory that gives identity to youths during early adolescence, includes at least three grades for stability, and brackets those grades in which significant numbers of pupils reach pubescence.[1]

From evidence presented in Part II, it is clear that the present authors feel that a 5–8 grade organization will enroll more of the youth in transition from childhood to adolescence than will any other grade grouping. The mere inclusion of these grades, however, does not constitute a middle school program, nor does the choice of some other age-grade arrangement disqualify a school from having a middle school program. Localized conditions may dictate a pupil age-grade grouping seemingly inconsistent with human growth and developmental stages, and yet through careful planning, a good program can be provided for all the youngsters. An example of a variant organizational pattern is the two-year (7–8) intermediate school frequently found in California. While most educators reject a two-year school because of the "revolving door" effect on pupils, who must always be either entering or leaving, sheer enrollment pressures in some districts dictate the creation of separate

[1]Mauritz Johnson, Jr., "The Magic Numbers of 7-8-9," *NEA Journal,* 52:50–51 (March 1963).

schools to house grades 7 and 8. In such cases it is still possible, though probably more difficult, to design a middle school program for the older children in the elementary building and the preadolescents in the intermediate building. The creative and cooperative planning necessary between staffs of the separate buildings could even result in a smoother transition and a higher degree of educational continuity than is usual between elementary and secondary units.

Other local considerations may lead a particular school district to decide to include pupils of ninth grade age in the middle schools. Planners for a middle school in Dade County, Florida's Northwest Central District (Miami), felt that the social and cultural problems, and the special language and communications skills needs of the youth of the area, could be better met in a middle school program focused on self-understanding and basic skills development than in a high school program which would be more specialized and more technically oriented. Using data about the needs of the pupils and the availability of staff and facilities, it was decided to have at least initially a 6–9 middle school in one section of the district, and a 6–8 middle school in another section. Similarly, the decision as to what grades and ages are to be assigned to specific levels must be reached within each school district on the basis of local data and experience.

THE HORIZONTAL ORGANIZATION

The *horizontal* dimension of organization deals with how pupils are grouped for instruction and other school-directed activities. The typical horizontal organization in the elementary school is a self-contained classroom with one teacher responsible for all, or a major portion of, the instruction for a single group of pupils. The typical horizontal pattern at the secondary level is a departmentalized organization with a different teacher for each subject. The preceding two chapters in Part III described program features which require organizational arrangements quite unlike either typical elementary or secondary patterns as presently conceived. Middle schools currently in operation exhibit a variety of interesting and innovative approaches to horizontal organization.

Combination Self-contained
and Departmentalized

Many middle schools attempt to retain the advantages and overcome the disadvantages of both the self-contained and departmentalized plans by combining some departmentalization with some self-contained or block-time provisions.[2] This organization attempts to smooth the transition from the security of the self-contained classroom of the elementary school to the more impersonal departmentalized structure of the secondary school in well-planned stages. The usual pattern is for grades 5–6 to be essentially self-contained and grades 7–8 to be largely departmentalized. The Chippewa Middle School in Saginaw, Michigan is illustrative of this "planned gradualism." Pupils entering the fifth grade at Chippewa are assigned to a "home" in a self-contained classroom with one teacher. Framed partitions and a central utility core, including a toilet, closets, cupboards, and a sink, are used to separate each fifth-grade classroom from other areas, so as to maintain a self-contained, "home" atmosphere.

The second step in the transition is from fifth-grade "home" to sixth-grade "neighborhood." The principal of Chippewa describes this stage as follows:

In the sixth grade, the students begin to move into a different world, a situation more akin to a neighborhood than the home of their self-contained classroom. Here the teachers work in informal teams. The students, while assigned to one classroom and spending most of their time with one teacher, move about to a moderate degree in different sizes and types of groups according to plans worked out by the teacher teams as the needs of the students are recognized. The students themselves are involved in the process of planning activities to the extent that they assume increasing responsibility for their own and each other's welfare. A student becomes acquainted with several teachers and different groups of children while remaining essentially attached to one teacher and one room.[3]

Here also the building is used to facilitate the purpose of the grouping. In sixth-grade areas, space is provided for small study groups and individual study spaces for special help or independent study.

The next move is from the sixth-grade "neighborhood" into the seventh- and eighth-grade "society." The seventh- and eighth-grade pupils spend two periods a day with a homeroom teacher who is responsible for instruction in language arts and social studies, and for group guidance with the help of a professional counselor. The remainder of the day is spent in a departmentalized schedule with five or more different teachers.

The gradual change from self-contained classroom to departmentalization has been effected very simply in the Pleasant Hills Middle School, Clairton, Pennsylvania. Grade 5 is housed in a separate wing of the school plant, and all of the instruction is in the self-contained classroom except science, which is taught in a laboratory by a specialist. Special facilities in art, physical education, music, and other areas are made available to

[2]Educational Research Service Circular No. 3, *Middle Schools* (Washington, D.C.: American Association of School Administrators and Research Division, National Education Association, May 1965), p. 3.

[3]Jack D. Riegle, "Saginaw Township Community Schools" (mimeographed, April 1966).

fifth and sixth graders under the coordination of the classroom teacher. Seventh- and eighth-grade students have an increasing number of elective subjects taught by departmental specialists.[4]

The Meredith G. Williams Middle School in Bridgewater, Massachusetts, represents another approach to achieving a gradual transition. The plan for articulation was described by the school's former principal as follows:

As is true of all intermediate schools, articulation is one of the prime functions of our middle school. We consider articulation to mean relating what we do to what has already happened in our primary schools and to what will take place in the regional high school. Classrooms of our primary schools are virtually completely self-contained. The regional high school serving our children is departmentalized, and the pupils are grouped by subjects. To help achieve articulation, we have taken the following steps. In grades five and six pupils are assigned to one teacher for at least one-half our school day. In grades seven and eight, we are departmentalized. But since we do not group by subject, but assign pupils to homerooms supervised by teachers whom they have in academic subjects, we reduce the number of adjustments to be made by boys and girls.[5]

A primary concern of all these plans is to provide for students both the security of a home base and the stimulation and added depth of some specialization in important curriculum areas. The combination of elements of elementary and secondary organizational plans is a natural development for middle schools bridging the schools for childhood and the schools for adolescence. The obvious pitfall to be guarded against in such arrangements is too much separateness between the self-contained and the departmentalized components of the school. For instance, a middle school with essentially self-contained grades 5–6 and departmentalized grades 7–8 may have as many articulation problems as separately organized elementary and junior high schools.

Team Teaching in the Middle School

Team teaching as an organizational alternative to the single teacher classroom is exciting much interest at all educational levels. Certainly, the functions ascribed to the emergent middle school throughout this book demand a cooperative approach which team teaching may facilitate. In this section team teaching is defined, patterns of team organization are discussed, and illustrative models of team teaching are presented.

[4]See Judith Murphy, *Middle Schools* (New York: Educational Facilities Laboratories, 1965), for a description of the Pleasant Hills physical plant.

[5]Paul J. Zdanowicz, "The Meredith G. Williams Middle School," *Educational Horizons*, 41:47–49 (Winter 1962).

What Is Team Teaching?

In practice, team teaching plans range from loosely structured, informal arrangements with teachers in adjoining or nearby rooms, with occasional combining or swapping of their classes as the desire strikes them, to highly formal arrangements with hierarchical staff patterns and definite large and small group instructional schedules. Some authorities would question the use of the label "team teaching" for the informal, permissive arrangements which may cease to function at the whims of individuals. Robert H. Anderson has recommended the use of the generic term "cooperative teaching" for all teacher collaboration including team teaching, and that the "team teaching" label be reserved for defined formal organizations.[6] Our own preference is for a broad definition of team teaching which encompasses even the informal plans, but specifically calls for joint planning and evaluation at the classroom instructional level. Such a definition has been proposed by Judson T. Shaplin:

Team teaching is a type of instructional organization, involving teaching personnel and the students assigned to them, in which two or more teachers are given responsibility, working together, for all, or a significant part of the instruction of the same group of students.[7]

Teachers have always worked together in groups and committees at the task of developing school-wide or grade-level curriculum plans, but have typically worked in isolation at the task of making instructional plans for a single class group. Only when the competencies of two or more professional staff members are combined in the tasks of planning, conducting, and evaluating instruction for and with particular student groups *at the classroom level* is the use of the term "team teaching" justified.

Patterns of Team Teaching

Although many different team teaching plans are possible under the broad definition proposed above, two basic patterns emerge in practice: the *interdisciplinary team* and the *single-subject team*.

Interdisciplinary team. The interdisciplinary team, as its name suggests, is a combination of teachers from different subject areas who plan and conduct the instruction in these areas for particular groups of pupils. The aim of the interdisciplinary team approach is to promote communi-

---

[6]Robert H. Anderson, "An Overview of Team Teaching," in *Team Teaching at the Elementary Level* (Report of an Invitational Workshop Sponsored by the Perkins and Will Partnership, Architects, May 1964), pp. 10–11.

[7]Judson T. Shaplin and Henry F. Olds (eds.), *Team Teaching* (New York: Harper & Row, Publishers, 1964), p. 15.

cation, coordination, and cooperation among subject matter specialists so that students benefit from instruction planned by specialists, but lacking the fragmentation which characterizes many departmentalized plans.

The interdisciplinary team may consist of as few as two teachers, representing related subjects, such as language arts and social studies, with an extended block of time to use as they see fit with their assigned students; or the team may combine representatives of all the areas of study in the school for a large group of students. The team decides on the instructional strategies for the different members of the group. The School Organization Committee of Baltimore County, Maryland, prepared a report in 1961, including descriptions of several alternative organizational patterns for middle school planners to consider. The description of a model of an interdisciplinary team illustrates the dominant features of this plan:

Instructional groups will be developed each of which combines four homeroom units and their teachers for cooperative planning and instruction in the general education areas. The pupils in the instructional group will be in the same year in school. Four homeroom teachers, each representing a special competence in one of the general education areas of language arts, social studies, science, and mathematics will meet regularly to plan cooperatively the instruction for the 100 pupils in the instructional group. Following a general county curriculum plan, the instructional group will devise the specific learning opportunities for particular groups of pupils, decide who is responsible for different aspects of instruction, procure the materials to be used, and select the evaluative procedures to be followed.[8]

Single-subject team. The single-subject team combines two or more teachers in the same subject matter area. The single-subject team plan fosters greater depth in the subject, provides an inservice experience for beginning teachers, and exposes a given teacher's talents to a larger number of students. Perhaps the greatest advantage of the single-subject team is that pupils may be more readily placed at appropriate achievement levels, thereby facilitating more continuous pupil progress. The Baltimore County report, cited above, provides a model of a single-subject team which summarizes the organizational characteristics of this plan:

1.   A team consisting of 2-6 teachers who represent special competence in a single subject area will work with pupils from one or more grade levels. As many teams can be formed as there are subjects in the curriculum with a sufficient number of teachers.

    a.   Each team will meet on a regularly scheduled basis to exchange ideas, develop common policies and purposes, develop and tailor the program to fit

[8]From mimeographed materials prepared by the Committee and provided the authors by Norris A. King, Director, Baltimore County, Maryland, Public Schools (March 1967).

the needs of the pupils, and share information regarding the pupils on their teams.

    b. Each teacher will assume responsibility for specializing in subject matter and for aiding in various team activities, including remedial instruction whenever necessary.

    c. Each team will concentrate not only on organization of material and high level instruction, but also on problems confronting individual pupils such as low motivation, poor study habits, and unwholesome behavior.

    2. A single subject team may include only teachers on a single grade level or may include teachers from several or all of the levels in the school.

    3. The team may arrange for some of the instruction to be in large groups and some of the work to be in small groups for discussion, and instruction in the basic skills.[9]

Administration of Team Teaching

Basic decisions about the assignment of leadership responsibilities on the team must be made. One model of team teaching is built on a hierarchical structure with a status leader who may receive a salary supplement or equivalent recognition for his administrative and leadership duties. There may be other categories of rank on the team such as master teacher, senior teacher, associate teacher, assistant teacher, intern teacher, and assorted teacher aides. The hierarchical team claims the advantage of offering reward and recognition for special professional competencies at the classroom teaching level. A teacher does not have to leave the classroom and "move up" into administration to make career advancement. Furthermore, the hierarchical team structure fixes definite responsibility for initiating team planning meetings, evaluating team efforts, scheduling the use of facilities and materials, and all the other assorted chores which must be performed for smooth operation of the team.

Another approach to team organization is the "emerging leadership" model, which envisions the team as a federation of equals, with each member assuming responsibility for those functions for which he is the most qualified person on the team. Proponents of this model claim that morale is higher and individual involvement is greater when the contributions of each member receive equal reward and recognition. It is claimed that the "emerging leadership" pattern is more consistent with the actual situation in most schools, with different teachers possessing special competencies in different areas of the curriculum, but essentially equal in value to the team.

Neither the formal hierarchical structure nor the completely informal emerging leadership plan is likely to prove successful in most middle schools. The hierarchical team imposes an organizational structure on a

[9]Baltimore County, Maryland, Public Schools.

group and defines responsibilities of the members. Any formal definition of responsibilities is a limiting device and may inhibit creative and free-flowing interchange, which is so highly desired among professionals. A formal, organizational chain of command almost invariably results in a degree of absolvement of responsibility on the part of the lower-ranked members. On the other hand, the "emerging leadership" plan, with no formal leadership arrangement, almost invariably suffers from lack of organization. If no one is responsible for initiating meetings, important planning purposes may not be attended to. Many routines such as scheduling joint meeting rooms, procuring needed materials, and deciding on appropriate next steps may not be effectively managed.

Most middle schools will follow a plan somewhere between the two extremes described above. A promising alternative is the semihierarchical team, with members of the team officially joined together in a close-working relationship. Each member has a formal obligation to assume responsibility for leadership in a given area of the curriculum, or in some other appropriate way. One member of the team is elected or appointed to serve as chairman or coordinator, with responsibility for seeing that the administrative and organizational functions of the team are properly executed. This position may rotate from member to member, or the member with an appetite and the talent for these duties may serve permanently. This plan has the advantage of fixing definite responsibility for administrative routines without seeming to make administration of the team more important than teaching on the team.

It is important that team teaching be seen as a way of organizing personnel, students, and teaching resources to accomplish educational goals. Team teaching is not a standardized approach, nor is it an end in itself. Viewed this way, school staffs are free to experiment with a variety of cooperative arrangements in an effort to find an approach which is comfortable to the participants and consistent with the goals of the school.

Middle School Examples
of Team Organizations

The team teaching plans of the University of Florida P. K. Yonge Laboratory School and the Dover, Delaware, Special District Middle Schools illustrate adaptations of the basic team patterns discussed above. The P. K. Yonge 6–7 team is organized on an interdisciplinary, semi-hierarchical plan. The Dover middle schools utilize both single-subject and interdisciplinary teams. The leadership in the single-subject team is provided by an appointed coordinator with released time for administration. The leadership in the interdisciplinary teams follows "emerging leadership" principles. Essential features of these plans are described below.

The P. K. Yonge 6–7 Team.   The P. K. Yonge plan is an interesting example of a relatively sophisticated interdisciplinary team approach involving approximately 60 pupils of sixth- and 60 of seventh-grade age, four teachers, and a variety of auxiliary and supporting personnel. The teachers on the team were chosen to represent special strength in one of the subject areas of English language arts, social studies, mathematics, or science. One teacher was designated "team leader," with responsibility for scheduling planning meetings and coordinating the efforts of the auxiliary and resource personnel. Team teaching arrangements were designed to achieve the following broad objectives:

1. *Promote maximum development of self-understanding and self-respect.* To facilitate achievement of this objective, a strong teacher-pupil relationship was planned by having each teacher responsible for the guidance and coordination of all components of the curriculum for approximately thirty of the pupils on the team. The schedule was organized to provide the teacher extended periods of time with the group of pupils for which he served as "teacher-counselor." In addition to the personal and educational counseling opportunities afforded, the curriculum was planned to include units of work around broad themes dealing with issues associated with preadolescent development.

2. *Stimulate in-depth interest in the academic disciplines.* Each teacher was responsible for becoming especially competent in one of the basic subject areas of the curriculum and for developing procedures and program materials to foster independent study, inquiry, and discovery in the discipline.

3. *Promote maximum individual development in basic learning skills.* Through team teaching, pupils were scheduled with different teachers for remedial or developmental classes or laboratory sessions. Special skills development sessions were a part of the weekly schedule for every pupil.

4. *Achieve a high degree of integration among all aspects of the educational program for pupils.* The close relationship of the teacher-counselor with pupils in the homeroom group, the scheduling of blocks of time for general education, broad-theme units, and independent study assignments cutting across subject matter lines were all facilitated by the daily team planning sessions.

5. *Provide each pupil with a wide variety of personally rewarding exploratory experiences.* Four teachers working together were able to provide for a wider range of both short-term and extended special interest experiences for pupils than one teacher working alone. In addition to the usual

exploratory courses, time was scheduled regularly for students to participate in activities of their own choice.

A look at a typical weekly schedule of the P. K. Yonge team shows the
balance among curriculum goals achieved through cooperative team planning and teaching:

Composite Schedule—School Year 1966–1967

Time	Monday Tuesday Wednesday	Thursday	Friday
			Morning
8:30	Homeroom—pupil guidance, individual	General	
	conference	education	Special
		double	help aca-
9:30	General education: Broad theme units	period	demic work-
	correlating all subjects, independent	available	shops, and
	studies	for large	independent
9:35	Exploratory	group,	study projects
	Art, first aid, general music, instru-	small	
	mental music, shop, home living,	group,	
10:20	humanities, great books	cross-grade	
		work	
10:25	Mathematics		
11:10			
11:10	English language arts		
11:50			
11:55	Lunch and activities		
12:20			
12:25	Double Period		*Afternoon*
	Science Social Science	Social	Special
	Studies	Studies	interest
2:05			groups
2:10	Physical Education for pupils		
3:10			
2:10	Team planning for staff		
3:30			

The Dover Plan. The William Henry Middle School and the Central Middle School in Dover, Delaware, illustrate a simple team organization in grades 5–6, paving the way for more complex arrangements at the 7–8 level. Essential features of the plan are described below:

Grades 5–6
1. Two teachers are "teamed" and located in adjoining rooms with a shared "project area" room.
2. Each teacher conducts a "humanities" oriented language arts—social studies program for his "own" pupils for approximately one-half day. Developmental reading, creative and expressive arts are incorporated in this block. Special reading consultants and facilities are available.
3. Teacher "A" teaches all mathematics while teacher "B" teaches all science. Pupils in these classes are grouped according to achievement, needs, or interests as recognized by the team of two teachers.
4. The two teachers have fifty minutes of team planning time daily while their pupils are in physical education, art, or music. (These offerings are rotated throughout the year.)

Grades 7–8
Four teachers and 120 to 130 pupils form a team. Two of the team members represent the areas of the "humanities," a fused language arts—social studies program. One member is a mathematics teacher, and one is a science teacher. These four teachers meet regularly to plan the instructional program for the pupils with frequent regrouping of pupils as needs are determined. The pupils in the team have approximately two-thirds of their schedule with the four teachers on the team in a variety of instructional groupings. The remaining one-third of the pupils' time is spent in the exploratory and physical education programs.[10]

Which Horizontal Organization Is Best?

Earlier in this chapter, it was stated that research on school organization does not demonstrate the clear superiority of any one organizational arrangement over all others. A middle school staff may experiment with a variety of horizontal patterns to find one, provided that the school staff knows exactly what they expect to achieve as a result of the adoption of any particular plan, and that they devise means of gathering evidence of whether they are, in fact, achieving the desired results. In determining what organizational plan to use, such criteria as the following should be applied:

1. The plan should provide each pupil with a continuing relationship with one teacher who is responsible for personal and educational guidance and for coordinating all aspects of the pupil's total program.

[10]From undated, mimeographed materials furnished by Alexander M. Gottesman, Assistant Superintendent, Dover, Delaware, Special School District.

2.   The plan should bring each pupil into an instructional relationship with teacher specialists in a variety of major curriculum areas on a regularly scheduled basis.

3.   The plan should provide for maximum professional interchange on the part of all staff members working with pupils through scheduled joint planning and evaluation.

THE VERTICAL ORGANIZATION

The vertical dimension of organization deals with policies for moving pupils upward through the program from entry until school departure. The American educational system places almost complete reliance on a *graded* school as the vehicle for vertical progression. The basic assumption underlying the graded system is that the amount of work to be done in a school year can be identified and packaged in first, or second, or any of the following grades through high school. If at the end of the school year instructors determine that the pupil has completed a fixed proportion of the work, he is passed or promoted to the next grade; if not, he may be required to start over on the same material at the beginning of the next school year. The alternative to a graded system is a nongraded, or multigraded, or continuous progress system, or a system in some way combining these plans. The graded system and all its accouterments of graded textbooks, report cards, grade level expectations, promotion or retention policies, and graded achievement tests are so much a part of our educational heritage that American schools persist in following the system in spite of convincing evidence of its inconsistency with current psychological insights, as described in Chapter 2. Goodlad and Anderson summarize several important generalizations regarding pupil realities, questioning the appropriateness of the rigidly graded system. They assert that:

1.   Children enter the first grade with a range of from three to four years in their readiness to profit from a "graded minimum essentials" concept of schooling.

2.   This initial spread in abilities increases over the years so that it is approximately double this amount by the time the children approach the end of the elementary school.

3.   The achievement range among pupils begins to approximate the range in intellectual readiness to learn soon after first-grade children are exposed to normal school instruction.

4.   Differing abilities, interests, and opportunities among children cause the range in certain specific attainments to surpass the range in general achievement.

5.   Individual children's patterns differ markedly from learning area to learning area.

6. By the time children reach the intermediate elementary grades, the range in intellectual readiness to learn and in most areas of achievement is as great as or greater than the number designating the grade level.[11]

In short, pupils start their formal schooling at different levels of readiness, and they progress at different rates through the programs. Goodlad and Anderson conclude that:

By the fourth or fifth year of school, more than half the achievement scores in a class are above and below the grade level attached to the group. There is, then, no such thing as a fourth-grade class or a fifth-grade teacher, regardless of the labels within our conventional graded structure.[12]

The National Committee of the NEA Project on Instruction made the following recommendation concerning vertical organization:

The vertical organization of the school should provide for the continuous, unbroken upward progression of all learners, with due recognition of the wide variability among learners in every aspect of their development. The school organization should, therefore, provide for differentiated rates and means of progression toward achievement of educational goals.[13]

Nongraded, Multigraded, and Continuous Progress Plans

Almost from the inception of the graded system, plans for modifying the system were organized. Saylor and Alexander summarize the salient features of many of these plans beginning with the Pueblo, Colorado, plan of 1888. They mention "subgroups within a class, multiple textbooks in some of the school subjects, particularly reading, and more flexibility in the assignment of content to each grade level."[14] These modifications, however, were usually made within the framework of graded expectations. Many recent innovations in the vertical school organization have been called, variously—and often erroneously—"nongraded," or "multigraded," or "continuous progress" plans. These recent innovations are descended from the earlier efforts to break the "lockstep" of the graded system. All of these plans attempt to provide for the "differentiated rates and means of progression" called for by the NEA Project on Instruction

---

[11]John I. Goodlad and Robert H. Anderson, *The Nongraded Elementary School* (New York: Harcourt, Brace & World, Inc., 1959), pp. 27–28.

[12]Goodlad and Anderson, p. 28.

[13]Project on Instruction, *Schools for the Sixties* (Washington, D.C.: National Education Association, 1963), p. 78.

[14]J. Galen Saylor and William M. Alexander, *Curriculum Planning for Modern Schools* (New York: Holt, Rinehart and Winston, Inc., 1966), pp. 340–341.

volume cited above. Aside from this one common characteristic, the plans are as varied as the number of schools following them. The essential features of each of these plans are discussed below.

Nongraded. The nongraded organization does away with grade level designations and classifies students as being in the "primary" or "intermediate" block, or in the "first year" or "third level" in the school. The curriculum is said to be "learner centered" rather than "subject centered." As John Goodlad puts it, "There are no 'minimum essentials' of subject matter laid out in advance to be 'covered,' although the bodies of knowledge are to be examined for their usefulness in promoting optimal development of the learners."[15]

In the nongraded plan, a system of reporting as fully as possible all of the aspects of a pupil's progress is substituted for marking by single-letter grade or percentage. Rather than receiving a grade of "A" or "95 percent," the pupil typically receives a narrative report detailing his achievement in specific skills, understandings, and content. The nongraded plan aims to eliminate the concept of "pass or fail" at the end of each school year. At the beginning of each school year, the pupil begins work at approximately the level he had attained at the end of the preceding year.

Multigraded. The multigrade plan is an attempt to provide for individual differences by combining pupils from two or more grades for instruction in given subjects. Sometimes students from two grades are combined for *all* of their work, with the grade range permitting intraclass groupings. More typical of recent multigrade plans is the rescheduling of pupils by grade level achievement within a subject area. For example, a student who may be classified as a seventh-grade student for most of his work may be grouped, because of his readiness level in these subjects, with a fifth-grade mathematics class and an eighth-grade social studies class. This plan keeps many of the features of the graded plan, but tries to overcome the disadvantage of keeping a student on the same grade level in all his subjects.

Continuous progress. The nongraded and the multigrade plans obviously are designed to promote continuous pupil progress. Few schools today can be described accurately as "nongraded" schools, although many can be classified in the category of "moving toward ungradedness." Some schools retain an essentially graded course of study but permit students to progress through the course at differentiated rates. In the continuous progress plan, the curriculum is typically comprised of "achievement levels" or "units of work." As a student completes a unit

[15]Project on Instruction, *Planning and Organizing for Teaching,* John I. Goodlad (Washington, D.C.: National Education Association, 1963), p. 66.

of work in a subject he moves on to the next unit. This plan utilizes programed and semiprogramed instructional materials, along with teacher-
made units. A shortcoming of this plan is that it may overemphasize
differentiation in rate *through* a program rather than differentiation *in* the
program. Some schools, in an effort to avoid the emphasis on rate alone,
use independent study plans and "depth study" phases to permit students
to go beyond the basic units of work.

An "Individualized Learning" Plan

A school in Iowa has been reported as having developed a plan stressing
"individualized learning." In accomplishing this task, the staff developed a
plan including many features discussed in the above sections on nongraded, multigraded, and continuous progress. An analysis of two days in
the schedule of "Tom," a typical ten-year-old "first year" student in this
particular middle school, is presented here. It is not likely that all of the
activities included in the example would occur in a two-day period. The
schedule compresses into two days, for illustrative purposes, the various
possibilities for individual instruction which in actual practice would be
utilized over a period of several days or weeks.

Composite Two-Day Schedule for "Tom"[16]
Monday
    8:45– 9:00   Diagnostic Test (comprehension) (Small Group)
    9:00–10:20   Study Center (Famous American Men) (Individual)
  10:20–10:40   Recess
  10:40–11:45   Math Class (Level G—Numeration; program materials obtained from study center) (Individual)
  11:45–12:45   Lunch
  12:45– 1:40   Inquiry Training (Film and discussion) (Small Group)
    1:40– 2:30   Science (Lab Work) (Small Group)
    2:30– 2:45   Social Studies (Film and Discussion—2 teachers) (Large
Group)
    2:45– 3:00   Social Studies (Note Study) (Small Group)
Tuesday
    8:45– 9:15   Study Center (Programed materials) (Individual)
    9:15– 9:45   Achievement Test and Study Center (Individual)
    9:45–10:20   Creative Writing (Large Group)
  10:20–10:40   Recess
  10:40–11:45   Math (Small heterogeneous group preparations for demonstrations of skills) (Small Group)
  11:45–12:45   Lunch
  12:45– 1:30   Science (Total class group) Rock study and classification
(Large Group)

[16]From Eugene R. Howard and Roger W. Bardwell, *How to Organize a Non-Graded
School* (Englewood Cliffs, N.J.: Prentice-Hall, Inc., 1966), pp. 22–23.

1:30– 2:00 "Famous American Men": Study center and activities area
(Individual)
2:00– 2:30 Social Studies (Lecture and activities or projects presentation
to 60) (Large Group)
2:30– 3:30 Half of above 60 continues with teacher regarding projects. Tom
to study center to initiate project. (Individual)

An examination of Tom's schedule reveals certain assumptions about
vertical progress of pupils. The way these assumptions are met in the
schedule is discussed below:

*Assumption 1. Pupils will progress at varying rates in different areas of
their program.* Tom works at a highly accelerated rate in his social
studies class; he is scheduled in a basic skills and special-help mathematics
group, and he works individually or with a very small group in the reading
class. He is not held back in an area of special competence because of
less able performance in another subject.

*Assumption 2. The grouping of pupils for instruction should be related to
the purposes of the grouping and not necessarily tied to chronological age,
number of years in school, or a global-type test score.* Tom works with
a number of different student groupings in the course of a week. At times
he works with a group matched on performance on a reading comprehen-
sion test, at other times he joins a very heterogeneous small group for
discussion and sharing; occasionally, he is in a very large group for
demonstrations, viewing, or group testing. Tom's progress is geared to
his own rate, not the average rate of a group.

*Assumption 3. Pupils should be given increasing responsibility for man-
aging their own time in educational pursuits of their own choosing.* Approximately one-quarter of Tom's time is in individual study. Some of
the work is programed practice on needed but underdeveloped skills. A
portion of his individual study is on a social studies research project of
his own choosing in a study center staffed by a trained resource specialist.

Which Vertical Organization Is Best?

We like John Goodlad's conclusion that "There is no *best* pattern of
vertical school organization in the absolute sense. The best pattern in
the relative sense, is that which most efficiently serves the functions of
the school."[17] Clearly, the functions of the middle school we have been
describing will not be served by the rigid graded system which prevails in
elementary and secondary schools today. The vertical organization "best"
suited to serve the purposes of the emergent middle school will allow for
"optimum individualization of curriculum and instruction for a popula-

[17]Goodlad and Anderson, p. 69.

tion characterized by great variability" (see Chapter 1). In our opinion, some plan of nongraded, continuous pupil progress offers the greatest promise for the middle school. We recognize the difficulties involved in reorganizing an existent program away from a prevailing pattern with wide cultural acceptance, but if the aims for the middle school, enunciated in Chapter 1, are valid, serious modification of existing graded structure is essential.

Enlightened, cooperative planning within a graded school may indeed result in a superior program, and unthinking, premature adoption of a nongraded plan without the necessary understanding of its underlying assumptions may result in inferior programs. Organization per se does not guarantee anything. Our position, then, is essentially in agreement with the NEA Project on Instruction recommendation that:

Nongrading and multigrading are promising alternatives to the traditional graded school and should be given careful consideration in seeking to provide flexible progress plans geared to human variability.[18]

OTHER ORGANIZATIONAL CONSIDERATIONS

Aside from the major considerations of age-grade range of pupils, the manner of organizing groups horizontally for instruction, and ways of moving pupils vertically through the curriculum, a number of other organizational decisions affect the instructional program of a school. Such factors as size of the school, utilization of plant and facilities, and selection and deployment of staff will determine the kinds of teaching and learning opportunities to be provided.

Optimum Size for a Middle School

Discussion of the optimum size of schools is not receiving much attention in the current educational dialogue. True, authoritative recommendations are still occasionally made, but local demographic and economic factors, and especially political boundaries, are more often the actual determinants of size. While most authorities would agree that a school can be too small to offer an adequate program, or too large to be managed efficiently, there is no universally agreed-upon formula for optimum size. The problem of bigness is being solved in many instances by some form of a "school within a school." Judith Murphy reports in an Educational Facilities Laboratory publication that:

[18] *Schools for the Sixties*, p. 78.

Most of the sizeable schools profiled have taken pains to mitigate bigness by one device or another, in deference to their young inhabitants. Generally the schools are designed to some variation of the house plan—Bedford, Giano, and Mettlin, for instance, with separate houses: Barrington and Kennedy in a layout with separate wings—acting to give youngsters a sense of identity and administrators a sense of knowing them as individuals.[19]

Plans for a middle school organization developed by the authors suggest that students might profit from identification with groups of three different sizes. Each student would belong to a *homeroom unit* of about twenty-five to thirty students of approximately the same age and year level in school. A *wing unit,* made up of several homeroom units, would provide for cooperative planning and instruction and would aid students to make the transition to living and working with larger units. A still larger unit would be a *vertical unit,* which would combine several wing units representing all year levels of the school. A vertical unit would enroll approximately four- or five-hundred pupils and would constitute a "school within a school." Any number of vertical units could be accommodated within a large school. This organization would give the developing adolescent a wider community in which to live, explore, and gain new social understandings, and at the same time would be small enough to promote a sense of identity and belonging. Younger students have opportunities to work and play with and learn from slightly more mature students, and the older student has an opportunity to provide leadership within the vertical unit.

We believe that the most important considerations for each pupil are that he belong to at least one group in which he has a close relationship with a teacher, and that he be well known by a counselor.

Relationship of Organization to School Plant Planning

While school plant planning properly requires more extensive treatment than is possible for present purposes, the relationship between program and plant should be clarified. A school plant should be designed to accommodate an educational program; not the other way around. A promising development which is fast becoming widespread is the writing of educational specifications to guide architectural planning. Professional staff members, including administrative and instructional personnel, consider the objectives of their program and describe the facilities and types of spaces needed to attain their objectives. The following excerpts from the Cecil County (Maryland) specifications for a middle school illustrate this kind of advanced planning:

[19]Murphy, p. 16.

The objectives of the middle school will be attained more easily through the use of the new technologies of team teaching, programmed instruction and television education.

The school will be zoned to permit efficient and practical use of the building by pupils and adults for after-school activities. Each department will have its teaching stations located together so that regrouping of students can be done with ease. Each cluster of teaching stations will have an area for the storage of materials of instruction, supplementary books, and textbooks. . . .

Middle schools will need carrels for individual study, conference rooms for small groups from 3–20, and larger areas for groups of approximately 100.

This school must have a flexible plan so that instructional space can be added or reduced on short notice. . . .

Each school should have an activity suite consisting of one conference room, three-quarters of a general classroom with flexible room furniture, and a small auxiliary workroom. The remainder of the suite will be composed of two rooms approximately one-half general classroom size. . . .[20]

The practice of involving all of the professional staff in the development of educational specifications for new school buildings will result in both improved building plans and increased understanding of the relationships among many aspects of organization and instructional program goals. School staffs do not have to wait for construction of a new building to engage in a process of careful scrutiny of the program and thoughtful analysis of creative ways to utilize, or perhaps modify, existing facilities to achieve the program goals. Some schools have effected an inexpensive metamorphosis in the conventional library to a resource and individual study center by including microfilm readers and films, more vertical file material, study carrels, and audio and video booths. A conventional classroom can be converted into a basic skills laboratory through the simple expedient of securing suitable tables and laboratory type materials. Indeed, if the curriculum plan calls for emphasis on basic skills development, such a change in facilities may stimulate efforts to schedule pupils' time in this important phase. The establishment of middle schools in many communities has sparked an interest in arranging the building to suit the program rather than planning a program to suit the building. Teachers and students alike have been pleased, even elated, at the creative solutions reached in meeting this new challenge.

STAFFING THE MIDDLE SCHOOL

Many local factors will determine the actual assignments of staff positions to particular schools, and no one pattern of staffing can be recom-

[20]*General Educational Specifications: Middle School* (Elkton, Md.: Cecil County Public Schools, 1966), pp. 1–3.

mended for all schools. Some middle schools will, out of necessity or choice, follow the conventional practice of employing grade level or subject area teachers and then, by redefining their roles and relationships to each other, attempt to accomplish the functions of the reorganized schools. Other schools may have the opportunity to create new staff positions designed to serve the new demands of the middle school program. In this section, some general guidelines for staffing the middle school are proposed, and various categories of staff positions needed to accomplish the objectives of the middle school program are discussed.

Guidelines for Staffing the Middle School

Rather than starting with a list of positions to be filled, planners of middle schools should develop a set of guidelines to govern staffing policies. We propose the following five general guidelines as starting points for individual middle schools to use in compiling a similar list:

1. *The functions which the school aims to serve should determine the qualifications and the categories of personnel to be employed.* While this is a most obvious consideration, we feel that it is so important that we state it at the risk of belaboring the obvious. A balanced professional faculty to staff all of the important curriculum areas of the school program is the first priority in assigning staff positions.

2. *Staff members should be assigned to the total middle school faculty rather than to fifth, sixth, seventh, or eighth grades.* While individual staff members may be given special responsibility for a particular phase of the program, *all* are jointly responsible for the total educational program of the school. Initial assignment should make this responsibility clear.

3. *Until preservice programs for middle school teachers are generally available, a realistic approach for most schools will be to employ a staff representing both elementary and junior high preparation and experience. Whenever feasible, arrangements which combine teachers from both elementary and secondary backgrounds for cooperative planning should be scheduled.* Care should be taken to avoid creating a separate "elementary" faculty for the younger and a "secondary" faculty for the older students in the school.

4. *The allotment of staff to the middle school should include sufficient auxiliary and special resource personnel* to serve the program and the pupils enrolled. A variety of teacher aide or paraprofessional categories may be used to extend the talents of the professional staff.

5. *Administrative staff personnel should be selected to perform these major tasks: (1) provide educational leadership to the school staff, student body, and school patrons; (2) serve the aims of the instructional program by providing services and resources for students and teachers; and (3) facilitate*

the work of the instructional staff by managing the business, financial, and routine housekeeping aspects of organization, so as to free staff and students to pursue educational ends. The administrative staff should represent both elementary and secondary preparation and experience backgrounds. It is desirable that the chief educational administrator have a background in both these areas.

It was observed in Chapter 5 that no one set of teacher characteristics or teaching behaviors could be identified as "best" for all instructional purposes. The middle school staff should be chosen to represent a variety of personality types and teaching styles. Perhaps one of the most significant variables to look for in selecting staff members is enthusiasm for and commitment to working with older children and younger adolescents. When a staff possesses these attributes, a well-planned and continuous inservice training program can develop most of the other desired qualities.

Staffing the Major Functions

There is no single formula applicable to all middle schools, but there are some identifiable categories of positions necessary to accomplish the broad functions of the middle school. While exact job titles are unimportant, these important roles must be considered when selecting the staff for the middle school.

Teacher-counselor. In the middle school program envisioned in this book, the teacher-counselor role is extremely important. The teacher-counselor will be expected to perform such duties as the following for an assigned group of middle school pupils:

1. Provide a secure and comfortable home-base environment for the assigned group;
2. Provide personal and educational guidance;
3. Plan and evaluate individual programs;
4. Coordinate all of the many parts of the total educational program for the students in the assigned group;
5. Develop with pupils a program of self-knowledge and understanding of the nature of adolescence.

While a background of preparation and experience in school guidance and counseling may be helpful, the essential qualifications for this position are an attitude of empathy and skill in working with many different types of pupil. The teacher-counselor should not be expected to replace the need for specialized guidance services in the school, but rather should facilitate these services by interpreting them to the pupils and their parents. Every middle school student should have a regular, continuing relationship with one teacher whom he identifies as "his" teacher. One teacher-counselor for every 25 or 30 pupils should be provided. Since this is near the usual teacher-pupil ratio allotment in today's schools, it is apparent that the teacher-counselor will also serve other roles in the school. For example, an individual might be assigned as a teacher-counselor for one-fourth of his time, and as a language arts specialist for the remainder.

Subject specialist. To assure every middle school student a degree of success in understanding the key ideas of the major disciplines and to promote maximum growth in basic skills, teachers should be selected for the middle school who have achieved competency beyond the beginning level in an academic discipline. In addition to giving instruction in his speciality, the subject specialist should serve as a resource person for other staff members in acquainting them with developments in his field. As was pointed out in Chapter 5, the middle school subject specialist need not be a renowned scholar or advanced researcher. Elementary teachers with a minor in a subject area and secondary teachers with a subject major or minor may become subject specialists by advanced study and through participation in the professional societies of the academic discipline. Some would prefer to name this position "subject generalist" to avoid the connotation of narrow specialization and fragmentation of the educational program of the students so often characteristic of the strict departmentalized organization associated with the use of subject area teachers. While some subject specialists may be assigned full-time loads in their special area, most will probably serve also as a teacher-counselor for one group of pupils. Organizational arrangements of the middle school should provide for inservice help for teachers to develop their abilities to perform both these functions.

Special learning resources personnel. The special needs of individual schools and the availability of qualified personnel will result in a wide variety of positions under this broad category, but one position which should be common, in broad outline, to all middle schools is that of *resource center librarian.* The person filling this position may be known by a variety of titles, but he should be skilled in the use of information retrieval procedures and should teach these skills to pupils and other teachers. The resource center librarian should be an individual who can serve as a resource aide for the student searching for materials for a class project or working on an independent study project. Many audio and video learning materials will be under the direction of the resource center, and ample assistants should be provided.

Other typical staff positions. All middle school staffs should include competent reading specialists and professionally qualified art, music, modern foreign language, home arts, and physical education resource teachers. Guidance specialists, including a psychologist and psychometrist, would be desirable; if not available at the school level, they should be provided in the district. Many middle schools will augment their full-time professional staffs by utilizing the part-time services of many well-qualified professional teachers who cannot accept full-time employment. Additionally, the use of paraprofessionals, including teacher aides, clerical aides, technicians, and intern teachers, will be characteristic of the emergent middle school.

Individual middle schools will work out widely divergent patterns for staffing the major functions of the middle school. This, we believe, is as it should be. The positions described in Chapter 5 and the guidelines proposed in this section are offered more in the nature of illustrations than as recommendations. Many staff decisions will be made at the system-wide level; however, it may be possible to make internal decisions as to the best use of the assigned personnel. For example, the whole matter of staffing instructional teams may in many instances evolve out of the cooperative efforts of the local school staff to provide better instruction for pupils. The needs of the specific school program will determine the specific staff needs within the framework of the broad functions described for the middle school.

In Summary

Throughout this chapter, we have developed three positions. First, we have maintained that while organization per se is no guarantee of improved teaching-learning opportunities, organization can be used to facilitate attainment of educational goals. We have stressed that organization is not an end in itself, but is a means toward the goal of improved teaching of and increased learning by students. Second, we have stated that local conditions significantly act to determine organizational policy: Local staffs should be involved in making organizational decisions. Finally, implicit in our treatment of the topic is the position that conventional organizational arrangements were developed for yesterday's schools—they must be modified to meet the needs of the emergent middle school.

PART IV

Establishing and Evaluating
the Middle School

Chapter 7

Evaluating the Middle School

American education has all too often been characterized by experiments which were really untested innovations. The junior high school came into being and flourished for decades without any systematic study to determine whether or not it did a better job for boys and girls than the 8-4 plan which it succeeded. Progressive education was already a waning movement when the Eight-Year Study was completed. Harold Fawcett's *The Nature of Proof*,[1] which indicated that considerable transfer of learning might be possible if plane geometry were taught for transfer, was an isolated study. Had innovations in medicine and pharmacy been fostered with equal carelessness, we would undoubtedly be worrying more about epidemics and less about the population explosion.

There are a number of reasons why this unfortunate situation has persisted. In the first place, tradition, common sense, intuition, and authority sanctioned existing practices. For generations, English-speaking schoolmasters knew that the best way to teach Latin was to beat it into pupils. Greek was best learned by first mastering Latin and then learning Greek from Latin; Greek could be learned only with great difficulty directly from English. The proper age to learn to read was six.

Second, the proper measuring tools and research designs for assessing educational practice are of very recent origin. There are still great gaps where the instruments do not exist. According to Ralph Tyler, "Test

[1]Harold Fawcett, *The Nature of Proof* (National Council of Teachers of Mathematics, Bureau of Publications, Teachers College, Columbia University, 1938).

practice and, to some extent, theory have been based on assumptions that are acceptable only for certain kinds of work."[2]

A third reason for the failure to rigorously test innovations is that there has been a lack of trained leadership to adequately evaluate changes. Only with the recent subsidies from federal agencies have enough persons been trained in the skills of test construction, statistical analysis, research design, and computer programing to provide necessary data.

A fourth reason is that adequate evaluation is often very expensive. There is the tradition of spending pennies per pupil for educational tests, having teachers spend long hours grading and recording results, believing that adequate tests could be speedily improvised by almost anybody. Possibly the best single work on the theory of test construction to date is *Educational Measurement,*[3] which was made possible with a grant of a few hundred dollars from a foundation and thousands of dollars of contributed knowledge from scholars in the field. Sixteen years later, when all external costs are included, it is difficult to design a study for less than $10,000 which would let a school system decide whether to use traditional grammar in the fifth and sixth grades of its middle school or a transformational grammar when the criterion is whether or not pupils can write better sentences after the period of exposure to the new grammar.

As suggested in Chapter 1, there are already several hundred middle schools operating, and the movement is receiving accelerating support. As additional systems consider the middle school, it is imperative that adequate plans be made for its evaluation. Before American education becomes completely committed to the middle school, would it not be well to look at its claims and find out whether or not they are supported by its practices and accomplishments?

WHAT IS EVALUATION?

"Evaluation" is more than the next to the most recent "in" term for testing, measuring, or grading (the most recent term is "feedback"). If man is viewed as an intelligent, choice-making creature, acting rationally at least part of the time, rather than functioning as a pawn of blind, external forces, motivated by unperceived, irrational impulses, then his behavior has purposes, and, within limits, he can control his behavior. Further, if his institutions exist to help him achieve his purposes better than he might in the primitive state of nature, then, to some degree, he

[2]Ralph Tyler, Robert Gagné, and Michael Scriven, *Perspectives of Curriculum Evaluation,* AERA Monograph Series on Curriculum Evaluation, No. 1 (Skokie, Ill.: Rand McNally & Company, 1967), p. 14.

[3]E. F. Lindquist (ed.), *Educational Measurement* (Washington, D.C.: American Council on Education, 1951).

can restructure his institutions. Evaluation, then, is the process by which he gathers information to find out how well he is achieving his purposes, how well his institutions are functioning, enabling him to modify his actions and his institutions in the future so that he may better achieve his purposes: "[E]valuation is the process of making meaning out of experience."[4] Evaluation can also include criticism, refinement, and modification of the purposes of the enterprise. When the enterprise being evaluated is an educational one, the evaluation should include a critical examination of the educational theory on which the enterprise is based. This examination can be both theoretical and empirical.

WHY EVALUATE THE MIDDLE SCHOOL?

Among the many possible purposes for evaluating the middle school, the following are important:

1. *To provide information on how well the purposes of the middle school are being achieved.* In Chapter 1, the authors stated as aims of the middle school: (1) to serve the educational needs of the "in-between-agers" in a school bridging the elementary school for childhood and the high school for adolescence; (2) to provide optimum individualization of curriculum and instruction for a population characterized by great variability; (3) in relation to the foregoing aims, to plan, implement, evaluate, and modify in a continuing curriculum development program, a curriculum which includes provisions for: a planned sequence of concepts in the general education areas; major emphasis on the interests and skills for continued learning; a balanced program of exploratory experiences and other activities and services for personal development; appropriate attention to the development of values; (4) to promote continuous progress through and smooth articulation between the several phases and levels of the total educational program; (5) to facilitate the optimum use of personnel and facilities available for continued improvement of schooling.

These purposes would not necessarily be the stated purposes of a system beginning to organize its own middle schools. For example, the New York City Board of Education, in beginning a middle school program, stated some different goals: "(1) to provide improved quality education; (2) to desegregate and integrate the middle school population." More specifically, these were:

1. To cultivate the abilities and encourage the self-fulfilment of students.

[4]Fred T. Wilhelms (ed.), *Evaluation as Feedback and Guide* (Washington, D.C.: Association for Supervision and Curriculum Development, 1967), p. 51.

2. To maintain pupil motivation by providing courses that are consistent with the pupil's ability, aptitude and need.

3. To achieve better ethnic distribution in the intermediate grades.

4. To improve the quality of human relations among students by providing them with ethnically integrated schools, and to improve pupil attitudes—especially in relation to self-image and other pupils of different ethnic, racial, religious, or social groups.

5. To improve academic achievement in relation to the rate of academic growth normally found among educationally deprived children in grades 5 through 8.[5]

There are both similarities and unique elements among the two sets of purposes. The second aim on the New York list is similar to the third purpose of the authors. Whether either of these sets of purposes or a different set were being used, evidence would still be required beyond assertions or testimonials that progress was being made toward the achievement of the objectives, or that the middle school organization represented a better way of achieving the purposes than the organization it was replacing.

Some purposes might be relatively easy to assess. For example, if agreement could be reached on what constituted "better ethnic balance," a census of pupils and staff could provide comparative data. To test a curriculum development program as to whether or not it improved academic achievement, a careful research design, collection of equivalent data over time, and somewhat sophisticated analysis of variance and possibly covariance to provide answers, would be required.

2. *To test assertions or hypotheses underlying the middle school.* The statements of purposes just listed do not necessarily give the kind of information needed to make judgments about how well the purposes are being achieved. For example, the statement, "To promote continuous progress through and smooth articulation between the several phases and levels of the total educational program" does not immediately provide such smooth articulation. What, for instance, constitutes the "total educational program"? In some fields, the smooth articulation might mean building courses of study which provide for sequential learning. A person who is expert in mathematics might look at the plans for the middle school mathematics program in relation to what preceded it and what is to follow it. He could seek to answer such questions as, "Does the middle school presuppose any mathematical concepts which are prerequisite to its program and which are not planned for during the middle school years?" and "Does the middle school program provide the necessary concepts which will enable its pupils to make normal progress in the mathematics they will encounter in succeeding grades?"

[5]E. Terry Schwartz, "An Evaluation of the Transitional Middle School in New York City" (mimeographed; New York: Center for Urban Education, 1966), p. 1.

Another interpretation of the above purpose could be that pupils would become oriented quickly to the middle school and would experience fewer academic, psychological, or social problems than pupils moving from regular elementary schools into the departmentalized, competitive, and adult-oriented junior high schools. The same smooth transition would be expected to occur as they moved from the middle school to the high school. These expectations form the bases of testable hypotheses.

3. *To provide feedback for improving practices in the middle school.* Fred Wilhelms asks in the opening chapter of *Evaluation as Feedback and Guide,* "Does the evaluation we have provide continuing feedback into the larger questions of curriculum development and educational policy?" and then answers with a resounding "No!"[6]

In the term "improving practices," the authors include what teachers do, how they do it, and all the courses, activities, and services provided for the children who attend the middle school. The authors have hypothesized that there will be significant differences between the curriculum in the middle school and what has preceded and what will follow it, as well as between the middle school and the upper elementary and junior high years it is intended to replace. It is further hypothesized that as a result of differences, consequences for children will be demonstrably better than in the traditional organization and that the new middle school will have an initial flexibility which will permit modifications dictated by evaluation.

4. *To provide psychological security to staff, pupils, parents, and school officials.* From the moment a child is born, parents want to know how he is doing. Gains in weight at monthly check ups are viewed with pride. A clinical thermometer is an early purchase and is used regularly. When the child gets to school, parents are even more eager to know how he is progressing. Teachers, often subject to criticism, like to know how their pupils are doing. School officials sponsoring innovations need evidence of how the new programs are succeeding. Pupils also like to know about themselves. An adolescent boy who is building muscles on a large frame will probably never be a successful jockey, but his size in eliminating him from one sport may eminently qualify him for many others.

All too often both conventional letter grades and written reports from teachers fail to tell anybody very much. A sixth grader whose grade equivalent has increased from a 4.0 to a 6.5 during a semester's work in a remedial reading class knows that he has made progress and may now have the confidence to attack academic tasks he has feared and avoided. Middle school mathematics teachers can stand up to criticism from high school teachers when they can point out that the pupils they are sending to high school are achieving at or above expectation on appropriate

[6]Wilhelms, p. 14.

standardized achievement tests. If a principal can show experimental evidence that thirty minutes of homework three times a week in an area significantly increases learning increments, as compared to no homework, and that doubling the time for homework does not appreciably further increase achievement, he is on sounder ground in supporting existing practice with both parents and teachers, who may want more or less homework.

5. *To provide a basis for expanding middle schools.* New developments in agriculture and medicine are carefully tested in the laboratory and then in the field. Usually a new hybrid corn does not become popular until it has been demonstrated that it resists disease and drought and gives a high yield of a grain with desirable characteristics. Doctors seldom start using new drugs just because of a rumor that "the Mayo brothers have been using this for a long time now." Educational innovations often spread for capricious reasons. Only occasionally do new practices get additional support because of evidence that they achieve a task better than existing practices. Sometimes we become enthused over a method, such as the most current approach to reading, and we attribute a change to difference in method when the pioneer's enthusiasm has been the actual determining factor.

It is hoped that if adequate evaluation is a part of developing middle school programs, there will be evidence available to show how well the middle school has overcome shortcomings of the present 6-3-3 organization. If the purposes are being achieved, if positive answers can be given to hypotheses underlying the middle school, and if evaluation can be used to refine and improve practices in the early middle schools, then we will have the best basis for a large-scale innovation that we have ever had in American education. We will not need fifty or sixty years in which to decide that the 4-4-4 plan was not the answer after all.

TYPES OF EVALUATION

There are a number of bases for classifying evaluation. Three of these are: when the evaluation is done, who does the evaluating, and what is evaluated.

Formative and Summative Evaluation

The two terms "formative" and "summative" have come into evaluation literature with increasing frequency as ways of distinguishing when the evaluating is done. With respect to the middle school, formative evaluation is that evaluation which takes place during the organizational and tryout phase of a new middle school or group of middle schools.

It could overlap the "who does the evaluating" and "what is evaluated" classifications.

Summative evaluation is the evaluation which takes place after the middle school is well launched. It would include finding out what happens to pupils as they go through the middle school and, particularly, what happens to them after they complete the middle school.

In September 1966, fourteen pilot intermediate schools began operation in New York City. Planning and preparation for launching these schools had taken many months. Evaluation was incorporated from the beginning into almost all aspects of both the planning and the initial operation. Workshops for teachers and other personnel were evaluated by participants and observers. Course outlines were reviewed and evaluated as to appropriateness for the listed intermediate school objectives by experts in such fields as social studies curricula, mathematics education, and home economics programs. Finally, a plan was developed to evaluate the operation of the schools during the first year:

Purposes of the Evaluation

The purpose of the present evaluation is to assess this plan as it functions in the fourteen pilot intermediate schools during its first year. The specific aspects of the plan which will be assessed are: ethnic balance and integration, school organization and services, school personnel and facilities, curriculum, pupil growth in self-concept, pupil performance and achievement, reactions of staff, pupils, parents and the community to the plan.

Plan of the Evaluation

The present evaluation is designed as a three stage procedure: initial status, process and products.

1. *Initial status:* This is the first stage whose purpose is to obtain a description of the school and the pupils at the beginning of the school year. Data concerning objectives, school personnel and facilities, school organization and services, curriculum, ethnic balance and integration, parents and community, and scores on citywide standardized tests provide the bench marks for determining growth and change.

2. *Process:* The second phase of the evaluation assesses the school in operation. The areas to be studied as ongoing processes are integration, curriculum, pupil self-concepts, school organization, services, and pupil performance.

3. *Products:* The outcomes of the project will be assessed at the end of the school year. School staff, pupils and parents will evaluate the effectiveness of various facets of the program; the holding power of the program for staff and pupils will be determined; and the achievement of pupils in academic and non-academic areas will be explored.[7]

---

[7]Edward Frankel, "Proposed Evaluation Design for: Grade Reorganization of Middle Schools in the Public School System" (mimeographed, New York: Center for Urban Education, 1966), p. 20.

The plan also includes the organization of the evaluation team, the target populations, the instruments and other data sources, and the handling of data collected.

It could be argued that some of the end-of-the-year evaluation was summative rather than formative. However, it is probable that data obtained during the first year will lead to more sweeping reorganization of the new program than is apt to occur at any other time.

What Is Evaluated?

After junior or senior high schools have made a self-study using *The Evaluative Criteria,*[8] visiting committees are accustomed to making judgments in terms of the stated philosophy and objectives of the school. Committees also judge the extent to which schools are meeting the needs of the enrolled students. Despite this custom, it is quite possible that goals or objectives are not above criticism. The Progressive Education Association was criticized for stating all of its purposes in terms of individual children and for having no social purposes. For a school to have a goal of giving each male pupil a salable skill in agriculture (one of the writers surveyed a school where all boys were required to take agriculture for three years) and no record of any graduate or dropout ever taking a job in agriculture (also true in the school) is obviously ridiculous.

Scriven points out that "if the goals aren't worth achieving, then it is uninteresting how well they are achieved. . . . An American History curriculum which consisted in the memorization of names and dates would be absurd. . . . A "Modern Math" curriculum for general use which produced high school graduates largely incapable of reliable addition and multiplication would be (and possibly is) simply a disgrace, no matter what else it conveyed."[9]

Goals which are so general that they permit practitioners to claim that whatever is done is consistent with the goals should be suspect. *To prepare pupils to be good citizens* is such a goal. It would be appropriate at any level and in the school system of any type of society—fascist, communist, or democratic. Certain terminal behaviors of the effective citizen in a democratic society—such as voting, holding office, serving on juries, bearing arms, being informed on issues, and obeying laws—must be defined.

Goals might also be criticized for lack of feasibility, for being inconsistent with what is presently known about how people learn, for being inconsistent with each other, for neglecting areas ordinarily judged to be important school functions, for being inappropriate for the pupil popu-

[8]*Evaluative Criteria* (1960 edition; Washington, D.C.: National Study of Secondary School Evaluation, 1960).
[9]Tyler, Gagné, and Scriven, p. 52.

lation or community served, for being trivial, or for being inconsistent with our democratic tradition.

In addition to examining the goals or objectives, the appropriateness of the curriculum should be evaluated in terms of the objectives and characteristics of the population served. Evaluative criteria have been developed in great detail for the present organization of schools, particularly the 6-3-3 plan, but such a complete set of criteria does not exist for a middle school. Using such an outline set of criteria as we presented in Chapter 4, a staff might examine the curriculum—its offerings, physical facilities, instructional staff, instructional materials and activities, and methods of evaluation. The guidance services, activity program, and health services, as well as the school plant, staff, and administration should also come under scrutiny.

Who Evaluates?

Evaluation can be internal, external, or a combination of both. It may be "amateur" or "professional." The self-study made by a school staff prior to initial or continued accreditation would be an example of internal evaluation. Evaluation and tryout activities of a state, regional, or national curriculum group in science, mathematics, or social studies made by the persons preparing the new program would be an example of internal evaluation. The visiting committee which follows the faculty self-study process and checks on its findings is, to the extent that its judgments are independently made, an example of external evaluation. Most faculty members participating in self-studies might be considered amateurs at evaluation as would most visiting committee members. Very few persons are trained in sophisticated techniques of evaluation in terms of the national need for such expertness. Even national curriculum projects have found it difficult or impossible to get staff members with appropriate evaluation skills. Some types of evaluation might be thought of as both "external" and "professional." These would include evaluative surveys of schools or school systems by trained and experienced members of consulting organizations or college faculties who do this kind of work on a full-time or nearly full-time basis.

Evaluation as Feedback

Yet regardless of whether the evaluation is formal or informal—and equally regardless of whether it is "good" or "sensitive" or "adequate"—it has one thing in common with every other system of feedback: When it has been blended into the background system of purposes and values and policies, *it controls the next step.* This is simply a fact of life; all our decisions are conditioned by perceptions of how we are doing in terms of what we hope to do. The purpose of this yearbook is to explore ways of developing systems of evaluation which will feed back to every level the kinds of data needed to improve these perceptions and, consequently, to improve all our educational decisions.[10]

The yearbook from which the preceding quotation was taken is intended to suggest specific ways by which much present grading, record keeping, and reporting can be replaced by cooperative procedures which will provide better measures of status and growth of pupils and which will give relevant information to both pupils and teacher on how well they are doing, how they might define both their common and individual goals more clearly, and how they might make steadier progress toward them.

Two chapters in this yearbook are of particular relevance to middle school faculties planning evaluation procedures to help strengthen curriculum and teaching: Chapter 6, "A Cooperative Evaluation Program," and Chapter 7, "Cooperative Evaluation in English."[11] While some consultative help might be desirable, these two chapters, and, in addition, an appendix on clear and simplified statistical procedures, are excellent and instructive, and the procedures suggested have been used successfully for two-year periods in three junior high schools.

EVALUATION AS HYPOTHESIS TESTING

Most of what has been said thus far about evaluation of the middle school has been directed toward clarifying objectives of the middle school, assessing progress toward achievement of the objectives, and providing information which can help improve both process and product. Everything suggested thus far could conceivably be accomplished, and the question of whether or not the middle school was providing a better education for its pupils than grades 5 and 6 in traditional elementary schools and grades 7 and 8 in our present junior high schools would be unanswered.

In order to find out whether there are differences, it is necessary to establish the conditions in which hypotheses can be formulated about pupils, teachers, parents, administrators, and school climate, and where data can be gathered to test the hypotheses. Ideally there should be control schools for the experimental middle schools, though many hypotheses might be tested without such controls. Two control schools would be necessary: grades 5 and 6 in elementary schools approximating the size of the middle schools and drawing upon similar attendance areas and grades 7 and 8 from junior high schools also serving populations of similar composition.

[10]Wilhelms, p. 3.

[11]Frances R. Link and Paul B. Diederich, Chapters 6 and 7, in *Evaluation as Feedback and Guide,* pp. 121–231.

Obviously, a thorough evaluation in which even the hypotheses to be listed in this section were tested would strain or be beyond the resources of most school systems. However, with state or federal help, a single system could give evidence on many or most of the hypotheses. It would be better, however, from the standpoints of both economy and sound research if a number of systems were to cooperate in testing these and perhaps additional hypotheses. If a dozen schools were involved, and if there were eighteen major hypotheses to be tested, then each school might test six of the eighteen. In this way, the opportunity to generalize results would be greatly increased, for each hypothesis would be tested four times in different schools.

Following are some of the possible hypotheses which might be tested. Brief explanations are given after each, with suggested types of data needed to test them and possible statistical procedures needed to analyze the data after it had been collected. (Brief information about many of the instruments suggested will be found at the end of this chapter.) Hypotheses relating directly to pupils follow:

1. *Pupils in the middle school will become more self-directed learners than pupils in the control schools.* The activities carried on by pupils would be cooperatively planned and tailored to the interests, ability, and present performance of the individual pupil. He would be responsible for the effective use of large blocks of time with a minimum supervision. Similar data would be collected in middle and control schools by interview, observation, and case studies. It would be expected that independent study would be used in a greater variety of ways, by a higher proportion of teachers, and would involve a higher proportion of students. It would be expected that more time would be spent in libraries, science laboratories, language laboratories, shops, and similar areas, and a lesser proportion of time in group instruction in classes by pupils in the middle school. Data would best be collected at three or four randomly spaced intervals throughout the school year in both middle and control schools. Chi-square tests might be used to analyze data, or proportions might be tested for significant differences.

2. *Pupils in the middle school will have fewer and/or less intense social and psychological problems than pupils in conventional schools.* The theory of the middle school minimizes pressures for growing up very rapidly, for competitive athletics, for early dating, and for similar activities characteristic of contemporary junior high schools. The theory emphasizes a program of variety and depth for children which is not necessarily geared to eventual work in the graduate school. Hence it is believed that the social and psychological pressures will be lessened. A common problem of many parents today is the youngster of junior high school age or younger who is in rebellion against going to school at all. It is believed

that the middle school will be a place children in the ten to fourteen age group will want to go.

Records would be kept of referrals to guidance counselors and psychologists and of diagnoses of problem cases. Many school systems today have school psychologists and school social workers to work with problem cases. They keep systematic records which would be available, on a confidential basis, for research purposes. In addition to these records, random samples of pupils (stratified by sex and grade level) would be drawn from time to time and given projective tests such as the Combs Picture Story Test. These are often indicators of psychological problems. Chi-square tests and analysis of variance might be used to test for differences by grade level, sex, and type of school.

3. *Achievement of middle school pupils on standardized tests will equal or exceed that of pupils in conventional schools.* Pupils in both middle and control schools would be participants in the testing program of their school systems at the same time of year. It would also be desirable to have pupils take group tests of mental ability. Use could be made as well of such information as chronological age and social class background. If pupils differ significantly on three such variables, achievement may be affected. Fortunately, combining analysis of covariance with analysis of variance can provide a statistical control for these differences and give a more accurate estimate of variance between schools.

There are ways besides standardized tests of getting estimates of certain kinds of achievement. For example, it is possible to have pupils spanning several different grade levels write short papers. These are identified by number only. The papers may be combined, even between schools. If twenty teachers are involved, each receives one-twentieth of the papers. These can be ranked in the top fourth, middle half, and bottom fourth. They are then mixed, divided, and given a second reading. Ratings are combined and a table like the following, which shows the results for a senior high school, is prepared:[12]

| | Year in School (and Number of Pupils) | | |
Rating	10 (238)	11 (190)	12 (161)
High	22%	41%	53%
Middle	65%	52%	42%
Low	13%	7%	5%

These ratings are for "academic pupils." Their papers were mixed with those of "nonacademic pupils," not shown above. The table indicates that a higher proportion of pupils score in the top fourth of all pupils in grade 11 than in grade 10, and an even higher porportion in grade 12 than

[12]Information from a table in Link and Diederich, p. 196.

in grade 11. Likewise, the proportion of pupils rated "low" decreases with advancing grade level. A chi-square test would undoubtedly indicate that these differences are significant well beyond the statistician's one percent level of confidence. Diederich and Link report, "We have not yet tried this measurement procedure in grades 4-5-6, but friends tell us that gains at this level are equally impressive."[13]

4. *Middle school pupils will equal or exceed pupils in conventional schools on standard measures of physical fitness and health.* Since the middle school would emphasize health and fitness for all pupils and would not permit a few students to be exploited for interscholastic competition, it would be expected that significant differences might occur on such tests as the AAHPER Youth Fitness Test and the Health Behavior Inventory. Analysis of variance would be used to test for significance of differences.

5. *Pupils in the middle school will have more favorable attitudes toward school than will pupils in conventional schools.* Pupils develop attitudes toward other pupils, teachers, the principal, their program, and the school as a whole. The Battle Scale is a 60-item pupil attitude inventory, with items directed toward each of the attitudes just mentioned. Scores are additive, and analysis of variance can be used with them.

6. *Middle school pupils will hold more adequate "self concepts" than will pupils in the conventional schools.* While psychologists argue about the existence of a "self concept," and others argue that a "self-report" is often mistaken for a "self concept," there is still a growing body of evidence which indicates that the genuine feeling a person has about his individual worth, ability, and adequacy, how he perceives himself and his situation, is as good a predictor of academic tasks such as learning to read as is an intelligence test. However, the "self concept" cannot be estimated directly, but must be inferred from projective instruments like the Combs Picture Story Test or by observation from structured situations. Since inferring the "self concept" is time consuming and relatively expensive, stratified random samples could be drawn and tested and would give sufficient information for making comparisons between schools.

7. *Social acceptance among middle school pupils will be higher than among those in conventional schools.*

In another sense, however, this measure was unsuccessful because the teachers could not see any real use for it. (a sociometric measure) They said that they already knew which students were popular and which were unpopular, and the scores showed that they were right . . . Still, they did not see that they could do anything about the state of affairs revealed by this instrument.

This was shocking to the few who began teaching in the 'thirties when acceptance of and by others was an important value, and when we would worry and

[13]Link and Diederich, p. 197.

scheme for months over students with low sociometric ratings if they were hostile or unhappy. . . .

The intellectual atmosphere of the 'sixties seems to have eclipsed our earlier interest in the personal relationships of our students. We hope such interest will return. . . . One junior high school counselor related how the sociometric data led her to an early interview with a seventh grader, when she discovered the child had been checked as "unknown" by everyone in her section. The counselor assumed that the student was new to the district. When she discovered that the student had been with most of the group throughout elementary school, the counselor was alerted to a problem soon enough to do something about it.[14]

The experience of some of the authors in a project on high school evaluations and curriculum change has supported this finding in a number of schools. Pupils, parents, and teachers in some junior and senior high schools are almost unaware that certain pupils are there.

Some sociometric devices can be extremely complicated to use for research purposes, but there are other instruments which are easy to use and which give information not just about stars and isolates but about all pupils. One of these is the Ohio Social Acceptance Scale. Another is a simple and similar device recommended by Diederich and Link.[15] Analysis of variance can be used when making comparisons between grade levels or schools.

8. *The average daily attendance of middle school pupils will exceed the attendance of pupils in conventional schools.* School records of attendance, transfers, and withdrawals (withdrawals should be rare in the middle school) would provide data for testing this hypothesis. Since such records must be carefully kept for the purposes of getting state support funds and obtaining and maintaining accreditation, they should be comparable from school to school. Comparisons could be made by grade level and between schools, using significance of difference between proportions.

9. *Measures of creativity among middle school pupils will show an increase rather than a decrease during middle school years.* Scores on measures of creativity tend to decrease during the middle school years. Since the middle school program is designed to foster young people who act on individual initiative, and since such pupils have less regimentation and fewer pressures to conform to, it is believed that creativity, as measured by tests of creativity such as the Guilford tests (or Torrance's adaptation, when more suitable for younger children), will remain constant or increase. Tests would have to be given at least twice, with intervals of several months between, and they should be given, ideally, several times during the four years the pupil is in the middle school. Analysis of vari-

---

[14]Link and Diederich, p. 160–161.
[15]Link and Diederich, pp. 159–161.

ance could be used to assess the significance of changes and whether or not the changes are greater in middle schools than in conventional schools.

10. *Middle school graduates will compile better academic records in ninth grade than will ninth-graders from the control schools.* The middle school pupils, having long been responsible for their own learning, should possess more self-discipline, and have, therefore, the ability to cope with the attractions and opportunities of the senior high school more ably than control school students. It is also possible that the middle school students will resist learning in what could be for them a more stringently regulated system. To determine which, if either, of these conjectures would prove to be fact, pupils who have had two, three, and four years in the middle school would have to be compared with pupils who have gone from control schools to the ninth grade, academic records being determined by grades obtained in required courses, and comparisons being made through appropriate analysis of variance.

11. *Middle school graduates will drop out of senior high school less frequently than pupils who follow the traditional pattern.* School laws and accreditation standards ordinarily require that reasons why pupils leave school before graduation be categorized and recorded. The proportions in categories could be used to compare middle school students to control school students.

These are just a few of the hypotheses regarding middle school pupils which might be tested. Other comparisons could be made using additional measures of knowledge and understanding, motivation, other attitudes, and other noncognitive outcomes. Additional comparisons could be made, examining differences in such things as high school subjects, participation in the activity program in high school, leadership in clubs, dramatics, journalism, sports, student government and committees, type of education beyond high school, career choices, and age at marriage.

As well as considering the activities of pupils, the behavior and reactions of others involved in the middle school might also be studied as part of a comprehensive evaluation of the middle school. Some hypotheses about teachers, parents, and administrators follow:

12. *Middle school teachers will more often use practices which experts generally recommend as superior.* While the teacher's primary responsibility is to the pupil, teachers also participate in activities involving other teachers, administrators and supervisors, parents, as members of professional organizations, and for professional growth. The Mathews Teacher Activity Questionnaire is a 90-item check list which covers things teachers do in these different roles. Results are sufficiently reliable and valid for comparisons between faculties in different schools.

13. *Teachers in the middle school will experience a higher degree of professional fulfillment and self-satisfaction than teachers in conventional schools.* Among schools there are marked differences in teacher morale. One of the factors which should contribute to teacher morale and teacher satisfaction with the human relations aspects of his job is significant interaction with other teachers. The plan of the middle school is apt to call for this kind of interaction more often than teachers might experience it in conventional elementary or junior high schools. Two possible instruments for assessing teacher morale are the Organization Climate Description Questionnaire, developed by Halpin and Croft, and the Teacher Human Relations Scale, developed by Walker. These could be given at the same time of year to both experimental and control schools, preferably twice, and the results treated by analysis of variance.

14. *Teachers in the middle school will utilize a greater variety of learning media than will teachers in conventional schools.* Records of the media departments would be studied for frequency and variety of use. Spot checks could be made in classrooms at irregular intervals. It would be necessary to have equal access to the various media in both experimental and control schools.

15. *Teacher turnover will be lower in the middle school than in conventional schools.* It is anticipated that the middle school would have a career appeal which is found now in many elementary schools and high schools, but which is often lacking in the junior high school, where teachers are frequently eager to move either up or down. To determine whether or not this is true would be a long-term project, and care would need to be exercised to allow for other variables, such as age and experience of the teachers involved and operating pattern of the principals.

16. *Teachers in the middle school will be more open to change.* Since patterns in the middle school have not yet crystallized as much as in elementary and junior high schools, it is felt that teachers would have more interest in innovation and would be less influenced by the inertia of tradition. One possible instrument for assessing readiness for curriculum change is Duncan's Curriculum Improvement Measure. Analysis of variance or t-tests could be used to assess the significance of differences between teachers in experimental and control schools.

17. *Patrons of the middle school will hold more positive attitudes toward objectives and procedures of the school than patrons of conventional schools.* It is important for any faculty to know how parents feel about their schools. Parent satisfactions are sources of strength upon which to build. Parent dissatisfactions often indicate problems which must be solved. Sometimes the solution is accurate information or better dissemination of information. Sometimes the school must modify some of its practices. If a high proportion of parents feel that nobody in the school is interested in their child, or that discipline is poor, or that there is

too much homework of a trivial nature, or that the socioeconomic status of the parents influences how the child is treated, then the faculty should take a critical look at what it is doing.

One source of information about parent feelings is the Parent Attitude Scale developed at the University of Florida. By using stratified random sampling, a faculty can secure close to 100 percent returns on samples of one hundred or so, with a high probability that returns will correspond closely to what all parents would say if they were polled.

18. *Principals of experimental and control schools will have similar operating patterns within each school system.* Differences have been found among some schools regarding some of the hypotheses listed for testing, differences which seem to be due to different operating patterns or styles of school principals or of different organizational climates within different schools. Hence it would be desirable to study the ways in which principals operate as possible alternative explanations to differences found in the evidence for some of the preceding hypotheses. A number of useful instruments are available including: the Principal Behavior Check List, from the University of Florida; the Leader (also, Principal) Behavior Description Questionnaire, from Ohio State; Halpin and Croft's Organizational Climate Description Questionnaire; and the Executive Professional Leadership Scale, from Harvard.

SOURCES OF DATA

Many possible sources of data for testing the hypotheses listed above have been suggested, but the list is by no means exhaustive. Possible sources of data might be: school records; pupil cumulative folders; grades received by pupils; reports to parents; standardized test results; questionnaires and opinionnaires from pupils, teachers, and parents; interview data from teachers, principals, and other members of the school staff; and library records.

The recently published book *Unobtrusive Measures*[16] is highly suggestive of ways of getting information without testing or interviewing. For example, the cost of repairs to plumbing and fixtures in the restrooms may be indicative of comparative degrees of frustration. The cost of replacing broken windows may be highly correlated with student dissatisfaction.

The authors—Webb, Campbell, Schwartz, and Sechrest—suggest scores of "unobtrusive" methods of gathering data, many of which could be applied to educational research. They categorize these under physical traces: erosion and accretion; archives—running records, episodic records, and

[16]Eugene J. Webb, Donald T. Campbell, Richard D. Schwartz, and Lee Sechrest, *Unobtrusive Measures: Nonreactive Research in the Social Sciences,* (Skokie, Ill.: Rand McNally & Company, 1966).

private records; simple observations and contrived observation. Two of their examples are:

The floor tiles around the hatching-chick exhibit at Chicago's Museum of Science and Industry must be replaced every six weeks. Tiles in other parts of the museum need not be replaced for years. The selective erosion of tiles, indexed by the replacement rate, is a measure of the relative popularity of exhibits. . . .

The degree of fear induced by a ghost-story-telling session can be measured by noting the shrinking diameter of a circle of seated children.[17]

GATHERING DATA

Some kinds of data should be obtained from the complete population. These would include information about mental maturity, achievement, health, and physical fitness. For some pupils, obtaining diagnostic information could be very important as a basis for knowing how to begin appropriate treatment, but would probably be a waste of time with a pupil who seemed to be reading well, or who scored near the top of a standardized test in science or arithmetic.

It is an efficient procedure to attempt to fit any hypotheses testing into regular testing programs of schools. Sometimes minor modifications in these, if planned, can increase their usefulness for over-all research or evaluation. For example, differences in achievement between two schools may to a great extent be caused by differences in mental maturity of pupils in the same grade. It would be desirable to use the psychological examinations and achievement tests at about the same time. This can both save much work and produce more dependable data. When differences are found, it may be possible to allow for them through statistical controls such as analysis of covariance.

There are also occasions when gathering data from the complete population may be very difficult or very expensive. If it is needed for research purposes, it is quite possible that a representative sample will be satisfactory. Such a sample might be as small as 5 to 10 percent of the pupils in a large school. A large number of responses can be misleading if they are not representative of the population being studied.

A final world should be added about informal methods of data gathering. When Fawcett[18] was gathering information on the effectiveness of his method of teaching plane geometry so that pupils were able to think reflectively in a variety of situations, he did not set up a controlled experiment, but rather depended upon a variety of methods, all of which pointed in the same direction, on which to test his case. He kept anecdotal

[17]Webb, Campbell, Schwartz, and Sechrest, p. 2.
[18]Fawcett.

records on pupils. The class was observed frequently by university students. He asked for written reactions from them. During parent conferences or parent attendance at school functions, he recorded unsolicited comments from parents. He had pupils write essays, stories, and plays on the nature of proof and had English teachers make judgments about how well this was done. He also had some scores on tests of reflective thinking and on the Ohio Every-Pupil Test in Plane Geometry.

All of these are possible methods when they are systematically employed for determining whether or not certain goals of a school program are being achieved. Does the boy who earns a Boy Scout merit badge in cooking ever cook at home? Do the girls (or boys) who have work in home economics take better care of their rooms and clothing than before, and how does the improvement compare with the performance of those girls or boys who have not had the homemaking experience? Often, the easy way to find out something is just to ask the persons most closely involved. It has been reported that during World War II, after several months spent developing tests intended to select persons for training for Arctic warfare and desert warfare, some radical finally came up with what proved to be the best solution: Ask the trainees whether they like cold weather or hot weather best.

SOME USEFUL MATERIALS FOR THE EVALUATOR

The following suggestions may be useful to middle school personnel interested in evaluation:

1. Write to Dr. Edward Frankel, evaluation director, intermediate school evaluation, Center for Urban Education, Educational Practices Division, 33 West 42d Street, New York, N. Y. 10036, for the set of mimeographed materials which the Center has prepared on the evaluation of the New York City experimental middle schools.

2. *Evaluation as Feedback and Guide,* the 1967 Yearbook of the Association for Supervision and Curriculum Development, should be read with care by any person involved in middle school evaluation. Chapters 6 and 7, cited previously, should be especially helpful.

3. *Perspectives of Curriculum Evaluation* is the first of an AERA series on Curriculum Evaluation. While all of it is relevant to a group planning a new curriculum, the papers by Gagné and Scriven are worth particularly close study. Persons working in curriculum evaluation should be alert for additions to the series.

4. All persons involved in educational research or evaluation would do well to keep a copy of *Unobtrusive Measures* close at hand for ready reference.

5. Any person needing to prepare evaluative materials for parts of a course or a curriculum and needing help on stating instructional objectives in behavorial terms should consult Robert F. Mager's *Preparing Instructional Objectives*. (Palo Alto, Calif.: Fearon Publishers, Inc. 1962.)

6. The single, most helpful source for research on curriculum and teaching is the *Handbook of Research on Teaching*, N. L. Gage (ed.) (Skokie, Ill.: Rand McNally & Company, 1963). A long chapter on experimental designs for research by Campbell and Stanley is available in a separate paperback edition.

7. When hunting for tests for particular purposes or information about tests, consult first any of the *Mental Measurements Yearbooks*, O. K. Buros (ed.) (Highland Park, N.J.: Gryphon, 1938, 1940, 1953, 1959, and 1966).

SOURCES OF SOME TESTS SUGGESTED
FOR EVALUATING HYPOTHESES

1. AAHPER Fitness Test, American Association of Health, Physical Education, and Recreation, 1202 16th Street, N.W., Washington, D.C. 20036.

2. A Parent's View of the School (developed by Paul P. Williams and revised by Lee Henderson, L. E. Smith, and M. C. King), College of Education, University of Florida, Gainesville, Florida.

3. Combs Picture-Story Test, A. W. Combs, College of Education, University of Florida, Gainesville, Florida.

4. Curriculum Improvement Measure (developed by J. K. Duncan), College of Education, University of Florida, Gainesville, Florida.

5. Executive Professional Leadership Instrument, (developed by Neal Gross and Robert L. Herriott). Neal Gross, Graduate School of Education, Harvard University, Cambridge, Mass.

6. Health Behavior Inventory (developed by Sylvia Yellen, Albert D. Colebank, and Marion Pollock), California Test Bureau, Del Monte Research Park, Monterey, California 93940.

7. Minnesota Tests of Creative Thinking, now called the Torrance Tests of Creative Thinking (developed by E. P. Torrance), Personnel Press, Inc., 20 Nassau Street, Princeton, N.J. 08540.

8. Ohio Social Acceptance Scale for the Intermediate Grades, Ohio Scholarship Tests and Division of Elementary Supervision, State Department of Education, Columbus, Ohio.

9. Principal Behavior Check List (developed by Morton Alpren, E. B. Van Aken, Doc Farrar, and Floyd Newman), College of Education, University of Florida, Gainesville, Florida.

10. Organization Climate Description Questionnaire (developed by

Andrew W. Halpin and Don B. Croft), The Midwest Administrative Center, University of Chicago.

11.   Principal Behavior Description Questionnaire (developed by staff members of the Ohio State Leadership Studies, Bureau of Business Research, College of Commerce and Administration), The Ohio State University, Columbus, Ohio.

12.   Student Attitude Scale (developed by J. A. Battle), College of Education, University of Florida, Gainesville, Florida.

13.   Teacher Activities Questionnaire, (developed by Walter B. Mathews), College of Education, University of Florida, Gainesville, Florida.

14.   Teacher Human Relations Questionnaire (developed by R. W. Walker), College of Education, University of Florida, Gainesville, Florida.

Chapter 8

Moving toward a Real
Middle School

School leaders in many American communities are currently considering the possibilities of a school reorganization which will include an
emergent middle school such as described in this book. The authors
confidently expect that most school systems will, within the next few years,
debate the pros and cons of various patterns of organization. Many of
them will undoubtedly choose to move from their present 6-3-3 or 8-4 organization to a 4-4-4, 5-3-4, or other pattern that has a middle level different from previous ones. This chapter summarizes some of the issues
and guidelines that might be agenda items for discussion and planning in
these school systems.

THE BASIC ISSUES

Obviously, the first issue is that of whether an organization different
from the prevailing one is needed. If the consensus on this issue is affirmative, the question becomes one of organization.

Is a Different Organization Needed?

Various questions are being and should be considered by those who
have decisions to make regarding the type of vertical organization in a

particular school district. Some questions which seem especially critical are these:

1. Does the present organizational pattern create unnecessary and undesirable breaks in the continuity of schooling?
2. Does the present plan lack an educational program uniquely adapted to the needs of children in the transitional years from childhood to adolescence?
3. Does it inhibit experimentation? Would experimentation be facilitated by a new organization?
4. Can program changes be made more effectively in a new organization than in the current one?
5. Do school population trends, in comparison with existing facilities, make necessary and desirable a new pattern of organization?

If So, What Organization?

If the foregoing questions are answered affirmatively, the question of what organizational pattern would be better must be answered next. Various systems that may be considered are briefly identified in the following paragraphs.

Educational park for total program. A complex for providing a complete program of schooling from school entrance to school exit amasses in a very large unit a totality of educational resources. The decision-making group considering this possibility must weigh the advantages of resource concentration against the problems of transportation and size. Even in the park, there will still be levels of schooling with the limitations of each level to be decided upon, although movement between levels may be made considerably more flexible and convenient.

Ungraded plans. Various types of ungraded plans including either the whole period of schooling or some portions of it can also be considered. Conceivably, some plan of schooling might be developed which would provide for a system of individual pupil progress without relationship to age or grade. Practically speaking, this plan is likely still to include some division of students into separate facilities which are unlikely to differ greatly from present ones for younger children, older children, and adolescents.

Two-level plans. The characteristic 8-4 and 6-6 patterns may again be considered, with new arrangements for bridging the two levels. For example, if the two schools are nearby, some plan of sharing instructional personnel and facilities for the two grades at the point of break might be introduced. However, the two-level plan has long since been abandoned in most American school systems.

Three-level plans. School districts still having an 8-4 or 6-6 plan are especially interested in introducing an intermediate level. Their decision, generally speaking, is whether to make the middle school a three- or a four-year unit housing grades 6–8 or 5–8. In school districts now on a three-level plan, usually a 6-3-3 plan, and less frequently, a 6-2-4 pattern, the decision to be made is how to regroup these grades.

In Chapters 1–3 we reviewed the rationale for changing the three-level plan from 6-3-3 to 5-3-4 or 4-4-4, and, hence, now suggest review of the issues and trends discussed in these chapters. Among the questions which the decision-making group should consider in relation to what and how many grades to include in the middle unit are the following:

1.   How many years of schooling should be included in the elementary unit and how large should the school be? As years are added below grade 1, should higher years be moved into the middle school level?

2.   How many years of schooling are needed in the middle school to provide an adequate program and facility?

3.   At what age or grade level in the community does there seem to be need for a program different from that usually provided in the elementary school such as would be available in a middle school?

THE PROBLEM OF FEASIBILITY

The authors fully recognize that a local decision as to what organizational pattern should be implemented must be made in relation to the question of what is feasible as well as what is desirable. Three matters of feasibility seem especially critical.

First, a change in organizational patterns would not seem feasible unless it has a reasonable chance of acceptance by the people most concerned. Specifically, it is questionable whether any change in pattern should be attempted without some prior involvement and general approval by an adequate representation of the parents and faculties concerned. If involvement has been negligible, or if the reaction is negative or even just lukewarm, reorganization would seem impractical.

Second, can adequate preparation be made for reorganization? American educational history is dotted with so-called experiments and innovations that were abandoned because they were undertaken too hastily without adequate preparation and procedures for evaluation. An overnight middle school reorganization promises little success and should not be considered feasible.

Third, what organization do present and contemplated facilities permit? If an existing elementary junior high or high school is to be converted to a middle school, does it include the facilities desired for the middle school program? If a new building is to be constructed for the middle school, is funding adequate to provide the kinds of facilities desired? If reorganization is dictated by school population problems, is there time for re-planning programs before shifting populations? Unless such questions as these can be answered affirmatively, little may be gained by simply renaming a school level and shifting grades around.

PLANNING THE NEW PROGRAM

Once the decision is made to move into a middle school organization and program, the colossal job of planning must begin. Ideally, all or a substantial portion of each middle school faculty should have a year of full-time study with competent leadership and adequate funds for travel in order to develop an adequate and sound plan. Indeed a few school districts, several of them with the use of extra-district funds, have provided a period of planning which involves at least a nucleus of the middle school staff. Undoubtedly, most middle schools have opened without such extensive planning, and many more will operate under the same circumstances. We can only describe briefly some of the steps in planning that need to be taken by any group and in whatever time is available.

Defining the Needs of Middle School Learners

An extended study of the characteristics and educational needs of children of middle school age would be desirable for every faculty of a middle school. Possible short cuts to such study include the following:

1. A series of presentation-discussion sessions with a competent authority on the characteristics and educational needs of children in the between-age years.
2. Reading and discussion of such materials as presented and reviewed in Chapter 2 of this book.
3. Parent-teacher discussions of their observations of middle school children, perhaps with use of "in-between-agers" as panelists.
4. Examination of data on particular children to be enrolled in the middle school as available in cumulative records, test profiles, and other school sources.

Evaluating Present Programs for Children
of Middle School Age

An evaluation of the existing school program for children in the middle school years should reveal strengths and deficiencies of this program. Such an evaluation would logically be based on the needs of these children as defined in studies such as the one described. Particular curriculum opportunities in existing elementary or junior high schools that appear highly relevant to the needs of the "in-between-ager" would of course be continued. For example, many of the exploratory programs of the junior high school might be extended downward and modified in schedule; certainly they should be continued.

At the same time this evaluation should identify curriculum opportunities that are inappropriate or lacking. For example, it might be expected that many of the interscholastic athletic and the relatively sophisticated social programs borrowed by the junior high school from the senior high school would not be found appropriate for young people of middle school age. General observation also suggests that in many communities instruction in the skills of learning is lacking in the middle school years and would be noted as a shortcoming to be overcome in the middle school.

A thorough evaluation of the present program cannot be conducted wholly as an occasional discussion type of activity. The services of one or more full-time people for at least a short period might well be engaged to search out and analyze available data, to prepare instruments for collection of information and opinion, and to prepare agenda for evaluation discussions.

Studying Emergent Programs

As we see it, each middle school should have a program that reflects the best judgment of its faculty, the needs of its children, its school facilities, and other factors indigenous to the school. At the same time, the planning group might very well take advantage of the experience of other middle schools in identifying possible program features for the new school. As yet, there are relatively few schools that would be considered "model," although the number of emergent middle schools is steadily growing. We have presented several illustrations of program features in these schools, especially in Part III of this book. Interested faculties might find references herein to schools with which they could communicate or even visit. Frequently, planning groups for new schools find it both advantageous and economical to invite as a consultant a leader of some exemplary school in another community. Several of the school districts now opening up experimental middle schools are publishing descriptive materials about their schools which will also be useful to other school faculties studying program possibilities.

Developing Specific Program Plans

The planning process should result in program plans recorded so as to serve as guidelines in initial school operation. While they may well take different forms, such plans should, we believe, take into account:

1. Bases of classifying children for administrative and instructional purposes;

2. Instruction in the organized knowledge or common-learnings component of the curriculum, including description of the scope of instruction in each major area;

3. Instruction and guidance in their personal development curriculum area;

4. Instruction, including self-instruction, in the learning skills area;

5. Operation of the activity program;

6. Staff utilization with reference to instructional organization;

7. Individual pupil evaluation and progress;

8. Scheduling arrangements for the program of the school;

9. Arrangements for the use of learning resources and centers;

10. Articulation with the levels below and above;

11. Responsibilities of administrators and other special school personnel;

12. Plans for evaluation of the school program.

Some of these plans would be recorded in written guides, some in charts, some in schedule and personnel allocation tables, and some, perhaps, in recordings that can be used as a basis for later discussions. The aim is the production of such materials as are needed for the school faculty to proceed with the educational program when school begins. Such plans would be regarded as starting points rather than as inflexible, unchangeable operational procedures.

DESIGNING THE FACILITIES

Many middle school planning groups have opportunity to design new facilities. Their specifications should be determined by the program plans developed as suggested in the preceding section. Several implications of middle school program plans for facilities are suggested in the following description of a floor plan arrangement developed for one middle school:

The floor plan layout reflects a generally well-defined initial educational program but is a design with deliberate attention to maintaining flexibility to achieve full utilization of evolving teaching concepts.

The arrangement of facilities within the building is carefully planned to minimize waste space with specialized activities located to avoid conflictions relative to student traffic flow and noise.

Instructional space would be adaptable to cooperative teaching by virtue of direct accessibility of adjacent classrooms, central group activity space and teacher planning resource center. The central library study area is located to serve all academic departments with individual and group use at one time. Open interior court yards separate major functions creating opportunities for development into science gardens and study courts. Different sized spaces are provided for large and small group instruction and for different degrees of privacy. Areas are provided throughout for individual learning. Integration of the various subdivisions of the building, each designed to accommodate a specific program function, creates an interesting spatial variety that should, in a natural and efficient way, stimulate learning on both an individual and group level.

The overall design concept would permit conversion of space usage and addition of complete facilities such as an auditorium and would allow expansion of any teaching unit or departmental space to accommodate innovations in teaching methods or in population growth.[1]

In many other school districts the designing of facilities is at best a plan for alteration and utilization of existing facilities. In these situations program plans are more likely to be influenced by existing facilities than the reverse. In planning the use of existing facilities, however, efforts are made to identify in them, or to alter them so as to provide, arrangements such as these, which seem especially desirable in the middle school:

1. A learning resources center readily available to all other instructional spaces;

2. Rooms of varying size for use by large and small groups;

3. Spaces for individual study;

4. Spaces for private conversations between a teacher and pupil;

5. Spaces that can be used for special instructional centers or laboratories, as described in Chapter 4;

6. Adequately equipped rooms for instruction in the various exploratory or personal development areas described in Chapter 4;

7. For larger schools, wing, cluster, or other arrangements that will facilitate decentralization into little schools, such as described in Chapter 6.

---

[1] *Model Middle School: Involvement by Design* (Rockland, Me.: Maine School Administrative District No. 5, 1967), p. 29.

RECRUITING THE STAFF

Staffing of the middle school was discussed at some length in Chapter 6. Here we would only emphasize the problem of a lack of availability of faculty specifically trained for the middle school. This is not a new problem since, generally speaking, teachers have not been specifically prepared for the junior high school either. Hence, so far as the training criterion is concerned, the middle school administrator will have to choose between people trained for either elementary or secondary school work. Since neither preparation is likely to be adequate, he will have to make his choice on other bases. Probably the most likely candidate among novice teachers is the alert and personable beginner interested in teaching children of the middle school years and eager to continue his professional study while in service.

Regarding experienced teacher candidates, their experience record will provide the administrator with some basis for evaluating the quality of their teaching, their interaction with learners, and their interest in continued professional study, all factors of critical importance in the choice of middle school teachers.

Very frequently, the recruitment of teachers for the middle school will involve selection of faculty members from existing elementary and junior high schools from which the new middle school population is drawn. Our own experience suggests that the administrator would well confine his choice to those teachers who request transfer to the middle school. Arbitrary transfer of teachers who really do not want to change positions can easily handicap the new school.

ORIENTATION OF THOSE CONCERNED

Many groups and individuals must be oriented to the reorganization and to the new school. Hopefully, the school faculty will have participated in planning the school program in ways such as those described above. If so, faculty orientation involves only full explanation of the rationale and program to new faculty members who join the staff after the planning has been completed. Members of the original planning group should be especially effective in making these explanations. However, not all middle schools will open on the basis of plans made by a large faculty planning group. For these schools, a preschool workshop, of as long a duration as is possible, may be a very helpful device for studying such plans as have been made, as well as for formulating new plans. A six-week workshop for this purpose is none too long and could provide opportunity for fundamental, even if brief, preservice preparation for the middle school teacher.

The middle schoolers and their parents particularly need orientation to the middle school. This should begin no later than the year preceding pupil transfer to the middle school. If the middle school is still in the planning stage, parents, and to some extent their children, can be involved in the definition of the rationale and program of the school. P.T.A. meetings, homeroom meetings for the parents immediately concerned, school bulletins, press releases, and radio and television can all be used effectively to explain the new program.

Once the school has been launched, orientation is simplified by the opportunity for children and their parents to visit the school prior to transfer, with frequent parent visitations hoped for after their children are enrolled in the middle school. In any event, when the rationale focuses on doing a better job for individual children during the middle school years, little opposition to the middle school concept should be anticipated. Parents and children do want to know, of course, why they are leaving the elementary school; why there is a different instructional organization; why the name has been changed, if it has; why certain activities associated with high school have been eliminated; and how "to get ready" for the middle school.

There seems special need for orientation of faculty members in the other levels of the school system. The elementary teachers, whose students may move out of their classrooms sooner than they would have under the traditional system in shifting to the middle school, should understand the reasons for the reorganization and the expectations of the middle school faculty as to what will happen in the middle school. Similarly, the high school faculty should understand what different emphases there may be in a middle school as compared with a junior high school, why the ninth grade has been moved into high school, if it has, and what differences in the high school program should result from the new educational program of the middle school. Vertical curriculum planning organizations representing all levels of the school system should be very helpful in bringing about these understandings. In addition, there may be reason to have general faculty meetings, devoted to the reorganization, along with bulletins, tours, and various communication arrangements specifically planned for the professional faculty.

SAFEGUARDING THE EMERGENT SCHOOL

If the new middle school is to have a decent chance to survive and succeed, a number of practical measures seem essential. The following suggestions may merit consideration by groups establishing emergent middle schools:

1. *Interpret the change as frequently and as widely as possible as one to serve better individual children of middle school age.* Justifications based

on criticisms of existing arrangements, temporary problems of housing and population, and trends elsewhere may not be very meaningful or acceptable to parents and others involved.

2. *Probably both the idea of "adopting" a new organization and of "experimenting" with one should be avoided.* The former has a connotation of finality that may make a later modification of the reorganization that appears desirable more difficult. The latter approach may suggest to some that the reorganization is so tentative that children's education may be sacrificed. A better explanation might be phrased something like this: "We are moving into a new organization that we have studied very carefully and believe to promise better education for children in this school district. Although we expect the middle school to be as successful here as in other communities where it is already being used, we will evaluate it as fully as possible in this district so that we may continue to have the best school organization possible for our children."

3. *Do not: move into the new organization too rapidly and without adequate preparation; reproduce in the new school the very program the middle school seeks to improve upon; staff the school with persons who object to being there; expect every new idea and practice to be successful.*

4. *Plan from the beginning to evaluate the new program.* Extensive suggestions for evaluations were made in Chapter 7. From these and others that may occur to the planning group, an evaluation design should be on paper when school opens, and its steps taken as carefully and fully as possible.

PROVIDING FOR CONTINUING CHANGE

However carefully prepared the plan of the new middle school may be, it is certain that a careful, continuing evaluation will reveal needs for frequent modification of the program. A number of flexible arrangements in the beginning should facilitate a process of continuing change and improvement.

First of all, the existence of the evaluation design and its careful utilization should provide data which can be the basis of continuing change. Hopefully, the evaluation design will be complete enough to yield facts and judgments pertaining to every aspect of the middle school program. Periodically, as this evidence is compiled and analyzed, new decisions can be made as to curriculum opportunities, staffing arrangements, instructional organizations, schedule patterns, and other aspects of the school program. Conceivably, total evaluations over a period of years will lead to conclusions about further reorganizations, even new organizational patterns, so far as the relation between the various levels of schooling are concerned. The gathering of evidence, provisions for consultation regarding such evidence, and freedom to make changes on the basis of information obtained in this way are essential to the continuing success of any school program, including the emergent middle school. Perhaps the primary assurance of continuing change and improvement of the middle school is the appointment of an administrator who is himself open to change. An imaginative, experimental-minded school principal, encouraged by an equally open-minded central administration, flanked by a faculty receptive to change, will not let a particular school organization and program freeze. Such a leader should be counted on to maintain a climate in which criticism and innovation flourish.

Finally, the process of continuing change requires some organization for change such as that suggested at the end of Chapter 4. These suggestions include: a regular plan of group organization for systematic program review and evaluation, continuing services to assist teachers in keeping their own knowledge updated, and adequate coordination of middle school planning with that for the system as a whole. As the professional staff of the school and the system is encouraged to keep reaching for educational improvement, and as opportunity is provided for systematic exchange of views and implementation of accepted proposals, both the system and the school are certain to continuously improve.

PART V

A Survey of Organizational Patterns of Reorganized Middle Schools

The research reported herein was performed pursuant to a grant (Co-operative Research Project No. 7—D–026) with the Office of Education, U.S. Department of Health, Education, and Welfare. Contractors undertaking such projects under government sponsorship are encouraged to express freely their professional judgment in the conduct of the project. Points of view or opinions stated do not, therefore, necessarily represent official Office of Education position or policy.

Appreciation is due the principals of the 110 schools in the sample for their cooperation in completing the survey instrument, and also to the principals and staffs of the eight schools visited for additional, illustrative information. The assistance of state departments of education in compiling the original list of middle schools is also acknowledged.

A very special note of gratitude is due Ronald Kealy for his splendid services as graduate research assistant throughout the project. We are also indebted to two other graduate students, John Jones and Wesley Blamick, for their assistance with certain tasks in the study, and especially to Professor Vynce A. Hines for his contributions as statistical consultant.

—William M. Alexander, University of Florida, Gainesville, July 1968

Chapter 9

Middle Schools in 1968—
The Facts

OVERVIEW

Purpose and Method

This project was undertaken to provide bench-mark data regarding the current status of middle schools in the United States. Recent partial surveys and other data have indicated substantial interest in the reorganization of the now traditional school ladder arrangement of elementary-junior-senior high school (6-3-3). There has been lacking, however, any comprehensive data as to the number and location of reorganized middle schools, replacing the grade 7-9 junior high, and as to the organizational characteristics of the newer schools in the middle of the school ladder.

The data were secured by compilation from state departments of education and other sources, of a list of schools meeting the survey definition of "a school which combines into one organization and facility certain school years (usually grades 5-8 or 6-8) which have in the past usually been separated in elementary and secondary schools under such plans as the 6-3-3, 6-2-4, and 6-6." A survey instrument was used to secure detailed data from a 10 percent random sample stratified by USOE regions. Eight schools from the original list were also visited to secure other information illustrative of the various organizational patterns determined in the survey.

Highlights of the Findings

The findings from the initial listing and the survey instrument were compiled, analyzed, and are reported by categories of questions, as follows, with certain highlight data summarized here:

Number of schools and grade organization. A total of 1101 schools meeting the survey definition and having at least three grades and not more than five and including grades 6 and 7, were identified. The largest concentrations of these schools were in USOE Regions I, V, VII, and IX (see Table 1). Of the 110 schools in the sample, 60 percent had a grade 6–8 organization, and 27.3 percent a grade 5–8 organization, with the remainder including grade 4–8, 5–7, 6–9, and 4–7 plans.

Establishment. Only 10.4 percent of the schools in the sample had been established before 1960, and 42.9 percent were established in 1966 and 1967. The most frequently checked reason for the organization was "to eliminate crowded conditions in other schools" although program-related factors were also checked frequently. Preparation activities for opening the middle schools were most frequently of an occasional and inservice education type.

Schools whose reasons for establishment included "to remedy weaknesses of the junior high school" were as likely to have interschool athletics as schools not giving these reasons, and the instructional organization did not differ significantly between these two groups.

Curriculum opportunities. Language arts, mathematics, physical education, science, and social studies are constants in all middle school grades, with a scattering of electives and other curriculum opportunities. Music, art, home economics, and industrial arts are each also required in about half or more of the schools at some grade level, most frequently grade 7 and/or 8. The offering of electives and other opportunities is sparse in many schools and disappointing in terms of usual middle school objectives. Larger schools tend to have more offerings than smaller ones.

Instructional organization. The self-contained classroom organization tends to persist in grade 5, with a pronounced increase in departmentalization in grade 6 and thereafter. Of other instructional organizations, the block-of-time plan for language arts and social studies is most frequent with the use of team teaching patterns relatively infrequent. About 30 percent of the schools use some type of variable or modular scheduling different from the traditional daily periods of uniform length.

Individualization. Some 20 percent of the schools provide scheduled independent study time, and smaller numbers offer other independent study arrangements. A relatively large number of the schools use marking and reporting systems different from or in addition to the traditional single-letter grade pattern.

Reactions. The reactions of student body, staff, parents, and general public were reported as generally positive ("enthusiastic" or "favorable") toward the middle school. Among these four groups the staff was the one most frequently reported as "enthusiastic" (40 percent) and the general public the one most frequently as "indifferent" (16.4 percent). Of the 110 schools, 80 did not anticipate changing to a different organizational plan within the next two to five years.

General Conclusions

The survey data clearly confirm the existence of a recent and current movement toward a different grade organization of the school ladder. They also indicate that the new middle school organizations in general fail to provide a program and instructional organization differing very much from those in the predecessor schools, especially in the grade 7–9 junior high school. Obviously, critical evaluation of the emerging middle schools is needed to determine what improvements they are making and can make over prior organizations.

BACKGROUND OF THE STUDY

The Problem

The middle school organization seems to be rapidly developing as a major alternative to the junior high school in providing the link between the beginning school and the high school. A growing list of publications about middle schools, their popularity as a topic in national meetings, and recurrent inquiries to the authors indicate that middle school organizations are burgeoning. There is, however, no comprehensive list of middle schools now in operation to which educational researchers may turn to secure data as to the identification, number, and organizational patterns of these schools or to the reasons they have come into existence.

On the basis of the increasing interest and growing concern for needed innovations in the middle schools, it seems likely that extensive research and experimentation will be undertaken. Even periodic determination of trends awaits the establishment of base-line data. The problem of this study was to compile and report such foundational data.

Specifically, the survey was planned to secure data as to the current status of middle schools with respect to the following characteristics:

1.   Number, location by USOE regions, grades included, enrollment, housing, and plans for articulation with lower and upper schools.

2.   Establishment: dates, reasons, preparation.

3.   Curriculum plans: required and elective subjects, other curriculum opportunities.

4.   Instructional organization: incidence by grade level and subject of various patterns, plans of grouping, scheduling arrangements.

5.   Arrangements for individualizing instruction: independent study, marking and reporting progress, counseling arrangements.

6.   Reactions to the middle schools.

The survey findings are organized in accordance with the above categories.

Method of the Study

Development of instrument.   The survey instrument, "A Survey of Organizational Patterns of Reorganized Middle Schools," was prepared, tested with individual middle school principals, and printed after clearance with the USOE Regional Grants Officer.

Compilation of list of middle schools in the United States.   A letter explaining the aims and purposes of this project as well as a definition of the middle school—"a school which combines into one organization and facility certain school years (usually grades 5–8 or 6–8) which have in the past usually been separated in elementary and secondary schools under such plans as the 6-3-3, 6-2-4, and 6-6"—was sent to state departments of education in each state and the District of Columbia. A request was made for names and addresses of such middle schools and for names of persons who would have information pertaining to middle schools in the state. Follow-up letters and telephone calls were used to gain this information from each state department of education. State department contacts were followed up through identification of middle schools in state directories, correspondence with district superintendents reported as having unidentified middle schools, and telephone calls to state departments and local superintendents to identify middle schools. Additional middle schools were identified through a review of the literature and through personal contacts of the project director with persons in certain states known to be identified with the middle school movement. A card file of middle schools in the United States was compiled and organized by USOE regions and states. In addition to the definition of the middle school, the criteria of having at least three grades but not more than five grades, and including grades 6 and 7 were used in compiling the final listing. Information including name of school, grades included, and name of principal was entered on each card in the file.

Completion of instrument by a sampling of middle schools. A stratified 15 percent sample by USOE region was randomly selected, and letters sent to these schools requesting confirmation that they conformed to the criteria set forth with regard to the definition of the middle school and that they would provide descriptive information about their middle school organizations. As these confirmations were received instruments were sent out until a 10 percent stratified sample, by USOE region, was attained. A total of 145 instruments were sent out, and a total of 121 returned for a 83.4 percent return. Of the 121 instruments returned, 4 were unusable, and 7 were returned after the 10 percent sample had been attained. These 7 were scanned and their data were found to correspond to the overall findings of the survey. (A list of the schools in the sample is available from the project director.)

Compilation and analysis of data. The data from the instruments were put on punch cards, compiled by computer, and transcribed into tabular form. In addition, the following questions were posed, and answered through analysis of the data:

1. Do those schools which indicated "to remedy the weaknesses of the junior high school" as a reason for establishment have an interschool ahtletic program for boys?
2. Are there differences in grades 7 and 8 instructional organization between those schools which indicated "to remedy the weaknesses of the junior high school" as a reason for establishment and those schools which did not?
3. What is the relationship between middle school size and the number of elective offerings?
4. What is the relationship between school size and the number of "other curriculum opportunities"?
5. How does the grade 6 instructional organization in grades 5–8 middle schools compare with the grade 6 instructional organization in grades 6–8 middle schools?

Visitation of selected middle schools. Eight middle schools from the total listing were selected for visitation, using type of organizational pattern, indication of distinguishing characteristics, size and type of community, and geographic location as criteria for selection. These schools were visited, and interviews with principals, staff members, and students conducted. Details of these visits and descriptions of the illustrative middle schools are reported in Chapter 10.

THE FACTS

The findings of this project are reported in the following sections:

Number of middle schools; grade organization and related factors
Establishment of middle schools
Curriculum opportunities provided
Instructional organization
Individualization of instruction
Reactions to the middle schools

Number of Schools

The final tabulation of the 1101 middle schools identified as described above ("Method") is shown in Table 1 by states and USOE regions. The schools so enumerated were those corresponding to the definition utilized in the study—"a school which combines into one organization and facility certain school years (usually grades 5–8 or 6–8) which have in the past usually been separated in elementary and secondary schools under such plans as the 6-3-3, 6-2-4, and 6-6." Also, this enumeration excluded schools identified as not having at least three grades and those having more than five grades, and those not including grades 6 and 7.

Although this definition is not identical with that used in a 1965–1966 survey by Cuff,[1] the data are considered roughly comparable. He identified 499 middle schools (schools having grades 6 and 7 and not extending below grade 4 or above grade 8). Definitely, the present identification of 1101 middle schools in 1967–1968 indicates a marked increase in the number of such schools established in the past two years, a conclusion confirmed by data reported below as to the date of establishment.

Table 1 also shows the heavy concentration of middle schools in certain populous eastern states (Region I), midwestern states (Region V), and the far west (Region IX). It also shows the weighting of the total number and that in Region VII by the 252 Texas schools fitting the definition as a result of reorganization there especially of the 8-4 plan.

Grades Included

Grades included could not be determined for all of the original listing of schools since this information was not included in all of the state directories and other sources utilized in identifying the original population of middle schools.

[1]William M. Cuff, "Middle Schools on the March," *Bulletin of the NASSP,* 51:82–86 (February 1967).

Table 1.   Number and Distribution of Middle Schools
by USOE Region and State

Region I

Connecticut.	25
Maine.	3
Massachusetts	10
New Hampshire	0
Rhode Island	3
Vermont	0
Total	41

Region II

Delaware.	2
New Jersey.	91
New York.	92
Pennsylvania	25
Total	210

Region III

Kentucky	4
Maryland.	13
North Carolina.	8
Virginia.	0
West Virginia.	0
District of Columbia	0
Total	25

Region IV

Alabama	15
Florida	10
Georgia	24
Mississippi	3
South Carolina.	6
Tennessee.	3
Total	61

Region V

Illinois.	142
Indiana.	21
Michigan	97
Ohio	3
Wisconsin.	21
Total	284

Region VI

Iowa	3
Kansas	0
Minnesota	1
Missouri	5
Nebraska.	3
North Dakota	1
South Dakota	1
Total	14

Region VII

Arkansas	4
Louisiana	2
New Mexico	7
Oklahoma	0
Texas	252
Total	265

Region VIII

Colorado.	4
Idaho.	0
Montana	0
Utah	0
Wyoming.	0
Total	4

Region IX

Alaska	0
Arizona.	14
California	131
Hawaii	0
Nevada.	0
Oregon	30
Washington	22
Total	197
Grand Total	1101

Table 2.   Grades Included in Middle School Organizations
as Reported by a Stratified Random Sampling
of 110 Middle Schools in the Nine USOE Regions

USOE Region	Grades 6–8		Grades 5–8		Grades 4–8		Grades 5–7		Grades 6–9		Grades 4–7		TOTALS	
	No.	%	No.	%	No.	%	No.	%	No.	%	No.	%	No.	%
I	2	50.0	2	50.0	0	00.0	0	00.0	0	00.0	0	00.0	4	100.0
II	12	57.1	5	23.8	1	4.8	2	9.5	1	4.8	0	00.0	21	100.0
III	2	100.0	0	00.0	0	00.0	0	00.0	0	00.0	0	00.0	2	100.0
IV	3	50.0	1	16.7	0	00.0	0	00.0	1	16.7	1	16.7	6	100.1
V	18	64.3	7	25.0	2	7.1	1	3.6	0	00.0	0	00.0	28	100.0
VI	1	100.0	0	00.0	0	00.0	0	00.0	0	00.0	0	00.0	1	100.0
VII	20	74.1	7	25.9	0	00.0	0	00.0	0	00.0	0	00.0	27	100.0
VIII	0	00.0	1	100.0	0	00.0	0	00.0	0	00.0	0	00.0	1	100.0
IX	8	40.0	7	35.0	5	25.0	0	00.0	0	00.0	0	00.0	20	100.0
All Schools	66	60.0	30	27.3	8	7.3	3	2.7	2	1.8	1	00.9	110	100.0

The grades included in the sample population were determined and are shown by USOE regions in Table 2. Of the 110 schools, 66 (60 percent) had a grade 6–8 organization, and 30 (27.3 percent) had a grade 5–8 organization, with the remaining 14 (12.7 percent) including grade 4–8, 5–7, 6–9, and 4–7 organizations. The proportions of grade organizations in regions having 10 or more schools in the sample is similar to the total—and the approximate 2 to 1 ratio of grade 6–8 to grade 5–8 organizations seems descriptive of present status.

Four of the schools visited, with descriptions included in Chapter 10, are illustrative of the grade 6–8 organization (B, E, F, H); three are descriptive of the grade 5–8 organization (C, D, G); and one grade 6–9 organization was included (A).

Enrollment and Housing

Table 3 shows the range of enrollment in middle schools as from below 100 to more than 1300. Approximately 75 percent of the sample had enrollments of from 300 to 1000.

Table 4 indicates that the large majority (80 percent of the sample) of middle schools have separate plants without "little school" arrangements, with 7 of the 110 schools having the latter. Illustrative of the "little school" plan are two descriptions of schools visited—Schools A and F (Chapter 10).

Table 3.   Distribution of Total Enrollments of Middle Schools
as Reported by 106 Middle Schools*

Range	No.	%	Range	No.	%
1–100	1	0.9	701–800	9	8.5
101–200	11	10.4	801–900	3	2.8
201–300	10	9.4	901–1000	6	5.7
301–400	19	17.9	1001–1100	2	1.9
401–500	7	6.6	1101–1200	2	1.9
501–600	13	12.3	1201–1300	1	0.9
601–700	19	17.9	Above 1300	3	2.8
			Totals:	106	99.9

*Number reporting, 106 of 110.

Table 4.   Distribution of 110 Middle Schools
by Type of Housing Arrangement

Type of Housing Arrangement	No.	%
One plant only, without separate areas for "little schools"	88	80.0
Certain year in separate buildings on the same campus	8	7.3
Separate areas of the plant for "little schools"	7	6.4
Housed in a plant with lower and/or higher grades	5	4.5
Some students housed in building(s) on another campus	2	1.8
Totals:	110	100.0

Articulation Plans

Table 5 shows in order of frequency the number of schools reporting various means of articulation with lower and higher schools. These plans include extensive use of means to acquaint both faculty and students with the programs which precede and/or follow the middle school, although actual sharing of faculties and program opportunities between schools is relatively slight. Group planning for articulation ranks high as do inter-visitation and sharing of data about students and programs.

Establishment of Middle Schools

Table 6 shows by USOE regions the number and percent of schools established before 1955 and each year thereafter through 1967. Only 4 (3.8 percent) of the schools in the sample were established before 1955, and only 10.4 percent before 1960. Nearly half (42.9 percent) had been estab-

Table 5.   Number and Percent of Middle Schools Employing Certain Means
To Provide Articulation between the Middle School and Schools
with Higher and Lower Grades as Reported by Sample of 100 Schools

Means of Articulation	No.	%
Obtaining and providing data concerning students entering and leaving the middle school	99	90.0
Provision of joint workshops with teachers in higher and lower grades	74	67.2
Provision of program information to elementary and/or high schools	74	67.2
Provision of joint curriculum planning activities with teachers of higher and/or lower grades	73	66.3
Provision for visitation by high school representatives for the purpose of orientation	63	57.3
Provision for students to visit the high school(s) for orientation	61	55.4
Provision for visitation of middle school by students from feeder schools	57	51.8
Provision for middle school teachers to visit elementary and/or high schools	45	40.8
Provision for sharing faculty with elementary and/or high schools	39	35.4
Plans for middle school students to visit feeder schools to orient elementary students	17	15.5
Provision for middle school students to take advanced course work in the high school	14	12.7
Others	9	8.2

lished during the last two years (1966 and 1967)—a fact that seems quite consistent with the earlier comparison of this survey (1967–1968) with one of 1965–1966. Clearly, the expansion of middle school organizations is a phenomenon of the very recent and current period. Only in Region II were there as many in 1960 as 20 percent of the current number; 3 of the 21 schools in the sample from this region were established before 1955, but nearly half (10) were established in 1966 and 1967.

The principals of schools surveyed were asked to indicate all applicable reasons, from a checklist of possible ones, for the establishment of their schools. Table 7 shows, by order of frequency for all schools, the reasons reported. Thus, the elimination of crowded conditions in other schools was most frequently reported, but other reasons somewhat unrelated to program—"to utilize a new school building," and "to aid desegregation"—were much less frequently cited than the various program-related reasons.

Table 6. Distribution of 105 Middle Schools in Nine USOE Regions by Year in Which Their Present Grades Were First Included*

Year	I No.	I %	II No.	II %	III No.	III %	IV No.	IV %	V No.	V %	VI No.	VI %	VII No.	VII %	VIII No.	VIII %	IX No.	IX %	All Schools No.	All Schools %
1967	1	25.0	2	9.5	0	00.0	3	50.0	3	10.7	0	00.0	3	13.0	0	00.0	1	5.3	13	12.4
1966	3	75.0	8	38.1	2	100.0	3	50.0	6	21.4	0	00.0	8	34.8	1	100.0	1	5.3	32	30.5
1965	0	00.0	1	4.8	0	00.0	0	00.0	6	21.4	0	00.0	2	8.7	0	00.0	3	15.8	12	11.4
1964	0	00.0	0	00.0	0	00.0	0	00.0	4	14.3	0	00.0	1	4.3	0	00.0	4	21.0	9	8.6
1963	0	00.0	1	4.8	0	00.0	0	00.0	1	3.6	1	100.0	3	13.0	0	00.0	2	10.5	8	7.6
1962	0	00.0	0	00.0	0	00.0	0	00.0	4	14.3	0	00.0	1	4.3	0	00.0	3	15.8	8	7.6
1961	0	00.0	3	14.3	0	00.0	0	00.0	1	3.6	0	00.0	1	4.3	0	00.0	3	15.8	8	7.6
1960	0	00.0	1	4.8	0	00.0	0	00.0	2	7.1	0	00.0	0	00.0	0	00.0	1	5.3	4	3.8
1959	0	00.0	0	00.0	0	00.0	0	00.0	0	00.0	0	00.0	0	00.0	0	00.0	0	00.0	0	00.0
1958	0	00.0	1	4.8	0	00.0	0	00.0	0	00.0	0	0.00	0	00.0	0	00.0	0	00.0	1	00.9
1957	0	00.0	0	00.0	0	00.0	0	00.0	0	00.0	0	00.0	1	4.3	0	00.0	1	5.3	2	1.9
1956	0	00.0	1	4.8	0	00.0	0	00.0	0	00.0	0	00.0	1	4.3	0	00.0	0	00.0	2	1.9
1955	0	00.0	0	00.0	0	00.0	0	00.0	1	3.6	0	00.0	1	4.3	0	00.0	0	00.0	2	1.9
Before 1955	0	00.0	3	14.3	0	00.0	0	00.0	0	00.0	0	00.0	1	4.3	0	00.0	0	00.0	4	3.8
Totals	4	100.0	21	100.2	2	100.0	6	100.0	28	100.0	1	100.0	23	99.6	1	100.0	19	100.1	105	99.9

*Number reporting, 105 of 110.

Table 7.   Number and Percent of Middle Schools Indicating Certain
Reasons for Establishment as Reported by 110 Middle Schools

Reason	Schools Reporting No.	%
To eliminate crowded conditions in other schools	64	58.2
To provide a program specifically designed for students in this age group	49	44.6
To better bridge the elementary and the high school	44	40.0
To provide more specialization in grades 5 and/or 6	33	30.0
To move grade 9 into the high school	27	24.5
To remedy the weaknesses of the junior high school	27	24.5
To try out various innovations	26	23.6
To utilize a new school building	23	20.9
To use plans that have been successful in other school systems	14	12.7
To aid desegregation	7	6.4
Other	13	11.8

Since one of the frequently cited weaknesses of the junior high school is its interschool athletics program, the returns were analyzed to determine if schools checking as a reason "to remedy weaknesses of the junior high school" provided interschool athletics. The percent of such schools providing athletics was found to be about the same as that for schools which did not check this reason. It appears that interschool athletics was either not

Table 8.   Number and Percent of Middle Schools
Indicating Persons Involved in Deciding on the School Organization
as Reported by 110 Middle Schools

Persons Involved	No.	%
System-level administration	86	78.2
Principal	76	69.1
Teachers	51	46.3
Parents	24	21.8
Board of Education	13	11.8
State Department of Education	12	10.9
Survey by an outside agency	7	6.4
Accrediting bodies	3	2.7
Other	9	8.2

regarded as a weakness or for other reasons was not eliminated in about half of the schools seeking to improve on the junior high school weaknesses.

Another frequently cited weakness of the junior high school is its duplication of the senior high school pattern of departmentalization. Consequently, the data were analyzed to determine if schools reporting as a reason for their establishment "to remedy the weaknesses of the junior high school" were likely to have instructional organizations differing from schools not giving this as a reason. The percent of schools in both categories using departmentalization in grade 7, for example, in the required subjects (language arts, social studies, science, and mathematics) was quite similar, and a chi-square test of significance showed no significant difference even at the .10 percent level. Apparently, departmentalization was either not considered a weakness, or it was no more remedied in schools seeking to improve on the junior high school that in schools not giving this reason for their establishment.

Each respondent also checked the persons and groups involved in deciding on the establishment of his middle school. The replies are shown in Table 8. Clearly, agencies outside the school district were infrequently con-

Table 9.   Number and Percent of Middle Schools Using Certain Types
of Preparatory Activities Prior to Opening
as Reported by 110 Middle Schools

Activities	Schools Reporting	
	No.	%
Occasional planning sessions of prospective middle school faculty members	57	51.8
Visitation of schools with similar plans in operation, by representatives	42	38.2
Inservice meetings of faculty with consultants on middle school development	28	25.5
A year or more of full-time faculty study and planning, in the district	27	24.5
Summer faculty workshop prior to the opening of the school year	5	4.5
A year or more of full-time study of representatives at a university in a program of preparation for middle school teachers	2	1.8
Representation in a middle school planning project, specially funded	2	1.8
Other	18	16.4

sidered as responsible, and locally the administrators and teachers, especially the former, were more frequently considered responsible than teachers, parents, and the board of education. The decisions apparently involved most frequently the school staffs.

Table 9 shows in order of frequency the activities checked as preparatory to opening the middle school. The most frequently reported activities were of an occasional and inservice type, although it was reported for 27 schools that there had been a year or more of full-time faculty study and planning in the district. The descriptions of schools visited in Chapter 10 illustrate relatively extensive preparatory programs—see the descriptions of Schools A, D, and F.

Curriculum Opportunities Provided

Table 10 lists the number of schools in the sample requiring each of various subjects by grade and by length of the course, up to half-year or all year. As would be expected, language arts, social studies, mathematics,

Table 10.   Number and Percent of Middle Schools
Requiring Certain Subjects, by Grade Level,
as Reported by a Sample of Middle Schools*

Subject†	Grade 5			Grade 6			Grade 7			Grade 8		
	No.		%	No.		%	No.		%	No.		%
	$\frac{1}{2}$ yr. or less	All yr.	% Req.	$\frac{1}{2}$ yr. or less	All yr.	% Req.	$\frac{1}{2}$ yr. or less	All yr.	% Req.	$\frac{1}{2}$ yr. or less	All yr.	% Req.
Language Arts	0	38	100.0	0	104	99.2	1	104	99.2	0	102	99.1
Social Studies	0	38	100.0	2	103	100.0	1	105	100.0	0	103	100.0
Science	2	36	100.0	12	93	100.0	12	89	95.3	8	93	98.2
Mathematics	0	38	100.0	0	105	100.0	0	106	100.0	1	102	100.0
Physical Education	0	37	97.4	5	95	95.3	5	97	96.3	4	97	98.2
Art	4	27	81.7	25	53	74.3	30	39	65.1	18	33	49.5
Music	3	31	89.5	22	68	85.7	29	42	66.9	24	37	59.2
Industrial Arts	3	3	15.8	11	8	18.1	23	20	40.6	21	26	45.7
Home Economics	2	4	15.8	11	10	20.0	23	23	43.3	22	27	47.6
Foreign Language	0	10	26.3	4	30	32.4	8	23	29.2	7	27	33.0
Reading	1	5	15.8	7	17	22.9	6	20	24.5	6	18	23.3

*Number reporting: Grade 5, 38 of 42; Grade 6, 105 of 110; Grade 7, 106 of 110; Grade 8, 103 of 106.

†Other required subjects listed: health (8), library (6), guidance (4), speech (3), typing (2), enrichment (3), sex education (2), geography, humanities, agriculture.

science, and physical education are virtually uniformly required in all grades, with only the latter two at all frequently required on only a half-year basis. Music and art are required in half or more of the schools at each grade level, but quite frequently, especially in grades 7 and 8, on a half-year basis. Industrial arts and home economics are required, about equally as to half-year or full year, in almost half of the schools in grades 7 and 8. These two subjects are also required in 15 to 20 percent of the schools in grades 5 and 6. Foreign language and reading are required in some schools at each grade level, but in not more than one-third of the schools at any one grade.

Elective offerings by grade level and length of time are shown in Table 11. The scattering here reflects the varied practices as to what is required and elective, the offering of additional electives in a required subject field, and the range in number of electives offered by individual schools. Only

Table 11.   Number and Percent of Middle Schools
Offering Certain Electives, by Grade Level,
as Reported by a Sample of Middle Schools*

Elective†	Grade 5			Grade 6			Grade 7			Grade 8		
	$\frac{1}{2}$ yr. or less	All yr.	% Req.	$\frac{1}{2}$ yr. or less	All yr.	% Req.	$\frac{1}{2}$ yr. or less	All yr.	% Req.	$\frac{1}{2}$ yr. or less	All yr.	% Req.
Reading	0	9	23.7	3	15	17.1	2	16	17.0	2	17	18.4
Science	0	3	7.9	0	5	4.8	0	7	6.6	1	12	12.6
Social Studies	0	3	7.9	0	4	3.8	0	5	4.7	0	6	5.8
Creative Writing	1	1	5.3	1	2	1.9	3	3	5.7	5	4	8.7
Mathematics	1	3	10.5	1	4	4.8	1	5	5.7	1	9	9.7
Vocal Music	0	13	34.2	2	34	34.3	4	47	48.2	4	54	56.3
Instrumental Music	0	22	57.8	1	64	61.8	0	74	69.8	1	73	71.8
Typing	0	0	00.0	1	3	3.8	1	6	6.6	4	6	9.7
Art	1	5	15.8	8	13	20.0	6	25	29.2	5	34	37.9
Industrial Arts	0	3	7.9	2	8	9.5	4	14	17.0	5	21	25.2
Home Economics	0	2	5.3	3	6	8.6	4	16	18.9	4	24	27.2
Dramatics	0	0	00.0	1	9	9.5	2	14	15.1	3	16	18.4
Speech	1	2	7.9	3	6	8.6	3	14	16.0	6	14	19.4
Journalism	0	0	00.0	0	2	1.9	1	6	6.6	3	8	10.7
Foreign Language	0	2	5.3	3	8	10.5	2	21	21.7	3	27	29.1

*Number reporting: Grade 5, 38 of 42; Grade 6, 105 of 110; Grade 7, 106 of 110; Grade 8, 103 of 106.

†Other elective offerings listed: crafts (3), current events (2), study skills (2), physical education, guidance, literature, agriculture, library, survival methods.

the vocal and instrumental music offerings are available in more than one-third of the schools at each grade level. The typical aim of the middle school to offer many exploratory experiences is not reflected in the relatively low numbers of schools offering these subjects as electives at any grade level: reading, creative writing, typing, dramatics, speech, and journalism. Only two schools offer foreign language in grade 5 and only 11 in grade 6, with some increase, still to less than a third, in grades 7 and 8.

Data were also secured as to the provision of curriculum opportunities other than required and elective subjects, and are shown in Table 12. Apparently the middle school organization has not developed as many opportunities for children in grades 5 and 6 only as for grades 7 and 8 only, where they were already available in the junior high school organization. Relatively few schools offer any of these opportunities in grades 5 or 6, but several of them are offered by more than a third of the schools for all grades: intramural athletics, band, chorus, and student government. Interschool athletics for boys is offered by about half of the schools in grades 7 and 8; as already noted, this provision seems unrelated to whether the school aims to remedy weaknesses of the junior high school. Certain opportunities viewed as means of meeting individual needs and interests are offered by only a few schools at any grade level: speech, photography, recreational sports, recreational games.

Individual schools do offer programs with a wide range of elective subjects and extra-classroom opportunities; for example, see the descriptions in Chapter 10 of Schools D, E, F, and H. The offering of electives and other opportunities was expected to be related to the size of school, and the data were analyzed in terms of the size factor. Thus a comparison was made between schools enrolling less than 400 and those with more than 800 pupils as to the offering of certain electives in grades 7 and 8. The number and percent of the larger schools offering the electives listed were consistently higher although it is disappointing that these offerings are not available in even more of the schools.

A somewhat similar situation was found with respect to the provision of certain other curriculum opportunities. Intramural athletics, arts and crafts, student government, orchestra, dramatics, and photography are available to larger percentages of pupils, in grade 7 and 8 and in all grades, in the larger schools than in the smaller ones. However, boys' interschool athletics is more likely to be available in grades 7 and 8 of smaller than larger schools, undoubtedly because of such factors as the interest of small communities in athletics and the lack there of other activities.

Instructional Organization

Patterns by subjects and grades. For each grade, 5–8, respectively, the number and percent of schools using each of six instructional organiza-

Table 12.   Number and Percent of Middle Schools
Offering Certain Curriculum Opportunities
Other Than Required and Elective Subjects, by Grade Level,
as Reported by a Sample of Middle Schools*

	Grade 5		Grade 6		Grade 7		Grade 8		All Grades	
	No.	%	No.	%	No.	%	No.	%	No.	%
Intramural athletics (boys)	4	9.5	9	8.3	22	20.4	20	19.2	61	56.5
Intramural athletics (girls)	4	9.5	7	6.5	24	22.2	22	21.1	43	39.8
Interschool athletics (boys)	2	4.8	4	3.7	52	48.2	55	52.8	28	25.9
Interschool athletics (girls)	0	00.0	1	0.9	21	19.4	24	23.1	12	11.1
Band	3	7.1	9	8.3	17	15.7	16	15.4	84	77.8
Orchestra	0	00.0	2	1.9	5	4.6	5	4.8	20	18.5
Chorus	1	1.4	8	7.4	27	25.0	30	29.8	53	49.1
Student government	0	00.0	3	2.8	13	12.0	14	13.5	68	62.9
Student publications	1	2.4	4	3.7	19	17.6	26	25.0	32	29.6
Speech	0	00.0	1	0.9	7	6.5	14	13.5	11	10.2
Dramatics	0	00.0	7	6.5	17	15.7	22	21.1	9	8.3
First aid	1	2.4	5	4.6	8	7.4	10	9.3	2	1.9
Photography	2	4.8	4	3.7	9	8.3	9	8.7	6	5.6
Arts and crafts	1	1.4	8	7.4	20	18.5	23	22.1	20	18.5
Honor societies	0	00.0	2	1.9	5	4.6	6	5.8	6	5.6
Social dancing	0	00.0	5	4.6	33	30.5	38	36.5	8	7.4
School parties	4	4.5	26	24.1	32	29.6	33	31.7	28	25.9
Recreational sports	0	00.0	6	5.6	16	14.8	15	14.4	9	8.3
Recreational games	1	2.4	9	8.3	14	13.0	14	13.5	11	10.2

*Number reporting: Grade 5, 42 of 42; Grade 6, 108 of 110; Grade 7, 108 of 110; Grade 8, 104 of 106; All Grades, 108 of 110.

tions was determined for each of the various subjects. Half or more of the schools including grade 5 maintain the typical elementary school organization, the self-contained classroom (that is, the same teacher), for language arts, social studies, science, and mathematics, and some of these schools include art, music, physical education, and foreign language in the same teacher's responsibility. The four first-named subjects are taught in the typical secondary school departmentalized organization even in grade 5 in about one-fourth of these schools, and the shift from the self-contained to the departmentalized pattern for these subjects is pronounced at grade 6, and much more so at grade 7. About three-fourths or more of the schools use the departmentalized organization for all subjects in grades 7 and 8, although the percents are smaller for language arts and social studies, the subjects most frequently included in the block-of-time plan. Relatively few schools use back-to-back and other team teaching plans at any grade level, but the block-of-time arrangement is more frequent.

As reported earlier (see "Establishment of Middle Schools," above), the schools reporting as an aim of their middle school establishment the remedying of weaknesses of the junior high school did not differ markedly in their instructional organizations from schools not claiming this aim. An analysis was also made to determine whether the instructional pattern varied between grade 5–8 and grade 6–8 schools, by comparison of the grade 6 instructional organizations within the two groups of schools. The self-contained classroom organization was used in a slightly higher percent of the grade 5–8 schools in grade 6 for the four basic subjects, but the differences were small. Hence one wonders if most middle schools have simply adopted the pattern of their predecessor schools without deliberate effort to change.

Nevertheless, some of the new schools, especially those housed in new buildings designed for new middle school programs and organizations, do utilize patterns other than self-containment and departmentalization. See in Chapter 10 the descriptions of team teaching plans in Schools A and F and also that of a block-of-time arrangement for grades 6 and 7 in School B.

Grouping.   Table 13 reports the respondents' checks as to criteria employed in grouping students for homeroom, required subjects, and elective offerings. Over half of the schools apparently use some type of homogeneous grouping in required subjects, with teacher recommendations being the most frequent criterion, and IQ tests, achievement tests, and previous school marks also each checked as one criterion by half or more of the schools. Only six of the schools checked only a single criterion for grouping in required subjects, these being either achievement tests, teacher recommendations, or age; in the other schools a combination of factors was used.

Apparently a relatively small number of schools attempt homogeneous grouping in assigning students to homerooms and elective subjects. Teacher recommendation is again the most frequently used criterion for elective subjects and second only to age for homeroom groupings.

Large group instruction was used in a relatively small number of schools, but there is a perceptible increase from lower to higher grades especially in language arts, social studies, science, and physical education.

Table 13.   Number and Percent of Schools Employing Certain Criteria
in Assigning Students to Groups as Reported by 110 Middle Schools*

Grouping	Criteria Employed									
	IQ Tests		Achievement Tests		Teacher Recommendations		Age (no. years in school)		Previous School Marks	
	No.	%	No.	%	No.	%	No.	%	No.	%
Homeroom	18	16.7	26	23.6	33	30.0	36	32.7	18	16.7
Instructional groups for required subjects	55	50.0	71	64.6	78	70.8	27	24.5	57	51.8
Instructional groups in elective offerings	15	13.6	19	17.3	30	27.3	13	11.8	16	14.5

*Eight schools reported none at all.

Scheduling.   Table 14 shows the distribution of schools according to
types of schedules used, revealing that about 30 percent use some arrangement other than the traditional daily periods of uniform length. Five of the
schools in the sample utilize modular schedules. This type of scheduling is
illustrated in Chapter 10 by the descriptions of Schools A, E, F, and H.
Another variation of schedules is described for School C. Various comments entered in the instruments and made orally in the schools visited
further attest to wide interest in departures from conventional schedules.

Table 14.   Distribution of Schools
by Type of Daily Schedule Utilized
as Reported by 108 Middle Schools*

Type of Daily Schedule	No.	%
Daily periods uniform in length	76	70.3
Daily periods of varying length	17	15.7
Some periods uniform in length, some periods varying in length	10	9.3
Modular scheduling	5	4.6
Totals	108	99.9

*Schools reporting, 108 of 110.

Individualization

Three provisions for individualizing the middle school program, in addition to those already reported in relation to curriculum opportunities, were especially examined and are reported in this section. Readers are also referred to Chapter 10 for illustrations of provisions for individualization described for the various illustrative schools, A–H.

Table 15 reports the provisions of independent study by type and grade. The most common provision, although in less than 20 percent of the schools at any grade level, is that of scheduled independent study time. The number of schools providing for released time from classes for inde-

Table 15. Number and Percent of Middle Schools Using Certain Types of Independent Study by Grade as Reported by 110 Middle Schools*

	Grade 5		Grade 6		Grade 7		Grade 8	
	No.	%	No.	%	No.	%	No.	%
Some students released part of all of the time from one or more classes, for independent study	1	2.4	10	9.1	19	17.3	20	18.8
Groups of students with special interest in some curriculum area work as a seminar	0	00.0	4	3.6	4	3.6	6	5.7
Some students have individually - planned programs with regularly scheduled time for independent study	0	00.0	1	0.9	7	6.4	5	4.7
All students have some time scheduled for independent study	8	19.0	18	16.4	20	18.2	20	18.9
Some students have time scheduled for work experience with faculty supervision	2	4.8	4	3.6	8	7.3	10	9.4

*Percents based on schools having grade 5, 42; grade 6, and 7, 110; grade 8, 106.

Table 16. Number and Percent of Middle Schools Using Various Systems
of Reporting Pupil Progress as Reported by 110 Middle Schools*

System of Reporting Pupil Progress	No.	%
Letter scale (A to E, etc.)	95	86.3
Regularly scheduled parent conferences	46	41.8
Satisfactory-Unsatisfactory scale	28	25.5
Informal written notes	51	46.3
Dual system (compared with his group and his own potential)	15	13.6
Number scale (1–5, etc.)	14	12.7
Work scale (excellent, good, etc.)	7	6.4
Percentage marks	6	5.5
Other*	21	19.1

*Other commonly mentioned: conferences as needed (9), interim reports (8).

pendent study, and for work experience increases from lower to higher grades. Relatively few schools provide seminars and individually planned programs at any grade level.

Since marking and reporting systems also reflect concern for individual differences, the survey instrument also included questions as to these systems. Table 16 shows that the letter scale is the most common system, but it is noteworthy that 46 (41.8 percent) of the schools use regularly scheduled parent conferences. Even more relevant to individualization is the use by 15 (13.6 percent) of the schools of a dual system in which one mark is based on the individual's own potential, the other on comparative achievement.

Table 17 reports the number and percent of schools using each of various personnel for counseling pupils. Opportunities of teachers for counseling and thus for relating to individual pupils they also teach appear very

Table 17. Number and Percent of Middle Schools Utilizing
Certain Persons for the Counseling of Pupils
as Reported by 110 Middle Schools

Persons Responsible for Counseling	No.	%
Homeroom (home base) teacher	60	54.6
Full-time counselors	52	47.3
Regular classroom teachers	49	44.6
Part-time counselors	26	24.6
Others*	24	21.8

*Others reported: principals (20), assistant principals (8).

frequent; in fact, the most frequently reported person as one responsible for counseling is the homeroom teacher, and the number of schools designating classroom teachers as responsible is almost as large as that for full-time counselors.

Reactions to the Middle School

Table 18 reports the estimates of the respondents as to the reactions of various groups to the middle school. Noteworthy is the fact that only one school reported that a single group was opposed—in this case, the parents. Relatively low percents reported "indifferent" reactions, the percent (16.4) being highest for the general public. The respondents more frequently regarded staff reaction as "enthusiastic" than they did student body and parents. Table 18 shows the respondents' estimates that in general the reactions were highly favorable.

Reactions may also be implied from the open-ended item returns. In response to the request for a list of major problems encountered in establishing the middle school, many items were listed but the most frequent ones were teacher adjustment, facilities, finances, and excessive pupil populations. It is inferred from the absence of problem statements as to opposition and unfavorable reactions, that the chief barriers to effective middle schools were perceived as tangible ones in achieving goals rather than dissatisfaction with the goals themselves.

In response to the request for descriptions of plans for evaluating the middle school, numerous plans were listed, especially standardized tests, follow-up studies, accrediting evaluations, and self-study programs. Several respondents indicated need for additional evaluation plans and others that plans were in process. No respondent suggested that unfavor-

Table 18. Distribution of 110 Middle Schools Reporting Reactions of Certain Groups to the Middle School Organization

	Enthusiastic		Favorable		Indifferent		Opposed		Totals	
	No.	%	No.	%	No.	%	No.	%	No.	%
Attitude of student body	28	25.4	75	68.2	7	6.4	0	00.0	110	100.0
Attitude of staff	44	40.0	63	57.3	3	2.7	0	00.0	110	100.0
Attitude of parents	24	21.8	76	69.1	9	8.2	1	0.9	110	100.0
Attitude of general public	16	14.5	76	69.1	18	16.4	0	00.0	110	100.0

able evaluations had been made or that evaluations were being demanded by school critics.

Thus, so far as this survey determined, the reactions to the 110 middle schools included are favorable. In fact, 80 of the 110 replies were "No" to the question, "Do you anticipate changing to a different type of organizational plan within the next two to five years?," and no information is available as to the types of change anticipated by the other 30 schools. The present author is inclined to regard this situation as one of perhaps undue complacency and will note in the final section of this report some relevant conclusions and recommendations.

CONCLUSIONS AND RECOMMENDATIONS

This project accomplished its primary objective of determining benchmark data as to the identification and description of middle school organizations differing from the now traditional grade 7–9 junior high school pattern. A total of 1101 schools defined herein as middle schools were identified, and a 10 percent random sample (110 schools) was surveyed for organizational characteristics. From these data, viewed in the context of criticisms of the 6-3-3 school ladder and claims for the new middle school organization, the following major conclusions are drawn:

1. There is definitely a current movement toward grade 5–8 and 6–8 school organizations in the middle of the school ladder; of the sample, approximately 90 percent have been established in the 1960s, and nearly half (42.9 percent) during the last two years (1966 and 1967).

2. Aims generally stated, both in the literature and by the respondents for the schools in the sample, such as "to remedy the weaknesses of the junior high school" and "to provide a program specifically designed for this age group" are not generally reflected in the curriculum plan and instructional organization of the schools surveyed. The program of studies is generally comparable to that of these grades in predecessor organizations, with a relatively sparse offering of elective and other curriculum opportunities, especially for grades 5 and 6. Instructional organization for grade 5 is most frequently similar to that of the elementary school, with the departmentalization pattern of the junior high school introduced even here and becoming the predominant organization in the other grades.

3. Despite the marked tendency of the newer grade organizations to resemble in program of studies and instructional organization the predecessor organizations and especially the grade 7–9 junior high school, there are certain observable developments which could be forerunners of a more general movement toward middle schools that do indeed differ

from the prevailing junior high school pattern and, for grades 5 and 6, the elementary school as well. The following such developments are noted:

a. A sizable number (30 percent) of the middle schools are utilizing variable and modular schedules differing from the conventional uniform daily schedule of equal periods.

b. Independent study arrangements are being provided in some 20 percent of the schools.

c. Team teaching patterns are infrequently used but seem more frequent in schools recently established in new facilities, and numerous respondents indicated as plans for the future the development of such patterns.

d. Reporting and marking systems are not uniform, and many schools are attempting plans which reflect interest in individual progress.

e. Many larger schools do offer a wide range of exploratory curriculum opportunities, and several respondents expressed interest in developing expanded programs.

f. Answers to the open-ended items in the survey and interviews in the schools visited revealed considerable dissatisfaction with certain "inherited" arrangements, and various plans for future modifications designed to meet the needs of children of middle school age.

In light of this project and its conclusions, the following major recommendations are offered:

1. Critical evaluations, probably by comparative studies of the new and traditional organizations, are needed to determine how the new ones differ, especially in terms of educational results, and how the organizations might be improved. See Chapter 7 for suggested procedures.

2. School districts contemplating changes in their organizational ladder should carefully plan the programs and instructional organizations of new schools to relate to the educational purposes and pupil populations of the latter. Even if overcrowded conditions necessitate new organizations, the latter can be planned to provide for the unique educational needs of the new age range rather than merely copying patterns characteristic of predecessor grade arrangements. See Chapter 8 for more detailed recommendations and suggested ways and means.

3. Suspecting that a major reason for the lack of innovation in the new organizations is their transplanting of personnel from the old ones—and this explanation was frequently suggested by respondents and interviewers —a primary need is the training of personnel specifically for the new organization. Preservice and inservice education programs must be developed to provide an input of innovative programs and organizational practices, if the new organizations are to really differ from the old ones.

Chapter 10

Descriptions of Illustrative
Middle Schools

ILLUSTRATIVE MIDDLE SCHOOL A[1]

Background

Drew Junior High School, a 6–9 middle school organization in 1967–1968, is located in the north central section of Dade County, Florida, and is a unit within the North Central District, Dade County Schools. The total enrollment of 1685 students is served by 87 professional staff members. The facility is a new, two-story, air-conditioned and carpeted building, opened in 1967 and designed specifically to accommodate the middle school program. Extraordinary features of the building are a large auditorium which may be partitioned for use as large group instructional areas, independent study rooms and areas, and the "loft" area, a large open expanse in the center of the second floor which is equipped with movable partitions so that the area may be utilized in several different room sizes and arrangements.

The school complex, which includes a K–5 elementary school, is located in an all-Negro, low socioeconomic area, with most residents living in

[1]Drew Junior High School, 1801 N.W. 60th Street, Miami, Fla. Based on a visit by William M. Alexander and Ronald P. Kealy on May 15, 1968, and interviews with J. L. Jones, Principal; Joseph W. Sharron, Assistant Principal; Edward M. Trauschke, Curriculum Coordinator; and staff members and students.

187

compact apartments. The attitude of the community toward the school program is generally favorable.

Stated reasons for the establishment of the middle school program were to better bridge the elementary and the high schools, to remedy the weaknesses of the junior high school, to eliminate crowded conditions in other schools, to provide a program specifically designed for students in this age group, to try out various innovations, to use some plans which have been successfully implemented in other school systems, and to better individualize instruction. The decision to adopt this organization was made at the county and district levels. Since this is the first year of operation, the program is continually being evaluated and adjusted to meet the original goals. There is one other middle school in the district. Approximately 85 percent of the staff spent the summer of 1967 planning for the opening of the new plant. Staff members were enrolled and compensated for participation in a six-week workshop, during which a number of consultants appeared on the agenda. Several staff members participated in a year long middle school institute at the University of Florida during 1966–1967.

The staff is generally enthusiastic about the middle school program, with major problems being stated as the delayed completion of the building, excessive student population, and adjustment to team planning and teaching. Most of the staff interviewed would favor a 6–8 organization. The staff is a combination of teachers with secondary school background and a few with elementary school background. A few teachers have a dual certification. Special staff positions are one assistant principal (administration), one assistant principal (curriculum), one assistant principal (guidance), six full-time counselors, one curriculum coordinator, and eight Continuing Education Center consultants. The Continuing Education Center augments the regular teaching staff with people who are available for demonstration teaching, subject and interdisciplinary planning, cooperative team teaching, individual or group planning, and unit resources. Federal funds of this Center also make available such services as materials production workshop, special audiovisual equipment, additional instructional materials, and consultants. Ten noncertified personnel are employed regularly for clerical assistance to teachers, test scoring, operation of audiovisual equipment, monitoring large group instruction, and helping individual students.

Drew Junior High School is fed by eight elementary schools and in turn feeds three high schools. Articulation between Drew Junior High School and the elementary and high schools is provided for by joint curriculum planning activities, arrangements for interschool visitation, sharing of information about school programs, obtaining and providing data about incoming and outgoing students, and orientation programs for students.

Program of Studies

The course offerings for grades 6–9 are divided into three phases and are designated as Phases A, B, and C. Required subjects included in Phase A are mathematics and science, with these subjects as electives: art, industrial technology, home arts, clothing and textiles, foods and nutrition, and health and grooming. In Phase B, required subjects are English, social studies, and reading, with the electives including drama, graphics, typing, business education, speech, French, Spanish, communicative arts, directed study, and independent study. Phase C includes the required courses of physical education, music, and group guidance. Each phase of the curriculum basically represents one-third (two hours) of the total school day, excluding time for lunch and home station. Students may enroll in at least two electives from Phases A and/or B in addition to the required courses in each phase, the flexibility here permitting time in directed study or independent study as needed by the student. A breakdown of the approximate amount of time per week allocated to each subject is given in Table A-1. Other curriculum opportunities are intramural athletics, interschool athletics, band, orchestra, chorus, student government, student publications, speech, dramatics, photography, arts and crafts, social dancing, and school parties.

Table A-1.   Number Minutes per Week Scheduled
for Various Subjects*

	Required Subjects	Min		Elective Subjects	Min
Phase A	Mathematics	300	Phase A	Art	150
	Science			Industrial Technology	150
				Home Arts	150
Phase B	English			Clothing and Textiles	150
	Social Studies	300		Foods and Nutrition	150
	Reading			Health and Grooming	150
Phase C	Physical Education	300	Phase B	Drama	150
	Music	300		Graphics	150
	Group Guidance	Varies		Typing	150
				Business Education	150
				Speech	150
				Foreign Language	150
				Communicative Arts	150
				Directed Study	150
				Independent Study	150

*This is estimated time per week since flexible scheduling within each phase allows variation from week to week.

Instructional Organization and Arrangements

The school population is divided into three groups of approximately 560 students each. The youngest group is composed mostly of students who would normally be sixth- and seventh-graders, with a few eighth- and perhaps a few ninth-graders. This group of students comprise what is designated as Little School One. Similarly, a middle-age group of students, who would normally be mostly seventh- and eighth-graders with a few sixth- and ninth-graders, comprise Little School Two. A group of older students, who would normally be mostly eighth- and ninth-graders, with a few sixth- and seventh-graders, make up Little School Three. Initially, students are assigned to little schools on the basis of chronological age, but may be moved from one little school to another on the basis of physical, social, or emotional development. Interdisciplinary teams of teachers are assigned to each little school, the only exceptions being the teachers of special areas of instruction, such as art, business education, foreign language, in which there are fewer than three teachers in the given area. In these cases, teachers teach their subject in more than one little school on a departmentalized basis. Team planning is done by teachers within little schools, within phases, by subject area, and across phases. Each little school is divided into four sections of approximately 140 students each. Phase teams of 4–6 teachers work with these sections during a class period, exceptions again being those subject areas that are departmentalized. Large and small group instruction, with group size ranging from 5 to 80, is utilized in each section as the situation warrants. Each phase team works with each of the four sections of the little school during their schedule. Teachers have approximately two hours per day for use in team and individual planning. On alternating weeks, teachers are assigned to the directed study program for one half-hour of their daily planning time.

The school day is arranged into 27 modules of 15 minutes each, with students spending approximately eight modules in each of the three phases, two modules for lunch, and one module for home station. The amount of time spent in any given subject area is determined by the identified needs, interests, and abilities of the student and is adjusted cooperatively by the teachers within each phase as often as necessary. A typical student schedule may be seen in Table A-2.

Counseling of students is the responsibility of the home station teachers, regular classroom teachers, and the full-time counselors. The home station meets for 15 minutes daily. Two full-time counselors are assigned to each little school, and hold group guidance sessions regularly with groups of 10–15 students. These students are scheduled by their counselors to these sessions from their physical education and music classes. Each student is involved in group guidance approximately once every two weeks. These

Table A-2. Typical Student Schedule*

Module†		Module	
1	Home station	17	Physical Education
2	Math/Science (Phase A)	18	Physical Education
3	Math/Science (Phase A)	19	Physical Education
4	Math/Science (Phase A)	20	English/Social Studies/Read-
5	Math/Science (Phase A)		ing (Phase B)
6	Phase A elective	21	English/Social Studies/Read-
7	Phase A elective		ing (Phase B)
8	Phase A elective	22	English/Social Studies/Read-
9	Phase A elective		ing (Phase B)
10	Music	*23	English/Social Studies/Read-
11	Music		ing (Phase B)
12	Music	24	Phase B elective
13	Music	25	Phase B elective
14	Lunch	26	Phase B elective
15	Lunch	27	Phase B elective
16	Physical Education		

*The schedule within the Phase A and Phase B blocks of time is determined by the team and may vary from day to day.
†Each module is 15 minutes in length.

sessions are devoted to problems of self-appraisal, educational or vocational guidance, personal adjustment, and interpersonal relationships, and may include a variety of activities. Individual conferences are scheduled as the need arises and the counselors also administer the standardized testing program.

A dual system of reporting pupil progress indicates the student's progress as compared with his group and with his own potential, and utilizes a 1–3 number scale (1, satisfactory; 2, further effort necessary; 3, must improve, conference requested). This report, along with a report of citizenship, effort, and class attendance, is sent to parents each six weeks. Parent-teacher conferences are scheduled as necessary and informal written notes are also used. Pupil progress from year to year through the middle school is to be determined by general achievement and achievement in separate subject fields.

Approaches to Individualization

Small group and individual counseling, described above, is one approach to individualization, as is the wide range of electives provided in the program. The directed study program is designed to help students gain skills needed for independent study and to identify students' interests. This program is taught back-to-back with another Phase B elective, meeting three days one week and two days the next week, although a student needing this may have directed study daily or a student not needing it may take some other elective. Some skills taught in directed study are use of audiovisual tools, practice in alphabetizing, use of oral and written directions, working alone and in groups, and use of listening skills. Activities include discussion groups, plays, work with visual materials packets, use of films and film strips, guest speakers, and field trips.

Students are admitted to the independent study program on the basis of maturity and readiness. In this program, students engage in activities independent of other students and in large part independent of immediate teacher direction. Examples are reading, writing, research, conferences, and using teaching machines and other automated instructional devices. Flexible scheduling and grouping procedures by teams within little schools and phases are designed to allow teachers to attend to individual needs and interests of students. The nongraded, individualized approach allows the student to progress in each subject area at his own rate. Pupil progress is reported partly on the basis of comparison with the student's own potential.

Plans for the Future

Scheduled to be installed during the summer of 1968 is a $250,000 dial-access audio-visual-video system, featuring dial-access to programs provided through an Audio-Visual Control Center to group areas and individual carrels. Evaluations and adjustments in the middle school program are continually being made to promote the achievement of school objectives.

Summary: Distinguishing Characteristics

Drew Junior High School can briefly be described as a 6-9 nongraded middle school organization with three "little schools" incorporating team teaching and planning and flexible scheduling and grouping practices. Other distinguishing characteristics are the directed and independent study programs, the wide selection of electives, the three-phase approach to curriculum, the group guidance program, and the Continuing Education Center.

ILLUSTRATIVE MIDDLE SCHOOL B[2]

Background

Taylor Junior High School, a 6–8 middle school organization, is located in a residential suburb of Alburquerque and is a unit of the Alburquerque Schools. It has a total enrollment of 710 students who are served by 36 professional staff members. Within a section of the facility is also housed a 1–5 elementary school. The community served is predominantly middle and lower class with about 14 percent of the middle school students being classified as culturally deprived. The community, as a whole, is interested in the activities of the school.

The present 6–8 organization was initiated in 1966 to replace the previously existing 7–9 junior high school organization. Reasons given for this reorganization were to move grade 9 into the high school, to provide more specialization in grade 6, to better bridge the elementary and the high schools, to remedy the weaknesses of the junior high school, to provide a program specifically designed for children in this age group, to try out various innovations, and to use plans which have been successfully implemented in other school systems. Persons involved in deciding on the reorganization were principals, system-level organization, teachers, and parents with the principals and system-level administration being most influential. Two other middle schools were organized within the district, to be included in a three-year experimental program along with Taylor Junior High School. Preparation for the change was made through a full year of faculty study and planning, occasional planning sessions of prospective middle school faculty members, some visitation of schools with similar plans in operation, and inservice meetings of prospective faculty members with consultants on middle school development. The community was receptive to the new organization, although some parents were concerned about sixth graders being with older students and the fact that there was no interscholastic athletic program.

The staff is mainly composed of teachers with secondary preparation with the exception of the sixth-grade core teachers who have had an elementary school teaching background. Special positions include one assistant principal and two full-time counselors, one of whom also works with the elementary school. There are no noncertified personnel employed regularly in the school.

---

[2]Taylor Junior High School, 8200 Guadalupe Trail, N.W., Albuquerque, N.M. Based on a visit by Ronald P. Kealy on May 17, 1968, and interviews with Lionel O'Neal, Principal, and staff members and students.

Taylor Junior High School is fed by three elementary schools and in turn feeds one high school. Articulation between these schools is provided for by joint workshops for teachers of all levels, joint curriculum planning activities, occasional interschool visitation, some sharing of faculty, pupil data records, and orientation programs. More articulation occurs between the middle school and the elementary school in the same facility than occurs among other schools.

Program of Studies

Subjects required for a full year in all grades are language arts, social studies, and mathematics. Science, physical education, and art are required for a half-year in grades 6 and 7, music for a half-year in grade 6, industrial arts or home economics for a half-year in grade 7, and physical education for a full year in grade 8. Electives are instrumental music in all grades, foreign language in grades 7 and 8, and science, vocal music, art, industrial arts or home economics, and dramatics in grade 8. A remedial reading program, directed by a system reading specialist, is available for those students needing help in this area. A breakdown of amount of time per week devoted to the subject areas is shown in Table B-1. Other curricu-

Table B-1. Number Minutes per Week Scheduled
for Subject Areas by Grades

Required Subjects	Grade 6	Grade 7	Grade 8
Language Arts	500	500	250
Social Studies	250	250	250
Science	250 ($\frac{1}{2}$ yr.)	250 ($\frac{1}{2}$ yr.)	
Mathematics	250	250	250
Physical Education	250 ($\frac{1}{2}$ yr.)	250 ($\frac{1}{2}$ yr.)	250
Art	250 ($\frac{1}{2}$ yr.)	250 ($\frac{1}{2}$ yr.)	
Music	250 ($\frac{1}{2}$ yr.)		
Home Economics (girls)		250 ($\frac{1}{2}$ yr.)	
Industrial Arts (boys)		250 ($\frac{1}{2}$ yr.)	
Elective Subjects			
Science			250
Vocal Music			250
Instrumental Music	250	250	250
Art			250
Industrial Arts (boys)			250
Home Economics (girls)			250
Foreign Language		250	250

lum opportunities are intramural athletics, student government, student publications, social dancing, recreational sports, and first aid.

Instructional Organization and Arrangements

Language arts (English and reading) and social studies are taught in a core-type program by the same teacher in the sixth grade and language arts is taught in such a program in the seventh grade. Other subjects are taught on a departmentalized basis with some subject area classes being scheduled at the same time so that teaming may occur if the situation warrants. Usual class size ranges from 30 to 33 students. Homogeneous grouping is used for mathematics only, based on IQ tests, achievement tests, teacher recommendations, and previous school marks as criteria for placement in a three-level system. Large group instruction is sometimes used in the science classes and small group instruction is used within the various subject area classrooms.

Students have a similar schedule each day during the week. There are six periods per day, each 50 minutes long, plus an additional 50-minute period for lunch and recess. Each teacher teaches six classes per day. Typical student schedules are illustrated in Table B-2.

Responsibility for counseling is assigned to the homeroom teacher, the counselors, the principal, and the assistant principal. Counselors work with teachers in the area of guidance techniques and also counsel individual students upon recommendation of teachers. They also administer the standardized testing program.

Pupil progress is reported by an A–E letter scale each quarter and informal written notes are also used. Progress in citizenship, work habits, attitudes, and effort are reported as well as progress in subject areas.

Table B-2. Typical Student Schedule

Period**	Grade 6	Grade 7	Grade 8
1	English*	Home Economics	Mathematics
2	Reading*	Social Studies	Industrial Arts
3	Physical Education	Mathematics	Physical Education
4A	Lunch	Lunch	Social Studies
4B	Mathematics	Physical Education	Lunch
5	Social Studies*	English†	Science
6	Music	Reading†	Language Arts

* and †Taught by the same teacher in a core-type program.
**Each period is 50 minutes in length.

Parent conferences are scheduled as the need arises. Pupil progress from year to year through the school is based upon the student's general achievement as related to his ability to achieve. Approximately 5 to 8 percent attend this middle school for longer than the normal three-year period.

Approaches to Individualization

The various grouping techniques used have been described above. Some students are released part of the time from one or more regular classes for independent study, and some work on a class project basis in small groups in special areas of interest. Teachers are encouraged to provide some independent study time for all students.

Plans for the Future

An evaluation committee of system-level administrators is assessing the experimental middle school program in order to determine the direction to be taken by the system with regard to the middle school concept. At Taylor Junior High School, an effort will be made next year to strengthen the independent study program and to do more in the area of team teaching. Informal evaluation of how the sixth-grader adjusts to the reorganization will continue.

Summary: Distinguishing Characteristics

Taylor Junior High School can briefly be described as a 6–8 middle school organization with a basically departmentalized organizational pattern and utilizing a language arts–social studies core program in grade 6, and a language arts core in grade 7. The school operates on a nonvariable, six-period schedule, and is a part of a three-year experimental middle school program within the system.

ILLUSTRATIVE MIDDLE SCHOOL C[3]

Background

Del Norte School is a 5–8 middle school organization, located in West Covina, California, just west of Los Angeles, and is a unit of the West Covina Unified School District. The total enrollment of 691 is served by

[3]Del Norte School, 1501 Del Norte Street, West Covina, Calif. Based on a visit by Ronald P. Kealy on May 20, 1968, and interviews with Peter Masonis, Principal, and staff members and students.

25 professional staff members. The community in which the school operates has grown very rapidly in the last several years, is predominantly residential, and is mainly middle class. Minority groups represented are Orientals, Negroes, and Spanish-Americans, with the Spanish-American group comprising the largest total of these. The community, as a whole, has above average interest in the school program.

The school district converted from a K–8 elementary program to a K–5, 6–8 program in 1965. Del Norte School also houses grade 5 due to crowded conditions in its feeder elementary school, but this grade is not actually a part of the intermediate program. The other five middle schools in the district are 6–8 organizations. The reasons stated for the establishment of the middle school program were to provide more specialization in grade 6, to bridge better the elementary and the high schools, to provide a program specifically designed for students in this age group, and to better utilize the strengths and interests of teachers. Principals, teachers, system-level administration, and the state department of education were involved in the decision to reorganize, with the principals and teachers regarded as being the most influential. The community as a whole was receptive to this reorganization. Preparation for the change was accomplished by faculty study and planning groups who met often during the year previous to the change, some visitation of schools with similar plans in operation, and meetings with consultants on middle school development.

Approximately two-thirds of the staff are teachers with backgrounds in elementary teaching, most being retained from the previous K–8 organization. Teachers with secondary school preparation teach only seventh and eighth grade students due to state certification regulations. Most teachers teach six classes per day and at least two different subjects. Special staff positions are one assistant principal and one full-time counselor. The school does not employ any noncertified personnel.

Del Norte School is fed by one K–4 elementary school and in turn feeds one high school. Articulation between the schools is provided by curriculum planning activities and workshops for teachers at all levels, sharing of information about school programs, and a high school orientation program for outgoing eighth graders. Some cooperative planning is done between the fifth- and sixth-grade teachers at Del Norte School.

Program of Studies

Fifth-graders at Del Norte School, who are not actually a part of the middle school program, have language arts, social studies, science, mathematics, physical education, art, and music each day during the week. Required subjects for sixth-, seventh-, and eighth-graders are language arts, social studies, mathematics, physical education, foreign language

Table C-1. Number Minutes per Week Scheduled
for Various Courses by Grades

Required Courses	Grade 6	Grade 7	Grade 8
Language Arts	225	225	225
Social Studies	225	225	225
Mathematics	225	225	225
Physical Education	225	225	225
Science ($\frac{1}{2}$ year)	225	225	225
Music ($\frac{1}{2}$ year)	225		
Art (included in Social Studies)	45	45	45
Foreign Language	$112\frac{1}{2}$	$112\frac{1}{2}$	$112\frac{1}{2}$
Reading	$112\frac{1}{2}$	$112\frac{1}{2}$	$112\frac{1}{2}$
Industrial Arts ($\frac{1}{2}$ year)		225	225
Home Economics ($\frac{1}{2}$ year)		225	225
Elective Courses			
Vocal Music	225	225	225
Instrumental Music	225	225	225
Dramatics	225	225	225
Journalism		225	225
Art		225	225

(Spanish), and reading, each taken for the entire year. Required for one-half year are science and music in grade 6, and science and industrial arts (boys) or home economics (girls) in grades 7 and 8. Art is required for less than one-half year in grades 6, 7, and 8, and is taken from the social studies time periodically. The reading and foreign language programs are combined in grades 6, 7, and 8. Electives are vocal music, instrumental music, and dramatics in grades 6, 7, and 8, and art and journalism in grades 7 and 8. A breakdown of the instructional time per week in each subject is shown in Table C-1.

Instructional Organization and Arrangements

Grade 5 has a completely self-contained instructional organization since it is actually still a part of the elementary program. The average class size is 33. Grades 6, 7, and 8 are completely departmentalized with an average of 32 students per class. Grouping for required classes is done mainly by teacher recommendation with achievement tests also being used. Three-track grouping is utilized in mathematics, and reading groups are classified as either remedial or average-high. Small groups are used in the remedial reading classes and in the low-track mathematics classes.

Table C-2.   Typical Student Schedules

Period	Grade 6	Grade 7 or 8
8:15– 9:00 (1)	Drama-Speech	Journalism
9:04– 9:14	Homeroom	Homeroom
9:18–10:03 (2)	Science	Mathematics
10:03–10:13	Recess	Recess
10:17–11:02 (3)	Social Studies	Industrial Arts
11:06–11:51 (4)	Language Arts	Social Studies
11:55–12:30 (5/lunch)	Reading/Spanish	Lunch
12:34– 1:19 (5/lunch)	Lunch	Language Arts
1:23– 2:08 (6)	Mathematics	Physical Education
2:08– 2:18	Recess	Recess
2:22– 3:07 (7)	Physical Education	Reading/Spanish

Students who choose not to take an elective are on a six-period day, while those who choose an elective start their day one period earlier and have a seven-period day. Periods are 45 minutes in length. There is a homeroom period of 10 minutes each day for grades 6, 7, and 8, and a 40-minute lunch break. Students follow the same schedule each day of the week. Typical student schedules may be seen in Table C-2.

Pupil progress is reported on a 1–5 number scale which corresponds roughly to the A–E scale commonly used. Informal written notes are sent to parents as necessary and regularly scheduled conferences are held once each year by fifth-grade teachers and as the need arises by sixth-, seventh-, and eighth-grade teachers. Citizenship, work habits, attitudes, and effort are also reported to parents each quarter. Progress from year to year through the middle school is determined by general achievement and by achievement in separate subject fields. Very few (less than 1 percent) are retained at grade level, and only after an extensive case study and consultation with parents.

The self-contained classroom teacher takes basic responsibility for counseling in the fifth grade while the homeroom teacher and the full-time counselor have this responsibility in grades 6, 7, and 8, with help from the principal and assistant principal.

Approaches to Individualization

Grouping practices in reading and mathematics have already been described. Small group instruction is utilized in the remedial reading program and in the low-track mathematics groups.

Plans for the Future

Plans are being made for a five-period day with a possible language arts–social studies core pending the repeal of certain state requirements. With this adjustment will be an increase in staff size and a more flexible schedule.

Summary: Distinguishing Characteristics

Del Norte School can be described as a departmentalized middle school organization, with self-contained fifth-grade classes, not actually a part of the middle school program, housed in the same facility.

ILLUSTRATIVE MIDDLE SCHOOL D[4]

Background

Aspen Middle School, a 5–8 organization, is located in Aspen, Colorado, a small community of about 2000 population, and is a unit of the Pitkin County School District. The total enrollment of 282 students is served by 13 full-time and 5 part-time staff members. The school building is the old high school building, and a new middle school building is being planned for the future. The school operates in an essentially middle and upper class community with about 7 percent of the school population being from the rural area. The community is very interested in activities of the school and residents are highly vocal in their reactions to these activities.

The 5–8 organization was first utilized in the 1966–1967 school year, primarily because of the crowded conditions existing when the high school and middle school age students were housed in the same building. When a new four-year high school was completed, the 5–8 middle school organization was formulated. Reasons that have developed for the maintenance of the middle school are: to provide more specialization in grades 5 and 6, to try out various innovations, and to provide a program specifically designed for students in this age group. Preparation for the initiation of the 5–8 organization was made by occasional planning sessions by faculty members, inservice meetings, and a nationwide survey of several operating middle schools and visitation of these by the principal. Prospective middle school teachers had reading assignments pertaining to the middle school and made reports to the staff. A Title III (ESEA) funded six-week summer

---

[4]Aspen Middle School, Aspen, Colo. Based on a visit by Ronald P. Kealy on May 22, 1968, and interviews with Gerald DeFries, Principal, and staff members and students.

program (1967) was attended by about 50 percent of the teachers who worked mainly on designing educational objectives. Several consultants participated in this summer program.

There was some concern expressed by parents with regard to fifth- and sixth-graders "growing up too fast" in the presence of older students, reduction in the amount of time spent in college preparatory courses, and de-emphasis of vocational preparation type activities.

The staff is composed of both elementary-prepared and secondary-prepared teachers. An authorization for a three-year exemption from state certification requirements was obtained so that elementary-prepared teachers could teach seventh- and eighth-graders and so that secondary-prepared teachers could teach fifth and sixth graders. There is one half-time counselor in the school and no noncertified personnel are employed.

Aspen Middle School is fed by one elementary school, and in turn feeds one high school, these being the only other schools in the community. Articulation between the middle school and the elementary school is promoted by the sharing of some teachers, occasional visitation by the staff, an orientation day for incoming fifth-graders, and subject area curriculum planning. Articulation between the middle school and the high school is in the form of occasional teacher visitation, student use of some high school facilities, subject area curriculum planning, and the counseling of eighth-graders for entrance into the high school by the high school guidance counselors.

Program of Studies

The program of studies is similar for fifth- and sixth-graders. Their required subjects are language arts, social studies, science, mathematics, physical education, art, music, reading, library and individually designed instruction. During the individually designed instruction time, the student is assigned to the library, and may be scheduled for special reading, language, weight training, band, or other individual work with teachers in areas in which he is interested and/or needs individual help.

Electives for fifth- and sixth-graders are instrumental music and foreign language (Spanish and French). Table D-1 gives a breakdown of the amount of time per week allotted for each subject. Other curriculum opportunities include band, student government, social dancing, and "exploration," a program that will be described later.

The program of studies for seventh- and eighth-graders is similar, with some minor exceptions. Required subjects are language arts, social studies, science, mathematics, physical education, art, home economics, library, health, speech seminar, and creative writing. Speed reading is required for all eighth-graders and individually designed instruction is required for all seventh- and eighth-graders except for the middle eighth-grade section.

Table D-1. Hours per Week Scheduled for Subjects
by Grades and Sections (to nearest quarter hour)

| | Grade 5 | | | Grade 6 | | Grade 7 | | | Grade 8 | | |
| | Sections | | | Sections | | Sections | | | Sections | | |
	1	2	3	4	5	6	7	8	9	10	11
Mathematics	3¼	3¼	3¼	3¼	3¼	4	3¼	3¼	3¾	3½	3
Science	3¼	3¼	3¼	3¼	3¼	4¼	4	4	3¼	5½	4
English	3¼	3¼	3¼	3¼	3¼	*5¾	*5¼	4½	*5	*5¼	*4¼
Reading	3¼	3¼	3¼	3¼	3¼				¾	¾	¾
Social Studies	3¼	3¼	3¼	3¼	3¼	3¾	3¼	3¾	3½	3½	3¾
Phy. Ed. (boys)	2¾	2¾	2¾	2¾	2¾	4	4	4	5	5	6
Phy. Ed. (girls)	2¾	2¾	2¾	2¾	2¾	3	3	3	3½	3½	3½
Library (boys)	2	2¾	3¼	2¾	3	3	3	3	3½	3½	3½
Library (girls)	2	2¾	3¼	2¾	3	2½	2½	3	3	3	3½
I.D.I.† (boys)	3¾	3	2¼	3	2¾	2	3	3¼	1		½
I.D.I.† (girls)	3¾	3	2½	3	2¾	2	3	3¼	1		½
Art	1	1	1	1	1	1	2	1½	2½	2	2
Chorus	1	1	¾	¾	¾	¾	¾	¾			
Homeroom	1	1	1	1	1	½	½	½	½	½	½
Health						¾	¾	¾	¾	¾	¾
Exploration	1	1	1	1	1	1	1	1	1	1	1
Home Economics						1½	1½	1	2	1½	1½

*Includes creative writing and speech seminar.
†Individually Designed Instruction

Music is required in grade 7 and mathematics application, a course in practical applications of mathematics, is required in the low sections of grades 7 and 8. Electives are instrumental music, typing, and foreign language in grades 7 and 8, and vocal music and dramatics in grade 8. Other curriculum opportunities are intramural athletics (girls), interschool athletics (boys), band, student government, school parties, social dancing, and "exploration."

The exploration program is an activity period each Friday afternoon in which the student may elect some activity of his choice from a wide variety of opportunities. Teachers and members of the community select areas of their own special interest around which to design specific activity programs. Descriptions of these activities are presented to the students who may choose one area in which to participate. New activities are selected each six weeks. Some examples are: ice-skating, ski jumping, modern dance, bird watching, fly tying, Indian lore, synchronized swimming, photography, and mountain climbing.

Instructional Organization and Arrangements

All subjects in all grades are taught primarily on a departmentalized basis, with class size ranging from 4 to 60. Informal teaming is sometimes done between teachers of classes that meet at the same time. Team planning is done by fifth- and sixth-grade teachers and also the seventh- and eighth-grade teachers. Students are grouped for required subjects into sections on the basis of IQ tests, achievement tests, and teacher recommendations. There is a total of 11 sections: 3 fifth-grade, 2 sixth-grade, 3 seventh-grade, and 3 eighth-grade sections. Section 1 is the lowest fifth-grade section and Section 11 is the highest eighth-grade section. Students may be changed from one section to another during the course of the year upon recommendation of teachers. Grouping for elective offerings is done on the basis of student interest and teacher recommendation. Students are grouped heterogeneously for their homeroom, with fifth- and sixth-graders mixed, and seventh- and eighth-graders mixed. Grouping within the mathematics and reading classes is done on the basis of achievement. Small grouping is also utilized in the individually designed instruction periods, music, foreign language, and home economics. The schedule is variable with not all classes meeting daily and, as with the program of studies, the fifth- and sixth-grade schedule is similar, and the seventh and eighth grade schedule is similar. Fifth- and sixth-graders have a daily schedule with five periods of 40 minutes each and an additional five periods of varying length, ranging from 20 to 60 minutes. Seventh- and eighth-graders have three periods of 50 minutes each and an additional five periods of varying length ranging from 30 to 120 minutes. Typical student schedules may be seen in Tables D-2 and D-3.

S (strong progress), N (normal progress), and I (insufficient progress), are the grades used to indicate the teachers' evaluation of student progress in comparison with ability. Student ability is determined by standardized test scores, teacher observation, health records, and growth patterns. Citizenship, work habits, attitudes, effort, and subject area skills are reported also, and this report is sent to parents at the end of each nine-week period. Time for parent conferences is scheduled twice each year, in the fall and in the spring. Progress from year to year through the middle school is determined by age, general achievement, achievement in separate subject fields, and teacher day-to-day evaluation. Very few students (less than 1 percent) are retained at a grade level and only after considerable investigation of several criteria and consultation with parents.

Homeroom teachers and the half-time counselor are primarily responsible for guidance of the students although subject area teachers also counsel. Homeroom meets twice each week for fifth- and sixth-graders and once each week for seventh- and eighth-graders, each period being 30

Table D-2.   Typical Student Schedule
(For Fifth or Sixth Grade)

Time	Monday	Tuesday	Wednesday	Thursday	Friday
8:30 / 9:10	Reading	Reading	Reading	Reading	Reading
9:50	English	English	English	English	English
10:30	Soc. St.	Soc. St.	Soc. St.	Soc. St.	Soc. St.
10:40	Recess	Recess	Recess	Recess	Recess
11:20	Science	Science	Science	Science	Science
12:00	Math	Math	Math	Math	Math
1:00					
1:45	Phy. Ed.	Art	Phy. Ed.	I.D.I.*	Phy. Ed.
2:00					
2:15		Recess		Recess	Library*
2:30	Library*	Library*	Library*	I.D.I.*	
2:40					Expl.
3:00		Chorus			
3:30	Homeroom		Homeroom		

*During library and individually designed instruction periods special reading, language, weight training, band, and individual work with teachers will be specially scheduled for those students electing and needing this work.

Table D-3.   Typical Student Schedule
(For Seventh or Eighth Grader)

Time	Monday	Tuesday	Wednesday	Thursday	Friday
8:30 / 9:30	Math	Library*	Math	Art	English
10:00	Homeroom		I.D.I.*		I.D.I.*
11:00	Phy. Ed.	Soc. St.	Phy. Ed. / Band	Library*	Phy. Ed.
12:00	Soc. St.	Math. Apl.	Adv. Band		
1:00					
1:50	Health	Science	Science	Science	Math.
	English		English	Speech Seminar	Speed Reading
2:40					
3:30		English	Soc. St.	Soc. St.	Expl.

*During the library and I.D.I. periods special reading, language, band, and individual work with teachers will be specially scheduled for students electing and needing this work.

minutes long. Students are allowed to choose their own homeroom teacher, in most cases being able to get their first or second choice.

Approaches to Individualization

Grouping techniques for class sections and within the mathematics and reading classes have already been discussed and are used regularly. The individually designed instruction periods provide for additional work in areas of interest and need. Provision of considerable library time allows the student to work independently and prepares him for the high school independent study program. The exploration period provides many opportunities for the student to pursue areas of interest. Reporting of pupil progress is done on the basis of the student's capabilities. Small groups in several areas provide for more direct teacher-student contact. In some cases, the student has an opportunity to work with members of the community who are skilled in areas of his interest.

Plans for the Future

Aspen Middle School is progressing toward a nongraded organization with plans for team teaching to be incorporated to a greater degree than it is at present. Next year, more teaming will be used and the amount of unscheduled time (library) will be reduced somewhat. Seventh- and eighth-grade boys will have industrial arts, using high school facilities. There may be a change to the 6–8 organization in the future.

Summary: Distinguishing Characteristics

The organizational pattern of Aspen Middle School can best be described as a departmentalized instructional organization incorporated into a variable schedule with not all classes meeting daily and utilizing periods of varying length. Distinguishing characteristics are the individually designed instruction plan, the exploration period, a variable schedule, and the self-selected homeroom teacher.

ILLUSTRATIVE MIDDLE SCHOOL E[5]

Background

Skiles Junior High School, a middle school encompassing grades 6–8, is located in Evanston, Illinois, and is a unit of Cook County School Dis-

[5]Skiles Junior High School, 2424 Lake Street, Evanston, Ill. Based on a visit by Ronald P. Kealy on May 24, 1968, and interviews with Thomas A. Sinks, Principal, and staff members and students.

trict #65. The building, completed in 1958 with an addition completed in 1963, houses approximately 860 students who are served by 53 professional staff members. The school serves essentially two distinct populations, roughly 70 percent being predominantly upper middle class whites, and the remaining 30 percent being predominantly lower class Negroes. The community has generally high interest in the school's activities.

The sixth grade was added to the previous 7-8 organization in 1967 mainly to aid desegregation and to eliminate crowded conditions in other schools. Preparation for the change to the 6-8 organization was made the previous year by bimonthly staff study groups dealing primarily with integration and human relations. The change met slight resistance by parents who objected mainly to the bussing of their children over long distances and the breakup of the neighborhood schools.

Special positions in the school include one assistant principal and one full-time counselor. The school also employs five noncertified personnel: one full-time audiovisual operator, two clerical assistants to teachers, one clerical assistant for an experimental project, and one parent-helper in the science department.

There are three main feeder elementary schools for Skiles Junior High School, and it feeds mainly one high school, Evanston Township High School, as do the other three middle schools within the district. Articulation between the middle schools, the feeder elementary schools, and the high school is provided for through system-level subject area coordinators, a curriculum coordinator, various interschool workshops, occasional visitation in other schools by teachers, and orientation programs for the incoming fifth-graders and the outgoing eighth-graders.

Program of Studies

The program of studies for Skiles Junior High School is essentially the same for the sixth, seventh, and eighth grades. The basic subjects are social studies, language arts, mathematics, and science. The social studies and language arts are combined in a block called general studies. Other required subjects are physical education and health, allied arts, and a foreign language (Spanish, French, or German). Sixth-graders have library science for one module each week. The allied arts include four major areas: home arts, industrial arts, dramatics, and fine arts. Each pupil may choose two electives per semester from a wide selection including band, orchestra, glee club, Latin, physical education activities, meteorology, ceramics, astronomy, wood projects, and any of the subject areas in which he might wish to develop special interests. Table E-1 gives a breakdown of the amount of time per week allotted to each subject. Other curriculum opportunities include intramural and interschool athletics for boys, student government, student publications, recreational games, and school parties.

Table E-1.   Weekly Time Distribution

		Min/Week
Basic Subjects		1000
Social Studies		250
Language Arts		250
Mathematics		250
Science		250
Exemplars		615
Foreign Language		150
Allied Arts		180
Music		90
Physical Education and Health		195
Other		485
Electives		210
Lunch		150
Passing		125
	Total	2100

Instructional Organization and Arrangements

All subjects are taught on a departmentalized basis except language arts and social studies which meet as a block-of-time called "general studies." Class size ranges from 20 to 30 students per class. Pupils are assigned to class sections on a heterogeneous basis with the same group remaining together in most learning areas. Each class section is considered a homeroom and is scheduled with the block-of-time general studies each day with the homeroom teacher. Within the general studies block, students are grouped for reading instruction according to demonstrated achievement. Grouping on this same basis is done in the mathematics class. Some team teaching is done in a back-to-back science arrangement with multi-size groups being utilized. A large group room near the science area is used for this purpose.

A learning center with a full-time teacher in charge operates adjacent to the library. Students are cooperatively selected by the learning center director and the subject area teacher for directed independent study projects. These students are assigned to the learning center on a quarterly basis or until termination of their projects, being released from general studies or another subject area to work on their projects. The learning center contains various audiovisual materials and references, and the students may use the adjacent library. About 45 percent of the students have used the learning center this year and plans are being made for enlargement of both the facility and the program for next year.

Table E-2.   Typical Student Schedule*

Module	Monday	Tuesday	Wednesday	Thursday	Friday
1	All. Arts	All. Arts	All. Arts	Science	All. Arts
2	All. Arts	Phy. Ed.	All. Arts	Science	All. Arts
3	Gen. St.	Phy. Ed.	Gen. St.	Science	Science
4	Gen. St.	Math	Math	Math	Science
5	Math	Math	Math	Math	Math
6	Science	Gen. St.	Gen. St.	Gen. St.	Lunch
7	Science	Gen. St.	Gen. St.	Gen. St.	Phy. Ed.
8	Science	Gen. St.	Gen. St.	Gen. St.	Phy. Ed.
9	Lunch	Lunch	Lunch	Lunch	Gen. St.
10	F. Lang.	F. Lang.	F. Lang.	F. Lang.	F. Lang.
11	Gen. St.	Music	Music	Music	Gen. St.
12	Elect.	Elect.	Elect.	Elect.	Elect.

*Sixth-, seventh-, and eighth-graders have essentially the same type of schedule.

Modular scheduling is used, with 60 modules of 30 minutes each per week. The schedule varies from day to day during the week but the weekly schedule for each class section remains the same throughout the semester. Various combinations of modules are used to provide a school day divided into periods of differing length for separate subject areas. The first eleven modules of each day are used for the required subjects and lunch, while the last period of the day is used for electives. A typical student weekly schedule may be seen in Table E-2.

Pupil progress is reported each quarter by letter grades (A,B,C,D,E) in each of the subject areas and grades of O (outstanding), S (satisfactory), and U (unsatisfactory) in citizenship also in each of the subject areas. The homeroom teacher schedules one parent conference each year, and informal notes are sent to parents when necessary. A very small percentage (about .01 percent) of the students are retained, only after considerable investigation and consultation relating to such factors as achievement, ability, maturity, age, and attitude.

The homeroom teacher is the advisor of each student in the homeroom section and aids the student with problems or in adjusting to new situations. The full-time counselor works with individual students upon recommendation of homeroom teachers and in other referral cases and also administers the school standardized testing program.

Approaches to Individualization

Grouping techniques in reading, mathematics, and science already mentioned are utilized regularly. Also, the learning center program provides directed independent study for students with special needs and/or interests. The elective program provides a variety of areas for developing special interests of students.

An experiment in the effects of individualization of instruction has been in progress in Skiles Junior High School during the past year. One group of two seventh-grade sections is taking part in a planned program of individually prescribed instruction in the areas of language arts, social studies, mathematics, and science; while another group of two seventh-grade sections is covering the same subject matter in the usual fashion. The experimental group is using pretests of self-direction as an approach to individualization. A comparison of the achievement of these two groups will be reported by the principal.

Plans for the Future

A self-evaluation is planned for next year, using the North Central Association criteria, procedures, materials, and visiting team.

Summary: Distinguishing Characteristics

In summary, the organizational pattern of Skiles Junior High School can be described as a departmentalized instructional organization with a block-of-time plan for language arts and social studies, all incorporated into a modular schedule. Distinguishing characteristics of the program are the modular schedule, deliberate heterogeneous grouping, the allied arts program, the learning center, the elective offerings, and the experiment in individualizing instruction.

ILLUSTRATIVE MIDDLE SCHOOL F[6]

Background

Fox Lane Middle School is located on the Fox Lane Campus, near Bedford, New York, and is administered by the Bedford School District. The total enrollment of 974 students is served by 65 professional staff mem-

[6]Fox Lane Middle School, Bedford, N.Y. Based on a visit by Ronald P. Kealy and Wesley Blamick on June 5, 1968, and interviews with Peter Telfer, Principal, and staff members and students.

bers. The middle school campus, opened in September 1966, is adjacent to Fox Lane High School, and consists of three two-level buildings (academic houses) grouped around a three-story octagonal central facilities building. Nearby is a physical education building. The three academic houses are almost identical, all having divisible classrooms and large group instruction rooms, science laboratory-classrooms, sub-libraries, teacher planning centers, and large, all-purpose spaces with tables, carrels, and folding partitions. The central facilities building houses the administrative offices, health areas, the educational media center, a little theater, the central library, and the unified arts studio. The school has a schoolwide electronics system which allows either student or teacher to dial an audio or video program for immediate use. Throughout the school are 30 group viewing stations and 30 carrels for one or two students with monitors and earphones. Production and utilization are coordinated through the educational media center. Programs are available originating from video tape recorders, film chains, multiplex film strip and slide projectors, audio tape decks and live camera. UHF and VHF television and AM-FM radio are available directly off the air. About 15 percent of the programs are produced by the Bedford Staff.

The school serves the four small communities of Bedford, Bedford Hills, Pound Ridge, and Mt. Kisco. This combined population represents a wide range of socioeconomic levels, and, in general, has a high interest in the school program.

The reorganization of the previous 6-6 system took place in 1966. The reasons for the establishment of the 6-8 middle school were to provide a program specifically designed for children in this age group, to eliminate crowded conditions in other schools, to provide more specialization in grade six, to better bridge the elementary and the high schools, to try out various innovations, to use plans which have been successfully implemented in other schools, and to promote unification of the four communities served. Those involved in deciding on this reorganization were principals, teachers, system-level administration, the school board, parents and Educational Facilities Laboratory, Inc., which cooperated in organizing a two-day planning conference of distinguished representatives of the fields of teaching, psychology, architecture, industrial design, city planning, programmed learning, school administration, library science and teacher training. A second conference with four consultants and local staff members participating planned the school design. Other planning activities were occasional planning sessions of prospective middle school faculty members, visitation of schools with similar plans, inservice meetings with consultants, and a four-week summer faculty workshop attended by approximately 80 percent of the teachers, who focused on the study of nongradedness and team teaching. The community as a whole was receptive to the new organization, although some persons expressed opposition to the nontraditional program and to the expense of the new facility.

The teaching staff of Fox Lane Middle School reflects both elementary and secondary preparation. The school system was granted a five-year waiver of certification requirements for the middle school teachers, qualifying as an experimental program. The staffing of each academic house includes 14 teachers: three English, three social studies, three mathematics, three science, and two foreign language. For the entire school, there are five unified arts teachers, two librarians, and four physical education teachers. Special positions include a head teacher and a guidance counselor for each of the three academic houses, one department chairman (unified arts), and an audio visual specialist. There are 16 noncertified personnel employed regularly in the school, performing duties such as clerical assistance to teachers, assistance in the library, preparation of instructional materials, operation of audiovisual equipment, general aid to teachers. In addition, six parent volunteers are utilized as tutors in grade 6, and twelve parent volunteers are utilized in the library from time to time.

Fox Lane Middle School is fed by four elementary schools and in turn feeds one high school. Means of articulation between the schools in the system are joint curriculum planning activities, student data records, sharing of information pertaining to school programs, and orientation programs.

Program of Studies

Each pupil spends two-thirds of his day in his academic house. This time, split into two-hour blocks, is devoted to mathematics and science in one block, and English and social studies in the other. More specific scheduling is done by teachers within these time blocks. The remaining two-hour block of the pupil's time is almost entirely spent out of his academic house in either the central facilities building or the physical education building. It is devoted to music, unified arts, and physical education. Foreign language is also scheduled in this block, in the academic houses. A skills laboratory for individual help in problem areas is scheduled for those students who are not in the foreign language program. The unified arts program is organized to bring each student to an understanding of the interrelationship of design, technique, and materials. All students, boys and girls, work in an open studio containing equipment appropriate to work in textiles, ceramics, foods, wood, graphics, metal design, and crafts. The unified arts program is divided into three phases: the sixth-grade orientation phase, in which the student is introduced to each of the eight areas; the seventh-grade pre-independent phase, in which the student

Table F-1. Time per Week Scheduled for Each Subject Area

	6th Grade	7th Grade	8th Grade
	(Min)	(Min)	(Min)
English–Social Studies	600	450	450
Mathematics–Science	450	600	600
Physical Education*	188	188	188
Unified Arts*	113	113	113
Music*	113	113	113
Foreign Language*	188	188	188
Skills Lab†	188	188	188

*Time per week for these subject areas is an average since their schedule alternates from week to week.

†Taken by those students not in the foreign language program.

learns problem solving methods; and the eighth-grade independence phase, in which the student works as an independent researcher and learner on self-selected projects. Other curriculum opportunities are intramural athletics, limited interschool athletics (seventh- and eighth-graders), band, orchestra, chorus, student government, student publications, speech, dramatics, social dancing (eighth-graders), school parties, recreational sports and games, Coin Club, Library Club, and AV Club. A breakdown of the amount of time per week spent in each subject area may be seen in Table F-1.

Instructional Organization and Arrangements

Teachers are not administratively assigned to teams but are jointly responsible for a given group of students, usually 25–30 in each class group. The scheduling pattern permits either individual or shared teacher efforts in the disciplines which fall within their two-hour time block. It also permits, as the need arises, the flexible regrouping of students according to ability, achievement, interest, learning activity, or maturation. The unified arts program is planned and executed by a team of five teachers, one of whom is designated as a head teacher or team leader. Foreign language, music, and physical education are taught basically on a departmentalized basis. Deliberate heterogeneous grouping is used to assign students to each of the academic houses so that in each are students from all four communities, in all three grades, and of all abilities and attitudes. Within the academic houses, basic assignment of students to mathematics-science and English-social studies blocks is by grade level, and various grouping practices are utilized by teachers within these time blocks. Large group in-

Table F-2.   Typical Student Schedule

Module*	Monday	Tuesday	Wednesday	Thursday	Friday
	Homeroom	Homeroom	Homeroom	Homeroom	Homeroom
1	F. Lang.	Un. Arts	F. Lang.	Un. Arts	F. Lang.
2		Music		Music	
3	Phys. Ed.		Phys. Ed.		Phys. Ed.
4		F. Lang.		F. Lang.	
5	Math-Sci.	Math-Sci.	Math-Sci.	Math-Sci.	Math-Sci.
6					
7	Lunch	Lunch	Lunch	Lunch	Lunch
8	Math-Sci.	Math-Sci.	Math-Sci.	Math-Sci.	Math-Sci.
9					
10	English-Soc. St.	English-Soc. St.	English-Soc. St.	English-Soc. St.	English-Soc. St.
11					
12					

*Each module is 30 minutes in length. On alternating weeks, the module 1–4 schedule as it appears here for Monday-Wednesday-Friday would be in effect on Tuesday-Thursday; and, likewise, the Tuesday-Thursday schedule as it appears here would be in effect Monday-Wednesday-Friday.

struction (50–60 students) is used as the situation warrants in all subject areas and each academic house has a large group instruction room. Small group instruction (2–10 students) is also used in all areas for various types of classroom activities.

The schedule is variable with not all classes meeting daily and is based on a school day of 12 modules of 30 minutes each. As has been mentioned above, the student's day is divided into three blocks of time of two hours each, one for mathematics-science, one for English-social studies, and one for unified arts, music, physical education, and foreign language or skills laboratory. A 30-minute lunch period is taken from the mathematics-science block in grade six, and from the English-social studies block in grades seven and eight. A typical student schedule may be seen in Table F-2.

Responsibility for counseling students is assigned to the full-time counselor in each of the academic houses. Some counseling is done by the regular classroom teachers.

Pupil progress in subject areas is reported by percentage marks, except for the unified arts area which uses a satisfactory-unsatisfactory scale. Conduct and effort grades are also reported. Time for parent conferences is scheduled twice during the year, and mid-period notices are sent to parents if the teacher feels a need to communicate in this manner. Pupil progress from year to year through the middle school is determined by age, general achievement. achievement in separate subject fields, and teacher recommendation. Only a very small number of students are ever retained at a grade level for more than one year.

Approaches to Individualization

In all grades, some students are released part or all of the time from one or more regular classes for independent study. Also, groups of students may work together in some area of special interest as a seminar. Study carrels, for one or two students, are available in each academic house and in the central library for use in special assignments, independent study, and make-up work. As noted before, 30 of these carrels are equipped with dial-access information retrieval stations. The presence of a guidance counselor in each of the academic houses gives the student more of an opportunity for individual guidance than in a normal school situation. The academic house arrangement retains a small school atmosphere so that teachers have a greater opportunity to know each student and work with them as individuals. Much of the unified arts program operates on an individual project basis so that each student may use procedures appropriate to his individual interest and ability level.

Plans for the Future

Plans are being made for 1968–1969 for the use of interdisciplinary teams, with common planning time, who will present mathematics, science, English, and social studies to groups of students in seven module blocks of time. Eventually, a completely nongraded organization is hoped to be achieved. More extensive and varied use of the dial-access information retrieval system is also planned, with the possibility of coordination of the library, communications, and classroom activities by a curriculum specialist. Next year, there will be a revision of the method of reporting pupil progress, introducing a dual system which indicates the student's progress as compared with his own potential as well as with his group, and doing away with percentage marks. More parent conferences will be scheduled to complement this grading system.

Summary: Distinguishing Characteristics

Fox Lane Middle School can briefly be described as a 6–8 middle school organization in which students are divided, by deliberate heterogeneous grouping, into three academic houses, each being a 6–8 "little school" organization. Within the academic houses, students are taught mathematics-science and English-social studies in a pair of two-hour blocks of time, the other subject areas being taught in the remaining two-hour blocks with students from the other academic houses. Other distinguishing features are the facility itself, with the modern five-building campus, and the dial access communication system, the team-taught unified arts program, the skills laboratory, wide use of noncertified personnel, varied grouping procedures, independent study, and the modular schedule.

ILLUSTRATIVE MIDDLE SCHOOL G[7]

Background

Fair Haven Middle School, a unit of the New Haven City Schools, is located in the Fair Haven section of New Haven, Connecticut. This 5–8 middle school is housed in a large four-story structure and has a student enrollment of 914. A staff of 74 works in the school. The Fair Haven Middle School serves a community of people rich in ethnic backgrounds. First, second, and third generation Italians, Slavs, Poles, Puerto Ricans, and Irish comprise the majority of the population. About 24 percent of the population is Negro. About 78 percent of the people belong to the Catholic church. Semiskilled workers predominate in this lower-middle class community. Although the school is classified as inner city, the community of Fair Haven is somewhat isolated from New Haven proper by the Quinnepiac River. Many of the citizens of this island community prefer to be considered as residents of Fair Haven rather than as residents of the city of New Haven. Community support and cooperation have been effectively cultivated by the professional staff of the middle school. Foundation support and money for community schools have enabled school professionals to plan, develop and implement community-wide programs for youngsters and adults after school hours in the afternoon and evening. These programs emphasize leisure time and recreational activities. Satellite programs for young people and adults are also being established in

[7]Fair Haven Middle School, 164 Grand Avenue, New Haven, Conn. Based on a visit by Wesley Blamick and Ronald P. Kealy on June 6, 1968, and interviews with Charles Flynn, Principal, and staff members and students.

elementary feeder schools. Church groups as well as other community groups and organizations are encouraged to use school facilities and to participate in school programs. School-community relations are considered as very important determinants in planning, developing, and implementing the curriculum of the Fair Haven Middle School. An illustration of this concern for community problems is the language program which has been developed specifically for foreign-born students.

The Fair Haven Middle School had previously been organized as a 7-9 junior high school but in 1965 grade 9 was transferred to the high school and grade 6 was added to the middle school. In 1966, grade 5 was added to form the present 5-8 middle school. Although the Fair Haven Middle School is the only 5-8 school now in the district, the reorganization of this school is part of a systemwide program to implement the 4-4-4 organizations throughout the system. This type of organization permits students from neighborhood schools to attend school with students from other neighborhoods at an earlier age than would occur under a 6-3-3 organization. Stated purposes of the reorganization suggested that grade 9 would be better served in the senior high school and more specialization could be provided for grades 5 and 6 if these became a part of the middle school. Planners expect that the fifth- and sixth-graders in the reorganized schools will have greater opportunities for acceleration.

Preparation for reorganization involved visitations to an area middle school by the administrative staff. Community members were informed about the reorganization through systemwide and local school information dissemination. Reactions from involved personnel indicated a lack of well-organized advance planning. This lack of planning resulted in administrative and instructional problems. It was stated that much more should have been done and could have been done to integrate fifth-graders into the total middle school program. Reports indicate that fifth-graders have had much difficulty in adjusting to the program and facilities of the middle school. A cleavage in walking patterns in the halls between fifth-graders and other students was noted. Fifth-graders had difficulty in eating lunch in the allotted 20-minute period. Consequently, their lunch period was extended to 29 minutes. Elementary school personnel, however, were reported to be pleased to have the extra space made available by the movement of the fifth and sixth grades to the middle school. Generally, the reaction of the student body and staff to the reorganization was favorable while the reaction of the parents and public was considered enthusiastic.

Elementary teachers have been teaching in the fifth and sixth grades, while secondary teachers have been teaching in the seventh and eighth grades. The trend, however, seems to be toward the movement of more elementary teachers into the seventh and eighth grades. In addition to classroom teachers, the staff of the middle school includes a principal, two assistant principals, a guidance director, two full-time counselors and one part-time counselor. The efforts of teachers within each department are coordinated by a teacher-coordinator. Former students now attending college often come back to serve as substitutes in the school.

Eight elementary schools serve as feeder schools for the middle school and, in turn, the middle school acts as a feeder to two high schools. Articulation with the elementary schools is managed through the use of records of students and orientation programs conducted by the counselors. A film entitled "A Day at Fair Haven" is used to introduce the elementary students to the middle school. Department heads from the middle school visit informally with the elementary schools. Area supervisors coordinate the programs of the elementary schools, middle schools, and the high schools.

Program of Studies

Required subjects for all students in all grades include language arts, social studies, science, mathematics, physical education, art, and music. Boys take industrial arts and girls take home economics. Elective subjects include instrumental music and foreign language. The number of periods per week devoted to each of these subjects is shown in Table G-1.

Other curriculum opportunities include: intramural and interschool athletics for boys of all grades; band, chorus, student government, and student publications for all students in all grades; photography for grades 7 and 8; social dancing and recreational games for grade 8; and woodwork for boys in all grades. These opportunities are provided during convenient hours of the day or after school and in some cases become a part of the community school program.

Table G-1.   Number Periods per Week
Scheduled for Each Subject by Grades

| Subject | Periods per week | | | |
	Grade 5	Grade 6	Grade 7	Grade 8
Language Arts	5	5	5	5
Social Studies	5	5	5	5
Science	5	5	5	5
Mathematics	5	5	5	5
Physical Education	2	3	3	3
Art	1	1	2	2
Music	1	2	2	2
Industrial Arts	1	1	2	2
Home Economics	1	1	2	2
Instrumental Music	1	1	1	1

Instructional Organization and Arrangements

In grades 5 and 6, language arts, social studies, mathematics, and science instruction are taught by the same teacher in a self-contained classroom plan. Art, music, physical education, industrial arts, and home economics are taught departmentally. In grades 7 and 8, all subjects are departmentalized. Class size varies from 25 to 27 in all grades. Large group instruction is used in all grades for physical education. Remedial reading, art, and music may be taught in small groups in seventh and eighth grades. Language for foreign-born students is taught in small groups in all grades. Ability grouping is used in all grades. A special group for multi-problem students has been established in each grade. In fifth and sixth grades, seven daily periods vary in length depending on the needs of the students. In grades 7 and 8, there are six periods each 47 minutes in length. The schedule for all grades may vary from day to day during the week. Sample schedules are shown in Table G-2. Much of the counseling done in the fifth and sixth grades is done by the homeroom teacher with help on particular problems being given by counselors. In seventh and eighth grades, each student is interviewed by a counselor. Follow-up interviews are conducted when necessary. Students are invited to participate in the parent conferences which are held with the counselor. Pupil progress is reported by letter grades. Reports to parents also include

Table G-2.   Typical Student Schedules

| | | Boy—Grade 5 | | |
Periods	Monday	Tuesday	Wednesday	Thursday	Friday
1	Lang. Arts	Lang. Arts	Lang. Arts	Lang. Arts	Lang. Arts
2	Social St.	Social St.	Social St.	Social St.	Social St.
3	Science	Science	Science	Science	Science
4	Math	Math	Math	Math	Math
5	Elective	Phys. Ed.	Phys. Ed.	Elective	Ind. Arts
6	Art	Elective	Elective	Music	Elective

| | | Girl—Grade 8 | | |
Periods	Monday	Tuesday	Wednesday	Thursday	Friday
1	Social St.	Social St.	Math	Lang. Arts	Math
2	Lang. Arts	Lang. Arts	Lang. Arts	Social St.	Lang. Arts
3	Science	Math	Science	Science	Science
4	Home Ec.	Elective	Phys. Ed.	Phys. Ed.	Phys. Ed.
5	Math	Science	Elective	Math	Social St.
6	Elective	Home Ec.	Social St.	Music	Music

information concerning citizenship, work habits, attitudes, and effort of the student. Warning of failure slips are mailed to the parents before the close of each marking period. Referral files, indicating teacher referral of students to administrative offices, are kept on students.

Approaches to Individualization

Some students are given special tutorial work in languages or other subjects. In the fifth and sixth grades, the last period of the day is usually used for this purpose. Students with emotional and mental problems receive individual help. Opportunities are provided for able students to work for the school during and after regular school hours.

Plans for the Future

Plans for the future are contingent upon renovation of the school building including the completion of the auditorium renovation project and continued refurbishing of classroom facilities. Consideration has been given to making the sixth grade completely departmentalized.

Distinguishing Characteristics

Basically, the instructional organizational pattern of the fifth and sixth grades for major subjects is the self-contained classroom. The seventh and eighth grades are departmentalized. Homogeneous grouping according to ability and emphasis on academic progress are utilized. The community school concept has a great influence on the program of the school.

ILLUSTRATIVE MIDDLE SCHOOL H[8]

Background

Fort Couch Middle School is located in a residential suburb of Pittsburgh and is a unit of the Upper St. Clair School District. The total enrollment of 1107 students is served by 55 professional staff members in a school building that was originally designed for a K–9 program and more recently had housed grades 6–12 until the new high school was completed. The present 6–8 organization was initiated in 1962. The community is pre-

---

[8]Fort Couch Middle School, 515 Ft. Couch Road, Pittsburgh, Pa. Based on a visit by Ronald P. Kealy and Wesley Blamick on June 7, 1968, and interviews with Donald H. Eichhorn, Assistant Supervising Principal for the district; John Wasson, Principal; and staff members and students.

dominantly upper-middle class and is highly interested in school activities. Approximately 75 to 80 percent of the students go on to college.

Stated reasons for the establishment of the 6–8 middle school organization were mainly to provide more specialization in grade six, to provide a program specifically designed for students in this age group, and to serve the interest in a four-year high school. Other considerations were the opportunity to bridge better the elementary and the high schools, to try out various innovations, to remedy the weaknesses of the junior high school, and to use plans which have been successfully implemented in other school systems. Persons involved in deciding on this reorganization were the principal, system-level administration, and teachers, with the principal and the system-level administration being most influential. Preparation for the reorganization was in the form of three years of administration and faculty study and planning, visitation of schools with similar plans in operation, and inservice meetings of prospective faculty members with consultants on middle school development. Community reaction toward the reorganization was generally favorable although some parents had aversions to the elimination of interschool activities and removal of sixth graders from the self-contained classroom. The staff, in general, is enthusiastic about the new organization. The limitations of the facility are voiced as a problem.

Sixth-grade teachers usually have an elementary school background, while seventh- and eighth-grade teachers have mainly secondary backgrounds. Applications for available positions are numerous and hence the school can afford to be highly selective in appointments to these positions. Certification requirements are very flexible in Pennsylvania for the middle school since it is classified as an experimental program so this poses no problem in staff selection and utilization. Special positions are one assistant principal, one full-time counselor, and four department chairmen. There are no noncertified personnel regularly employed by the school.

Fort Couch Middle School is fed by three elementary schools and, in turn, feeds one high school. Articulation between these schools is provided by district workshops, limited interschool visitation, some sharing of faculty members, student data records, and orientation programs.

Program of Studies

Required subjects for grade 6 are language arts, social studies, mathematics-science, physical education, art, music. Students are selected for foreign language or enriched studies, a program of special help in language arts and mathematics-science. In seventh and eighth grade required subjects are language arts, social studies, science, mathematics, physical education, and music for a full year each and home economics (girls) or industrial arts (boys) for a half-year. Seventh-graders have a half-year of art and eighth-graders have a half-year of health. Seventh- and

Table H-1.   Amount of Time per Week Scheduled
for Various Subject Areas by Grades

Required	Grade 6	Grade 7	Grade 8
	(Min)	(Min)	(Min)
Language Arts	500	300	300
Social Studies	250	300	300
Science	200	160	160
Mathematics	200	250	250
Physical Education	100	100	100
Art	50	250 ($\frac{1}{2}$ yr.)	
Music	50	50	50
Home Economics (girls)		200 ($\frac{1}{2}$ yr.)	200 ($\frac{1}{2}$ yr.)
Industrial Arts		200 ($\frac{1}{2}$ yr.)	200 ($\frac{1}{2}$ yr.)
Reading	(In Lang. Arts)	100	100
Special Interests	120	120	120
Health			250 ($\frac{1}{2}$ yr.)
Homeroom	130	130	130
Others			
Foreign Language*	120	150	150
Enriched Studies	90	60	60
Study Hall	var.	var.	var.

*Students are selected for foreign language; some start in sixth grade, some start in seventh grade.

eighth-graders are selected for foreign language or enriched studies. Sixth-, seventh- and eighth-graders are involved in a "Special Interest Program." This program provides opportunities led by appropriate staff members for pupils interested in these activities: art, audiovisual, beginning chess, chess, Collectors Hobby Club, crafts for girls, current world affairs, dramatics, educational games, girls' games, golf, cooking, sewing, Junior Red Cross, library, marionettes, mathematics, reading for pleasure, school newspaper, knitting, boys' physical fitness, school service group, girls' activity training group, band, and chorus. Intramural athletics are also provided.

A breakdown of the amount of time per week for each subject area is shown in Table H-1.

Instructional Organization and Arrangements

The instructional organization at Fort Couch Middle School is mainly departmentalized with the exception of the mathematics-science block and the language arts block in the sixth grade. Back-to-back scheduling in some areas allows for team teaching situations as the need arises. Class size ranges from 19 to 36 in grade 6, an average of 28 in grade 7, and an average of 32 in grade 8. Students are grouped for required subjects by IQ tests, achievement tests, and teacher recommendations. For the homeroom, which meets for two periods each week as well as for a short period at the start of each day, students are grouped heterogeneously. Large group instruction is being used on an experimental basis in some social studies classes and small group instruction is used in the enriched skills program. Flexible grouping procedures are used within the classroom as the situation warrants.

The school operates on a modular schedule with 37 modules of 10 minutes each per day, plus a 40-minute period daily used for the special interest program and homeroom. The schedule is variable with not all classes meeting daily. Typical student schedules may be seen in Table H-2.

Table H-2.   Typical Student Schedule

Module	Monday	Tuesday	Wednesday	Thursday	Friday
	Homeroom	Homeroom	Homeroom	Homeroom	Homeroom
1					
2					
3			Science	Science	Science
4					
5					
6	Art	Art			Study Hall
7				Music	
8			Art		
9					
10					
11					
12				Soc. St.	Soc. St.
13	Reading	Reading	Soc. St.		
14					
15					
16					
17	Lang. Arts	Lang. Arts			
18					
19			Lang. Arts	Lang. Arts	Lang. Arts
20	Study Hall	Study Hall			
21					

Table H-2. Typical Student Schedule (Continued)

Module	Monday	Tuesday	Wednesday	Thursday	Friday
	Homeroom	Homeroom	Homeroom	Homeroom	Homeroom
22 23 24	Soc. St.	Soc. St.	Study Hall	Lunch	Lunch
25 26 27	Lunch	Lunch	Lunch	Enrich. St.	Enrich. St.
	Special Int.	Special Int.	Homeroom	Special Int.	Homeroom
28 29 30 31 32	Social Sci.	Science	Math	Math	Math
33 34 35 36 37	Math	Math	Phy. Ed.	Lang. Arts	Phy. Ed.

Teachers are given approximately 30–35 modules per week for planning and preparation.

Counseling is done by the homeroom teacher, regular classroom teachers, the full-time counselor, the principal, and the assistant principal. Homeroom meets for two 40-minute periods each week as well as for one 10-minute module at the beginning of each day. The full-time counselor works with teachers regarding methods of guidance, counsels students on an individual basis as the need arises, and administers the standardized testing program.

Pupil progress is reported each quarter on an A–E scale, and citizenship and effort are also reported at this time. Conferences with parents are scheduled by teachers as the need arises. Pupil progress from year to year through the middle school is determined by age, general achievement, achievement in separate subject fields, and socioemotional development. Very few students (less than 1 percent) are retained at a grade level for more than one year.

Approaches to Individualization

The Special Interest Program provides an opportunity for students to meet in the activity of their interest for three periods each week. These groups are sponsored by staff members qualified and interested in leading in some worthwhile activity. (See list in "Program of Studies" above.) Other approaches to individualization are the grouping procedures already described and the enriched studies program.

Plans for the Future

An extensive remodeling of the school facility will begin next year, the result of which will increase opportunities to incorporate more flexible scheduling and grouping procedures. Another middle school is scheduled to open in the area in September of 1969. More extensive use of team teaching is proposed for next year.

Summary: Distinguishing Characteristics

Fort Couch Middle School can briefly be described as a basically departmentalized 6–8 middle school organization incorporating a variable, modular schedule. A language arts core and a mathematics core in grade 6 is the only exception to this departmentalized instructional pattern. Other distinguishing characteristics are the special interests program and the enriched studies program.

Illustrative Materials from Middle Schools

MODERN SCHEDULING FOR MODERN SCHOOLS*

"What subject do you have during the twelfth period? If you overhear your child asking this question of a friend, please don't assume that the Middle School has extended the day till past your dinner time. For when school opens September 8, the Middle School will introduce a new concept in scheduling—a modular schedule which features twelve periods, each twenty-five minutes in length, and a schedule which changes daily."

This was the way we introduced our new schedule to our parents and pupils last summer in the district newsletter. Naturally, many questions were raised: What is a module? How can you accomplish anything in twenty-five minutes? Won't the children be confused with a different schedule each day? How will teachers organize their day with classes meeting at different times and for different durations? Won't there be chaos with Middle School youngsters wandering around the school every twenty-five minutes? How will you, the Principal, know where children are located? What's wrong with the old seven period day? Well, here it is spring and we have survived; and, more important, we have created a schedule which contributes to our pupils' education.

The key to a quality school is certainly not the schedule alone, yet it can, and does, facilitate learning. Here in Pearl River, as throughout the nation, we are attempting to upgrade our educational program: we are convinced that we can do a better job. At a faculty meeting last year, our whole philosophy of education was questioned. Various issues were debated and ultimately someone asked: "How can we make better use of our staff and pupil time?" We asked ourselves if there was any reason why all subjects should be taught for equal lengths of time? Was there any evidence to support our current scheduling practices? Are there certain times of the day that are more productive? Evidence seems to indicate that both children and adults are more alert at the beginning of the day and become restless towards the lunch hour and at the end of the day. If this is so, what happens to the pupil who has math during the last period of the day? Science just before lunch? Someone said, "But somebody has to be scheduled during these times," and then, the question—why?

Once this magic word "why" has been uttered, we were on our way. We decided to find the answers to our questions. Of course, our search led to more questions. Finally, after many weeks of investigation and study, we decided that we would construct a more realistic schedule—a flexible schedule based on the principle of modules of time. Our teachers were asked to tell us exactly how much time they wanted for their subject.

---

*From duplicated material provided the authors by Raymond J. Gerson, Principal (Pearl River Middle School, Pearl River, New York, March 24, 1966).

Did they want to meet their classes daily? Did they want certain classes to be longer than others? Should bright children and slower learning children receive identical allotments of time? Answers to the above questions determined the schedule, not some preconceived notion that all pupils should have the same program.

After seven months of operating under a modular schedule, we can identify many distinct advantages. The entire atmosphere of the school has changed, simply because everyone realizes that we all are involved in a significant innovation. Science teachers are now able to plan for more meaningful experiments: they are not concerned about the bell interrupting their class. The same advantage holds true for the industrial arts and art teachers: they don't have to waste valuable time setting up and putting things away seven times a day. The home economics teacher reports that time is now available to demonstrate a new operation on the sewing machine and ascertain that her girls have sufficient time to practice and master the newly learned skill. Gym classes are more effective since enough time is allotted for changing clothes, showering, and participating in a full, meaningful program. Academic teachers, incidentally, note that pupils coming from physical education classes are far more punctual than in the past. Staff members report that they are now able to accomplish much more with their pupils because on certain days, at least, they don't have to be concerned that a bell will interrupt the lesson. Teachers have been able to schedule field trips and invite outside speakers without disturbing other classes. Our corridors are less congested since only a part of the school moves at any given time. We have increased instructional time since our pupils actually average only four moves a day and we have reduced the passing time because the halls are not crowded. Teachers and children are most pleased with the opportunity of meeting each other in "prime" time; no one has the same class at the end of the day. A recent survey indicated that the vast majority of our pupils prefer the modular schedule to the traditional schedule. They reported that their day was more interesting because each day was so different. When asked to react to the new schedule, our faculty overwhelmingly supported the change and only one teacher recommended a return to the traditional schedule.

Naturally, there must be some problems; if the modular schedule is such a good idea, we should have had flexible scheduling a long time ago. Well, we haven't found the problems where one would expect to find them—although we have discovered some new areas to study. We find, for example, that a bell ringing every twenty-five minutes does not interfere with the learning process. Pupils know, instinctively, when the bell is for them. At other times, the signal is ignored. Pupils are not confused with a different schedule each day, nor for that matter are teachers. The largest problem, and probably the one hindering most schools from constructing the schedule, in developing the master program is not significant—it just takes much more time. But, it is time well invested. The foremost problem is the teacher use of the new schedule. It takes time for teachers to orient themselves and to plan for different kinds of activities, for different blocks of time. Only through experience will a faculty learn the "ideal" number of modules to accomplish their goals.

We have discovered much about learning these past months. Already, work is going on to evaluate our program and plan for next year. In all probability we will increase the number of modules and shorten their length. Why? Because, by following this proposal, we will be able to offer more flexibility—we will be able to offer more time to teachers when they want the time. A flexible modular schedule, we are convinced, allows a school to govern itself by the needs of the curriculum and the pupils, rather than by the artificial demands of seven or eight look-alike periods.

TEACHING TEAM*

Four academic teachers are assigned 100 students. Each team has a block of time composed of 168 minutes. The teachers decide how this block of time will best be utilized to serve the individual student.

The following diagram shows only a few of the possible flexible arrangements:

Various Possible Team Schedules

Time Block	Mon	Tues	Wed	Thurs	Fri
42 min	English	English	Math	Math	English
42 min	Math	English	Soc. St.	English	Math
42 min	Soc. St.	Math	Soc. St.	Science	Soc. St.
42 min	Science	Soc. St.	Science	Science	Science

Teachers planning together enables each to better see the total picture. Associative teaching and a better understanding of each child are easier to accomplish.

A guidance counselor, librarian, reading consultant, and nurse are assigned to meet with each teaching team, on a regular basis during the team planning period.

*From duplicated materials provided the authors by South Ocean Avenue Junior High School (Patchogue, New York, undated).

THE LEARNING CENTER*

The heart of Barrington Middle School is the 7000 square foot Learning Center, the hub of self-initiated student learning activities. Located near the building's center, this area serves as a ready access library and research and study facility for all students. A teacher who knows the children is always available to answer questions and give meaningful help. Because of its location, students pass through and by it when enroute from one wing to another. It was purposely designed without barriers and doors so it appears open and inviting to the students. Each student spends some time each week working in this area, and by using it often, the children develop a natural sense of responsibility for their own learning process. Also available in the Learning Center are a listening center, visual equipment areas, a project center, a meditation area and individual study carrels.

Planetarium and Other Areas

An open stage, for theatrical and special projects and student presentations, inter-connects the Learning Center with the Activity Center. This activity area serves as an assembly room, a lunchroom, a theatre, a study area and can be used for group seminars, special projects and student displays. The Activity Center is a further expression of the intent for students to be actively and personally engaged in their daily learning.

The Nova Planetarium is integrated with the over-all science program, and is in keeping with space-age developments. This facility is available to all students in the Barrington School Districts.

ORGANIZATIONAL PLAN FOR A LARGE SCHOOL†

While certain phases of the educational program need to be centralized, others clearly need to be decentralized. A single administrator is clearly responsible for the centralized needs of staff, budget, curriculum, and school-wide pupil services.

Certain other needs require decentralization. Guidance-oriented pupil service and individualized needs of all kinds are of this nature. An organization which sees the pupil in smaller groups can best serve this purpose.

*From *Barrington Middle School: A Report 1966* (Barrington Public Schools, Barrington, Illinois: 1966).

†From "Considerations For a 6-7-8 Junior High School," duplicated material provided the authors by John P. Lovetere, Principal (Old Orchard Junior High School, Skokie, Illinois, March 10, 1967).

Sub-administrative units based on some logical division and grouping offer one avenue.

These units should include all three grade levels, be essentially self-sufficient regarding staff and services, should retain the student through his three years, have their own administrator, and be large enough to be a viable grouping population.

A "house-plan" meets all these requirements and more if the instructional team concept is incorporated. Each house would be made of 3 teams, one at each grade level. The size of these teams vary from 150–180 and therefore the size of the house from 450–540 (the size of the school from 1350–1620). These figures cover the range of the population presently in grades 6–7–8 (1340) to the number which can be expected in the foreseeable years. Students from the four K–5 schools would be randomly assigned to each house.

Each house would be headed by an assistant principal responsible for the overall administration of his house and for coordinating the guidance and instructional needs of that house. The three ITCs in each house would continue to attend to duties ITCs presently handle.

Clearly then, the organizational structure can meet certain of criteria referred to earlier.

Ungradedness, variable group sizes and increasing self-responsibility for learning as well as responsive homogeneous grouping can be met by overlaying the instructional teams with a team teaching setup. The team teaching overlay might be met by subdividing each instructional team within the house into two groups of 75 to 90 students. This would give each house six groups of 75 to 90 students—2 at the sixth-grade level, 2 at the seventh and 2 at the eighth-grade level. These groups would be heterogeneous and could be programed as units into a modular schedule. Each unit would be team taught by the three appropriate subject matter teachers in the house. For example, a sixth-grade group would be taught by all three Math teachers, with one of the Math teachers serving as instructional leader for the group. The three teachers would have the other five groups for math too. Students could be regrouped daily in each subject during their three (or so) -year stay. These three teachers would best know each student's math capability and performance and best meet his needs by constantly regrouping. They would also know best whether he should spend two or four years in the junior high school, rather than three.

To recap the organizational structure, from the viewpoint of where the student fits, each student would be part of an instructional team varying from 150 to 180 students. Each house would be comprised of three such instructional teams, one at each grade level. The school would be made up of three houses.

GUIDANCE: STUDENT ORIENTATION*

Meeting Needs

Guidance in the middle school is concerned with meeting the personal, social, emotional and educational needs of children of varied maturity levels. Its purpose is to help each child make a satisfactory adjustment to life, both in school and out. This service is provided for all children, not only for those who have behavior problems, learning difficulties and deep-seated emotional disturbances. Normal well-adjusted children also need to be guided in their thinking, their attitudes and their personality development. All children are often in need of special help in gaining social approval and in finding suitable outlets for their interests.

Differences

Because of the diversity of the middle school with students in different rates of maturation, both within and between youngsters, the program must be flexible and devote much attention to the individual differences among its students. Therefore, the guidance program must focus on each child in relation to his total experience, helping him develop realistic goals based on the best possible understanding of himself, the world, and the tremendous changes taking place in both.

Thus, the purpose of guidance at the middle school level is focused on assisting pupils to integrate such primary group forces as the home, the school, the church, and peer relationships. These are the forces which form the basis for the pupil's adolescent and later years. The aim of guidance, then, is to blend those forces into a harmonious whole.

Personnel

The school's guidance team should consist of the principal, nurse, social worker, guidance specialists and classroom teachers. Team work and cooperation is necessary for an effective and efficient guidance program.

Key Person

The key person in the middle school guidance program is the classroom teacher. Because of the close daily contact with the children, he has an

*From *Model Middle School: Involvement by Design* (Rockland, Me.: Maine School Administrative District No. 5, 1967).

excellent opportunity to know each child well and to observe children closely, and being familiar with their usual appearance and knowing their normal reactions and responses in various situations, he is able to recognize any deviation from the normal. He can thus watch all indications of growth or failure to grow socially, mentally and physically. Add to this our goal of teacher cooperation and we multiply the effectiveness of the teacher's part.

Even though classroom teachers do much individual counseling, a fulltime counselor is essential to an adequate guidance program. The counselor coordinates and provides leadership for the guidance activities of the entire school. The counselor must be aware of the total educational program, helping to bring more complete understanding between the whole staff in relation to each child and himself.

Orientation

An explanation of the total guidance program and printed material on its various services will be given to students as they enter the program. Parents will be visited whenever necessary and possible in order to promote understanding of the educational system and guidance services for all students. Grade warnings will clear through the guidance office. Notes may be added or other appropriate action taken.

Individual Counseling

Counseling will be carried on with individuals whenever necessary in an effort to enable them to gain the self-understanding and confidence in themselves so that they may be able to cope effectively with their personal problems. Individual counseling will also attempt to guide him in vocational and educational planning, as well as toward better social relationships with people around him. Pupils will be free to visit the guidance office whenever they desire to talk with the counselor about an individual problem since immediacy of action is important to this age level.

TWO-PHASE SCHEDULING*

Our scheduling for students is carried on in two separate phases. We believe that teachers and students should have an important part in the

*From duplicated material provided the authors by Jack D. Riegle, Principal (Chippewa Middle School, Saginaw, Michigan, undated).

planning of the schedule. Schedules that are completed and rigidly organized within the confines of the administrator's office are usually lacking essential elements that only the people who put the schedule into operation can add.

After all curricular studies have been reported the first phase of the scheduling begins. The scheduling team (in our case the principal, assistant principal and two teachers) schedules all classes that meet in specialized or limited facilities. Then students are scheduled into classes in groups and assigned to teams of teachers. Each student has a teacher or a room that he reports to at the beginning of the school term. The teachers and students then work together to plan a meaningful schedule.

An example of this second phase of the scheduling would perhaps clarify the role of teacher and student in scheduling.

John has been assigned in phase one to Language Arts–Social Studies–Core in room 112 with Mr. Pitts. John reports to this room and begins the school term. He will have 135 minutes of time in this block and Mr. Pitts will work with the speech teacher to schedule John into Speech II, which he elected to study. After a few days John expresses an interest in a study project concerning Ponce De Leon. Other students in other sections of the group of approximately 100 students have expressed a similar interest. The teaching team then plans for this group to meet as a committee and thereby meets the individual interests of a group of students.

This example could be used in Unified Arts, Science, or other subject areas. The reason for grouping could be need as well as interest. Ability is often used as a means of grouping for a lesson. The basic group of 100 students is heterogeneous.

No administrator could possibly schedule his school to meet this type of need on an ever changing basis. No computer or so called flexible schedule can meet the test of flexibility and human involvement that this type of two phase scheduling has met.

The important caution for people doing phase one scheduling is: *Don't over schedule.* Keep as much flexibility in your teaching team, time block, subject groupings, etc. as possible. An important caution for people involved in phase two would be: *Don't get stereotyped.* Always involve as many people as practical and use as wide a range of techniques as possible.

Two phase scheduling puts the priority on the human element of our school. Schools are people and our interest should always be in people and what we are doing to them and for them.

BIBLIOGRAPHY

RATIONALE AND STATUS

Alexander, William M. "The New School in the Middle," *Phi Delta Kappan*, 50:355–357 (February 1969).

Alexander, William M. "What Educational Plan for the In-Between-Ager?" *NEA Journal*, 55:30–32 (March 1966).

American Association of School Administrators and Research Division, National Education Association, "Middle Schools," *Educational Research Service Circular*, No. 3 (May 1965).

Berman, Sidney. "As a Psychiatrist Sees Pressure on Middle Class Teenagers," *NEA Journal*, 54:17–24 (February 1965).

Blackburn, Jack. "An Unfinished Dream: The Junior High School," *High School Journal*, 49:209–212 (February 1966).

Boutwell, W. D. "What's Happening in Education? What Are Middle Schools?" *P.T.A. Magazine*, 60:14 (December 1965).

Brod, Pearl. "Middle School: Trends toward Adoption," *Clearing House*, 40:331–333 (February 1966).

Buell, Clayton E. "What Grades in the Junior High School?" *Bulletin of the National Association of Secondary-School Principals*, 46:14–22 (February 1962).

Coleman, James S. "Social Change: Impact on the Adolescent," *Bulletin of the National Association of Secondary-School Principals*, 49:11–14 (April 1965).

Committee on Junior High School Education. "Recommended Grades in Junior High or Middle Schools," *Bulletin of the National Association of Secondary-School Principals*, 51:68–70 (February 1967).

Compton, Mary F. "The Middle School: Alternative to the Status Quo," *Theory into Practice*, 7:108–110 (June 1968).

Cuff, William A. "Middle Schools on the March," *Bulletin of the National Association of Secondary-School Principals*, 51:82–86 (February 1967).

Curtis, Thomas E. "Administrators View the Middle School," *High Points*, 48:30–35 (March 1966).

Curtis, Thomas E. "Crucial Times for the Junior High School," *New York State Education*, 53:14–15 (February 1966).

Educational Facilities Laboratories. "Middle School: A Report of Two Conferences in Mt. Kisco on the Definition of Its Purpose, Its Spirit, and Its Shape," New York: Educational Facilities Laboratories, 1962.

Eichhorn, Donald H. *The Middle School*. New York: The Center for Applied Research in Education, 1966.

Friedenberg, Edgar Z. *The Vanishing Adolescent*. Boston: The Beacon Press, Inc., 1959.

Grooms, M. Ann. "The Middle School and Other Innovations," *Bulletin of the National Association of Secondary-School Principals*, 51:158–160, 162, 164, 166 (May 1967).

Grooms, M. Ann. *Perspectives on the Middle School*. Columbus, Ohio: Charles E. Merrill Books, Inc., 1967.

238 BIBLIOGRAPHY

Havighurst, Robert J. "The Middle School Child in Contemporary Society," *Theory into Practice*, 7:120–122 (June 1968).

Howard, A. W. "Which Years in Junior High?" *Clearing House*, 33:405–408 (March 1959).

Hull, J. H. "Are Junior High Schools the Answer?" *Educational Leadership*, 23:213–216 (December 1965).

Hull, J. H. "The Junior High School Is a Poor Investment," *Nation's Schools*, 65: 78–81 (April 1960).

Johnson, Mauritz. "School in the Middle—Junior High: Education's Problem Child," *Saturday Review*, 45:40–42, 56 (July 21, 1962).

Lerer, Lawrence. "A Critical Analysis of the Concepts and Patterns of Middle School Organization," Unpublished doctoral qualifying paper, Harvard Graduate School of Education, May 1966.

Lounsbury, John H. and Harl R. Douglass. "Recent Trends in Junior High School Practices 1954–64," *Bulletin of the National Association of Secondary-School Principals*, 49:87–98 (April 1965).

Lounsbury, John H. and Jean Marani. *The Junior High School We Saw: One Day in the Eighth Grade.* Washington, D.C.: Association for Supervision and Curriculum Development, 1964.

Madon, Constant A. "The Middle School: Its Philosophy and Purpose," *The Clearing House*, 40:329–330 (February 1966).

Mead, Margaret. "Early Adolescence in the United States," *Bulletin of the National Association of Secondary-School Principals*, 49:5–10 (April 1965).

"Middle School for Tomorrow, Successor to the Junior High School," *School Management*, 4:101–103, 105, 107 (November 1960).

Mills, George E. "How and Why of the Middle School," *Nation's Schools*, 68:43–53, 72, 74 (December 1961).

Mills, George E. *The Middle School.* Ann Arbor: Michigan Association of School Boards, undated.

Nickerson, Neal C. *Junior High Schools Are on the Way Out.* Danville, Ill.: The Interstate Printers and Publishers, 1966.

Powell, Richard H. and E. Wayne Roberson. "The Junior High 'School World': A Shadow Study," *Bulletin of the National Association of Secondary-School Principals*, 51:77–81 (February 1967).

Pumerantz, Philip. "Relevance of Change: Imperatives in the Junior High School and Middle School Dialogue," *Clearing House*, 43:209–212 (December 1968).

Riessman, Frank. "Low Income Culture, the Adolescent, and the School," *Bulletin of the National Association of Secondary-School Principals*, 49:45–49 (April 1965)

Sanders, Stanley G. "Challenge of the Middle School," 32:191–197 (January 1968).

Skogberg, Alfred H. and Mauritz Johnson, Jr. "The Magic Numbers of 7, 8, 9: Is This Structure Really the Best for Junior High Schools?" *NEA Journal*, 52:50–51 (March 1963).

"The Schools in Between," *Education USA*, April 17, 1967.

Treacy, J. P. "What Is the Middle School?" *Catholic School Journal*, 68:56–58 (April 1968).

Trump, J. Lloyd. "Junior High Versus Middle School," *Bulletin of the National Association of Secondary-School Principals*, 51:71–73 (February 1967).

Vars, Gordon F. "Change and the Junior High School," *Educational Leadership*, 23:187–189 (December 1965).

Vars, Gordon F. (ed.). *Guidelines for Junior High and Middle School Education*. Washington, D.C.: National Association of Secondary-School Principals, 1966.

Wattenburg, William W. "The Junior High School—A Psychologist's View," *Bulletin of the National Association of Secondary-School Principals*, 49:34–44 (April 1965).

Williams, Emmett L. "The Middle School Movement," *Today's Education*, 57:41–42 (December 1968).

Woodring, Paul. "The New Intermediate School," *Saturday Review*, 48:77–78 (October 16, 1965).

Wright, Grace and Edith Greer. *The Junior High School: A Survey of Grades 7-8-9 in Junior and Junior-Senior High Schools, 1959–60* (Bulletin 1963, No. 32, United States Office of Education). Washington, D.C.: Government Printing Office, 1963.

Wright, Grace and Edith Greer. "Survey of the Junior High School Curriculum," *Education Digest*, 43–45 (December 1963).

Zdanowicz, Paul J. "A Study of the Changes That Have Taken Place in the Junior High Schools of Northeastern United States during the Last Decade and the Reasons for Some of the Changes," Unpublished doctoral dissertation, Temple University, June 1965.

RESEARCH—NATURE OF THE LEARNER

Bayer, S. M. and Nancy Bayley. *Growth Diagnosis*. Chicago: University of Chicago Press, 1959.

Bayley, Nancy. "Individual Patterns of Development," *Child Development*, 27:45–74 (March 1956).

Dacus, Wilfred P. "A Study of the Grade Organizational Structure of the Junior High School as Measured by Social Maturity, Emotional Maturity, Physical Maturity, and Opposite-Sex Choices." *Dissertation Abstracts*, 24:1461–1462, University of Houston, 1963.

Flavell, John. *The Developmental Psychology of Jean Piaget*. Part II. Princeton, N.J.: D. Van Nostrand Company, Inc., 1963.

Gesell, Arnold, Frances L. Ilg, and Louise B. Ames. *Youth: The Years From Ten to Sixteen*. New York: Harper & Row, Publishers, 1956.

Harvey, O. J. and Jeanne M. Rutherford. "Status in the Informal Group: Influence and Influencibility at Different Age Levels," *Child Development*, 31:377–385 (June 1960).

Inhelder, Barbel and Jean Piaget. *Growth of Logical Thinking from Childhood to Adolescence*. New York: Basic Books, Inc., 1958.

Kagan, Jerome and Howard A. Moss. *Birth to Maturity: A Study in Psychological Development.* New York: John Wiley & Sons, Inc., 1962.

Kagan, Jerome and Howard A. Moss. "The Stability of Passive and Dependent Behavior from Childhood through Adulthood," *Child Development,* 31:577–591 (September 1960).

Laurendeau, Monique and Adrien Pinard. *Causal Thinking in the Child: A Genetic and Experimental Approach.* New York: International Universities Press, Inc., 1962.

Lynn, David. "Sex-Role and Parental Identification," *Child Development,* 33:555–564 (September 1962).

Meredith, H. "Changes in Stature and Body Weight in North American Boys during the Last 80 Years," in L. P. Lipsitt and C. C. Spiker (eds.), *Advances in Child Development and Behavior.* New York: Academic Press, Inc., 1963.

Schaefer, Earl S. and Nancy Bayley. "Consistency of Maternal Behavior from Infancy to Preadolescence," *Journal of Abnormal and Social Psychology,* 61:1–6 (July 1960).

Sutton-Smith, B., B. G. Bosenberg, and E. F. Morgan. "Development of Sex Differences in Play Choices during Preadolescence," *Child Development,* 34:119–126 (November 1963).

Tanner, James M. *Education and Physical Growth.* London: University of London Press, 1961.

Tanner, James M. *Growth at Adolescence.* Oxford: Basil Blackwell & Mott, Ltd., 1962.

Yamoto, Kaoru, Elizabeth C. Thomas, and Edward A. Karns. "School-Related Attitudes in Middle-School Age Students," *American Educational Research Journal,* 6:191–206 (March 1969).

Zander, Alvin F. and Elmer E. Van Egmond. "Relationship of Intelligence and Social Power to the Interpersonal Behavior of Children," *Journal of Educational Psychology,* 49:257–268 (October 1958).

RESEARCH—ORGANIZATIONAL PLANS FOR IN-BETWEEN-AGERS

Arvin, Charles L. "An Experimental Study of Programed Instruction in Multiplication of Fractions." Unpublished doctoral dissertation, Colorado State College, 1965.

Baum, E. A. "Report of the Individualization of the Teaching of Selected Science Skills and Knowledges in an Elementary School Classroom with Materials Prepared by the Teacher." *Dissertation Abstracts,* 26:898, Columbia University, 1965.

Broadhead, Fred C. "Pupil-Adjustment in the Semi-Departmental Elementary School," *Elementary School Journal,* 60:385–390 (April 1960).

Chapel, D. E. "The Relationship of a Programed Study Skills Unit to the Academic Achievement of a Selected Group of Eighth-Grade Students." *Dissertation Abstracts,* 26:3694, North Texas State University, 1965.

Gibb, E. Glenadine and Dorothy C. Matala. "Study on the Use of Special Teachers of Science and Mathematics in Grades 5 and 6," *School Science and Mathematics,* 62:565–585 (November 1962).

Goodlad, John I. "Experiment in Team Teaching," *Elementary School Journal,* 59:11-13 (October 1958).

Goodlad, John I. and Robert H. Anderson. *The Non-graded Elementary School* New York: Harcourt, Brace & World, Inc., 1963.

Harrison, J. E. "Achievement of Selected Types of Educational Objectives through Use of Programed Materials and the Relationship between This Achievement and Selected Aptitudes for Learning." *Dissertation Abstracts,* 26:159, University of Pittsburgh, 1964.

Howard, Arthur Eugene. "The Personal and Social Characteristics of Normal American Preadolescents as Revealed in Research Completed Since 1950." *Dissertation Abstracts,* 25:4477-78, North Texas State University, 1965.

Livingston, A. H. "Does a Departmental Organization Affect Children's Adjustment?" *Elementary School Journal,* 61:217-220 (January 1961).

Mann, Maxine. "What Does Ability Grouping Do to the Self-Concept?" *Childhood Education,* 36:357-360 (April 1960).

Morgenstern, Anne. "A Comparison of the Effects of Heterogeneous and Homogeneous (Ability) Grouping on the Academic Achievement and Personal-Social Adjustment of Selected Sixth-Grade Children." *Dissertation Abstracts,* 24:1054, New York University, 1963.

Sweet, R. and Peter Dunn-Rankin. "An Experiment in Team Teaching Seventh Grade Arithmetic," *School Science and Mathematics,* 62:341-344 (May 1962).

CURRICULUM AND INSTRUCTION

Alexander, William M. and Emmett L. Williams. "Schools for the Middle School Years," *Educational Leadership,* 23:217-223 (December 1965).

Anderson, Robert H. "Team Teaching in Action," *Nation's Schools,* 65:62-65 (May 1960).

Anderson, Robert H. "Team Teaching in the Elementary School," *Education Digest,* 25:26-28 (November 1959).

Association for Supervision and Curriculum Development. *Developing Programs for Young Adolescents.* Washington, D.C.: The Association, 1954.

Association for Supervision and Curriculum Development. *The Elementary School We Need.* Washington, D.C.: The Association, 1965.

Association for Supervision and Curriculum Development. *The Junior High School We Need.* Washington, D.C.: The Association, 1961.

Association for Supervision and Curriculum Development. *The New Elementary School.* Washington, D.C.: The Association, 1968.

Atkins, Neil P. "Rethinking Education in the Middle," *Theory into Practice,* 7:118-119 (June 1968).

Bahner, John M. "In Grades Four through Six," in *Reading Instruction in Various Patterns of Grouping.* Proceedings of the Annual Conference on Reading. Chicago: University of Chicago Press, 1959.

Bradley, Phillip. "Individualized Instruction through Cooperative Teaching and a Programed Text," *National Elementary Principal,* 43:46-49 (May 1964).

Bruntz, George G. "Team Approach to Social Science Teaching," *High School Journal,* 43:337-374 (April 1960).

Butterweck, Joseph S. "Teachers on a Team," *Pennsylvania School Journal,* 106:57 (October 1957).

Dunlap, J. M. "Gifted Children in an Enriched Program," *Exceptional Children,* 21:135–137 (January 1955).

Durrell, D. D. "Implementing and Evaluating Pupil-Team Learning Plans," *Journal of Educational Sociology,* 34:360–365 (April 1961).

Eichorn, Donald H. "Middle School Organization: A New Dimension," *Theory into Practice,* 7:111–113 (June 1968).

Empey, Donald W. "Students Self-Direction, Flexible Scheduling, and Team Teaching," *Bulletin of the National Association of Secondary-School Principals,* 47:118–124 (February 1963).

Flanders, Ned A. "Teacher and Classroom Influences on Individual Learning," in A. Harry Passow (ed.), *Nurturing Individual Potential.* Washington, D. C.: Association for Supervision and Curriculum Development, 1964.

Fogg, Walter F. and Hugh Diamond. "Two Versions of the 'House' Plan," *Nation's Schools,* 67:65–69, 94 (June 1961).

Gallagher, James D. "Research on Enhancing Productive Thinking," in A. Harry Passow (ed.), *Nurturing Individual Potential.* Washington, D.C.: Association for Supervision and Curriculum Development, 1964.

Gambold, Willard J. "Modern Teacher and New Media of Instruction," *Education,* 83:67–70 (October 1962).

Grambs, Jean and others. "Junior High School of the Future," *Education Digest,* 27:15–18 (September 1961).

Green, D. R. and Hazel W. Riley. "Interclass Grouping for Reading Instruction in the Middle Grades," *Journal of Experimental Education,* 31:273–278 (March 1963).

Hines, Vynce A. and William M. Alexander. "Evaluating the New Middle School," *National Elementary Principal,* 48:32–36 (February 1969).

Hooper, Ned E. "Training Process for Team Teaching," *Journal of Teacher Education,* 14:177–178 (June 1963).

Howard, Eugene R. and Robert W. Bardwell. *How to Organize a Non-Graded School.* Englewood Cliffs, N.J.: Prentice-Hall, Inc., 1966.

Keimel, M. Virginia. "Team Teaching: Pros and Cons," *Pennsylvania School Journal,* 3:382–387 (April 1963).

King, Arthur, R., Jr. "Planning for Team Teaching: The Human Considerations," *Journal of Secondary Education,* 37:362–367 (October 1962).

Klausmeier, Herbert and William Wiersma. "Team Teaching and Achievement," *Education,* 86:238–242 (December 1965).

Landers, J. and Carmela Mercurio. "Improving Curriculum and Instruction for the Disadvantaged Minorities," *Journal of Negro Education,* 34:342–366 (Summer 1965).

Lobb, M. Delbert, M. F. Moall, and H. L. Slichenmayer. "What Are Some Promising Practices in Team Teaching?" *Bulletin of the National Association of Secondary-School Principals,* 44:2–7 (April 1960).

Lord, J. C. E. "Team Teaching Should Be Tailored to the Individual School Situation," *Business Education World,* 43 (April 1963).

Miller, Richard I. (ed.) *The Nongraded School: Analysis and Study.* New York: Harper & Row, Publishers, 1967.

Morse, Arthur D. "Team Teaching in Action: The Franklin School in Lexington, Massachusetts," in *Schools of Tomorrow—Today.* New York: Doubleday & Company, Inc., 1960, 9–26.

National Education Association, Project on Instruction, *Schools for the Sixties.* Washington, D.C.: The Association, 1963.

Noall, Matthew G. and P. Wilson. "Paraprofessional Helpers in a Language Arts Program at the Logan City High School, Utah," *Bulletin of the National Association of Secondary-School Principals,* 44:172–177 (January 1960).

Ogle, A. V. "How Tulsa Teaches the Grades, Semi-Departmentalized Elementary Education Method," *American School Board Journal,* 136 (April 1958).

"Planning and Operating a Middle School," *Overview,* 4:52–55 (March 1963).

Popper, Samuel H. *The American Middle School: An Organizational Analysis.* Waltham, Mass.: Blaisdell Publishing Company, 1967.

Sanders, David C. "School Organization: How Do You Decide?" *National Elementary Principal,* 43:25–28 (September 1962).

Scanlan, W. J. "Increased Services of Master Teachers Assisted by Cadet Teachers and Clerical Help," *Bulletin of the National Association of Secondary-School Principals,* 41:265–267 (April 1957).

Schiffer, Arthur R. "Use of Science Teams," *Science Teacher,* 28:31 (February 1961).

Schwartz, E. Terry. "An Evaluation of the Transitional Middle School in New York City." Mimeographed; New York: Center for Urban Education, 1966.

Strickland, JoAnn and William M. Alexander. "Seeking Continuity in Early and Middle School Education," *Phi Delta Kappan,* 50:397–400 (March 1969).

Thelen, Herbert A. *Classroom Grouping for Teachability.* New York: John Wiley & Sons, Inc., 1967.

Wolfson, Bernice J. "Individualizing Instruction," *NEA Journal,* 55:31–33 (November 1966).

FACILITIES

Design for Learning: Learning Laboratories. Winnetka, Ill.: Skokie Junior High School, May 1964.

Educational Facilities Laboratories. "Schools for Team Teaching." New York: Educational Facilities Laboratories, 1961.

Educational Facilities Laboratories, "Two Middle Schools, Saginaw Township, Michigan," in *Profiles of Significant Schools.* New York: Educational Facilities Laboratories, September 1960.

Murphy, Judith. *Middle Schools.* New York: Educational Facilities Laboratories, 1965.

ILLUSTRATIVE MATERIALS PERTAINING
TO SPECIFIC MIDDLE SCHOOLS

"Amory's Middle School," in *Southern Education Report,* 1:27–28 (November–December 1965).

Barrington Middle School: A Report. Barrington, Ill.: Barrington Public Schools, 1966.

Brown-Bridgewater Project, Section II. "A Study of the 4-4-4 Arrangement: The Middle School," Providence: Brown University, 1960.

"Caudill Builds Two Middle Schools," *Architectural Record,* 132 (January 1961).

Cordry, Vernon. "More Flexible Schedule at Fremont," *California Journal of Secondary Education,* 35:114–116 (February 1960).

McCarthy, Robert J. *How To Organize and Operate an Ungraded Middle School.* Englewood Cliffs, N.J.: Prentice-Hall, Inc., 1967.

Model Middle School: Involvement by Design. Rockland, Me.: Maine School Administrative District No. 5, 1967.

"The Nation's School of the Month" (Barrington, Ill.: Middle School), *Nation's Schools,* 76:61–68 (November 1965).

"The Nation's School of the Month" (Hithergreen Middle School, Centerville, Ohio), *Nation's Schools,* 80:53–55 (August 1967).

Zdanowicz, Paul J. "The Meredith G. Williams Middle School," *Educational Horizons,* 41:45–52 (Winter 1962).

INDEX